HISTORY'S GREATEST HEADLINES

HISTORY'S GREATEST HEADLINES

Events that Shook the World

James Inglis & Barry Stone

PIER 9

CONTENTS

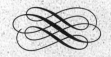

The Modern Times 260

INTRODUCTION

History is philosophy teaching by example.

DIONYSIUS OF HALICARNASSUS

The study of history represents a bulwark against the relentless march of time. The ceaseless flow of world events, both great and small, threatens to drown all but the most memorable and significant moments in a sea of obscurity. The historian's task is to rescue as many of these moments as he or she can, to lift them out of the past, to secure them and to bind them together in the printed word and in images—to turn them into the headlines of history—so that they will never be forgotten by a world obsessed with the present and the future, but all too often neglectful of its past.

So what is history? It is a composite—a mixture of events in time and the subsequent recollections and recording of those events. But if events are not recorded, can they be regarded as historical at all? Would the decline of the Roman Empire be considered a historical event if no one had written of its demise? 'History' is history that has been written down, events that have been retained and preserved in our collective conscience. History is not the countless global and personal incidents that occur in the broad sweep of humanity that slipped by us, unnoticed, incidents that nobody felt worthy enough to record. Those things, the 99.9 per cent of the daily comings and goings of human beings and their interactions with each other and their environment, their joys, their achievements, their insights, these things will never be known. They are forever lost to us.

There are all sorts of history. There is political history, military history, social history, medical history and the history of everyday things: sporting events and natural disasters, business news, the construction of a bridge, and the birth of a child. There isn't anything that has ever happened in the world that hasn't become a candidate for being considered a historic event the very moment after it has happened.

Historians are like investigative journalists: they glean what they can about past events, often through a trickle of evidence, some relic or fragment from ages past, that has survived, enabling them to decipher it, to gain insights and to draw conclusions. History is the accumulation and utilisation of documentary evidence. Everything depends upon the availability or otherwise of primary and secondary sources: documents, monographs, artefacts, tape recordings, pottery shards, petroglyphs or old coins, anything that provides the historian/journalist with information. Without these sources to illuminate the way, entire histories can be lost, which is why no one knows what really happened to the Aztecs. They left nothing behind to tell us.

It is wrong to think that history is simply the retelling of past events. It is wrong because almost nowhere does the historian find facts so meticulously, chronologically and unambiguously laid out that little or no interpretation is required. After all, the modern historian can only work from that which earlier observers themselves deemed worthy to select and preserve, and history cannot be retrieved or repeated once it has happened. Most often, by the time we have become aware of an event it is already long past us. The common thought among those who are not historians is that the writing of history is a relatively straightforward task involving timelines, quotes, facts, figures and commentaries from the past, and from all this the historian constructs a fairly predictable sort of narrative. It is assumed that any complexities in the text must have been introduced by the writer. But the writing of history has never been that simple.

Historians, like newspaper chief editors grappling with the week's lead story, are well aware of the shortcomings inherent in their craft, always struggling towards a better understanding of events, of sorting through history's complexities in the hope of better comprehending its causes and legacies. Often in a historical account of anything there will be contradictions, ambiguities, gaps in the narrative where there is a narrative, and statements that require interpretation—historians are always being accused of qualifying what they say and hedging their bets. Historians work with assumptions and likelihoods because often what is left for them to work with is a proverbial drop in the bucket compared with the information that could have been passed down but which instead was left unrecorded, forcing them to reconstruct events from the available data.

Historians, like feature writers, must also be critical and have the courage not merely to pass on data but to weigh up differing points of view, to reject accounts that might be considered tainted or self-serving. Often an identical set of facts will result in differing interpretations because historians are first and foremost individuals, who will look at facts in different ways and select different emphases. Historians, like us, can be guilty of approaching their material with all of the inbuilt prejudices and points of view of the era in which they live. And when a historian dares to at last write history instead of just study it, when they dare to emerge from the closeted world of academia and are rash enough to put their interpretations and conclusions on paper before their peers, they are offering themselves up for ritual slaughter.

Historians, argue with one another with a ferocity other professions can hope to match, with the possible exception of journalists. The arguments of both professional groups can be vicious and can destroy reputations. The writing of history's greatest headlines is not something for the faint-hearted.

Of course, history is not about the people who document it. It is about people who live it. History cannot exist without people. It is the recording of the chaos and the mess of life as it unfolds through the conduit of our shared humanity. And there is no end to it.

THE ANCIENT ANNALS

LEFT: Nineteenth century artist
James Hamilton's dramatic
interpretation of the destruction
of Pompeii in 79 AD.

1274 BC

CHARIOTS CLASH AT KADESH

The Second Battle of Kadesh between the Hittites and the ancient Egyptians is the first battle in history where enough historical evidence survives, from both sides, to paint a fairly accurate picture. The armies of these two empires were both massive, and it was probably the largest chariot battle ever fought, involving up to 5000 chariots. Rameses II, arguably Egypt's most powerful and celebrated pharaoh, led the Egyptian charge, and glorified his achievements on the battlefield in a breathtaking display of building works that survive to this day.

THE SECOND BATTLE OF KADESH AND THE LEGACY OF RAMESES II

He is [my] brother, and I am his brother, and I am at peace with him [forever. And] we will create our brotherhood and our [peace], and they will be better than the former brotherhood and peace of [Egypt with] Hatti.

HITTITE VERSION OF EGYPTIAN–HITTITE PEACE TREATY

Rameses II, also known as Rameses the Great, was the third king of Egypt's Nineteenth Dynasty, and one of the greatest. His rule from 1279 to 1213 BC was the second longest in the history of the Egyptian Empire and included some of the most extensive and magnificent building programs in its history.

Rameses' reign was also marked by conflicts with his neighbours—the Lybians to the west and the Indo-European Hittites to the north in an area occupied by present-day Turkey. His wars against the Hittites culminated in the Second Battle of Kadesh in 1274, the first battle in history with first-hand written evidence, and culminated in the world's first known peace treaty.

Rameses, meaning 'fashioned by Ra' (the sun god, one of Egypt's most revered deities), was born into a non-royal family. His grandfather Rameses I had attained power in 1293 BC, after a period of decline and loss of Egyptian influence under both Akhenaton and his son Tutankhamen. Akhenaton is best known for his highly individualistic religious beliefs, which focused on the worship of one god, Aton. His heir, Tutankhamen, died at eighteen; although his reign was brief, the splendours of his tomb were revealed to the world with its opening in 1922.

After some uncertainty and power-manoeuvring, the Rameses dynasty took over and set about the task of restoring the empire's status. Since the death of Tutankhamen, various nearby states (from the region extending from present-day Sudan to Syria) had begun to seek opportunities to extend their own territories. The Hittites, skilled in the military arts, had been particularly troublesome during this period, fortifying their southern border with Egypt and making continual speculative sorties into Egyptian territory. The city of Kadesh, a long-time Egyptian possession that had recently defected to Hittite sovereignty, now lay just inside the Hittite border. It was a location of extreme strategic import, lying directly on the vital trade route that connected Europe to the Asian and African states.

The young Rameses II

Two years after coming to power the elderly Rameses I installed his eldest son, Seti I, on the throne. Seti fought a series of partially successful wars against neighbouring countries in western Asia, Libya and Nubia (present-day southern Egypt and northern Sudan). He also managed to recapture Kadesh, which had repelled similar attempts by Tutankhamen and Horemheb (the last pharaoh of the Eighteenth Dynasty). Seti's son, the young Rameses II, was part of the victorious army, but the Egyptians did not sustain a permanent military occupation, and the Hittites reclaimed control within a few years. Hostilities ceased until after Seti's death in 1279, perhaps because Seti had reached an agreement with Hittite ruler King Muwatalli on the position of the border between their empires.

Seti provided Rameses with an opulent lifestyle, including a personal harem. The young prince accompanied his father on military sorties, so that when he came to rule in his own right he was already an experienced warrior. He was given the rank of army captain at the age of ten (the rank was probably honorific, but the experience enabled the king-in-waiting to observe tactics and receive military training). Seti nominated Rameses as his successor at the unusually early age of fourteen, probably to ensure that he would succeed him as king—and around the age of thirty Rameses became pharaoh of Egypt.

In 1274, five years into his reign, Rameses II set off into the Sinai desert across present-day Israel, Lebanon and into Syria towards Kadesh. His army comprised some forty thousand troops and two thousand chariots. The Hittites, however, possessed some technological and strategic advantages. Many of their new chariots carried three men, rather than the traditional two. More importantly, the Hittites had set a cunning trap, luring Rameses forward into an ambush and separating him from the bulk of his army.

March to Kadesh

The Egyptian army comprised four divisions, each named after an Egyptian god: Amon, Re, Ptah and Seth. Rameses sent a division of about five thousand men to capture the nearby port of Sumur before returning to link up with the main army. Meanwhile the majority of his army turned inland and marched towards Kadesh. As he drew near Kadesh, Rameses captured two Hittite spies who were masquerading as messengers, and extracted the 'information' that Muwatalli's army was situated at Aleppo, hundreds of kilometres to the north. In fact, the Hittites were concealed in nearby mountains and valleys, waiting in ambush. Emboldened, Rameses and his troops forded the river Orontes about 12 kilometres (7½ miles) south of Kadesh, only to find that their retreat had been blocked and their fragmented army was now surrounded and vastly outnumbered by a superior Hittite army of about twenty-seven thousand troops and three thousand chariots.

The Hittites had used propaganda (and the crucial element of surprise) to seize the advantage. Rameses despatched messengers to hasten the return of the division sent to Sumur, but as the Hittites attacked, the Egyptian forces panicked and retreated in disarray. Amid the general mayhem, Rameses was unable to communicate with his troops, while Muwatalli's soldiers, too preoccupied with plundering the Egyptian camps to maintain surveillance, failed to detect that Rameses' reinforcements were rapidly approaching from the north and east.

Rameses was left with a small corps of personal troops who fought desperately until his Sumur troops arrived and his reunited company embarked upon a headlong counter-attack. Knives, maces, swords, spears and longbows clashed as thousands of chariots engaged in battle. The Hittite three-man chariots, though more powerful and effective in open-plain combat, were now rendered vulnerable by their lack of manoeuvrability at close quarters, and suffered huge losses. Rameses retained control over the battlefield, but failed in his aim of taking Kadesh. Both sides had suffered failures of communication, and good and bad exercise of central command. By this stage, both armies had suffered enormous casualties—the next morning the two sides agreed to an armistice and the Egyptians returned home.

Over the next fifteen years the Egyptians and Hittites fought a series of inconclusive skirmishes in the Kadesh region. The failure of the Kadesh campaign inspired some of the Egyptian-controlled states in the region to rebel against the central government. Rameses was forced to fortify the borders of the empire's Asiatic and African dominions at the same time as dealing with the Hittites. Eventually, like his father before him, he found that he could not retain control over territory so far from home in the face of continual insurrections.

A peace treaty … and monuments in stone

Eventually concluding that the two kingdoms' mutual dreams of conquest were unattainable, Rameses and the new Hittite king Hattusili III, brother of Muwatalli, signed a peace treaty in 1259, the first in recorded history. It contained eighteen articles, including requirements that are still found in treaties today—an amnesty for all refugees, exchanges of prisoners-of-war, and an agreement not to form alliances with each other's enemies. Two versions were recorded, one in Egyptian hieroglyphs, the other in Hittite cuneiform script. Most of the text is identical, with the exception that the Egyptian version claims that the Hittites relented and sued for peace, while the Hittite version claims the opposite.

Rameses was a master of self-aggrandising propaganda. Scribes and poets accompanied him on his various military exploits—not to provide an objective, factual account, but to glorify his deeds and present them in the best possible light.

In an early display of propaganda, an Egyptian temple painting depicts Rameses II defeating the Hittites single-handedly.

Rameses II's imposing temple complex at Abu Simbel has stood for over three thousand years.

Although the 1274 battle ended in a stalemate, Rameses' version of events claimed that he had won a resounding victory. He made the vainglorious boast that, even though his cowardly army had deserted him, he was nonetheless able to defeat the Hittites almost single-handedly (not crediting the reinforcements whose timely arrival had, in fact, saved the day).

Rameses arranged for numerous rock carvings and papyrus scrolls to record this and other sometimes tenuous 'victories'. Such records are also found in the numerous temples that Rameses constructed—or co-opted from earlier times—to exalt his reign. Two major Egyptian narratives were made of the Battle of Kadesh. 'The Poem' (a verse of which is reproduced below) is inscribed in the temples of Karnak, Luxor, Abydos and the Ramesseum, while 'The Report', a shorter version, is found in Luxor, Abydos, the Ramesseum and Abu Simbel. A Hittite version was set down on tablets found in the Hittite capital Boghazkoy.

Then the king he lashed each horse,
And they quickened up their course,
And he dashed into the middle of the hostile,
 Hittite host,
All alone, none other with him, for he counted
 not the cost.
Then he looked behind, and found
That the foe were all around,
Two thousand and five hundred of their
 chariots of war;
And the flower of the Hittites, and their helpers,
 in a ring …

A Hittite bride for Rameses

With the peace formalities completed, the Egyptian and Hittite royal courts embarked upon a period of cordial relations. Rameses exchanged letters with Hattusili, discussing the possibility of a royal marriage to confirm the peace. In about 1245 a Hittite princess, given the Egyptian name of Maat-Hor-Neferure, arrived in Egypt to marry Rameses. This wedding was commemorated with inscriptions in numerous temples, including Karnak and Abu Simbel. It must have been a successful alliance, for Maat-Hor-Neferure was soon elevated to the status of Great Royal Wife, a title reserved for the highest ranked wife of the time (during his 66-year reign there were seven great royal wives).

Although incest was taboo in most ancient societies, including Greece and Rome, it was very common among Egyptian royalty. Rameses II is believed to have married several of his sisters and daughters. The major wives of kings were usually of royal blood, often their sisters or half-sisters. These marriages were profitable for several reasons. They blocked outsiders who might have designs on the throne, and produced royal children who would be eligible heirs. They also ensured that a suitably trained princess would be available to become queen—the most important role available to an Egyptian woman. While the king could marry whomever he wished, a royal female was not permitted to marry below her status, so the field of potential husbands beyond her brothers (or father) was very limited. Egyptian princesses were also forbidden from marrying foreign monarchs, for fear their husbands or offspring might later lay claim to the throne of Egypt.

A time of prosperity

Despite the rich repository of records of Rameses' public life and achievements, little is known about his personal life. His first (and apparently favourite) queen was Nefertari, whom Rameses immortalised in the smaller Abu Simbel temple. She bore him at least eight children in the more than twenty years of their marriage, and her ornate tomb in the Valley of the Queens at Thebes attests to her status. We know Rameses also married Isetnofret (among whose sons was Rameses' eventual successor, Merneptah) and Meritamun. The king maintained a large harem as well, comprising unattached female courtiers—including unmarried and widowed sisters, daughters and other relatives—foreign brides, upper class Egyptian women, and numerous consorts of unprivileged birth, including the servants of aristocratic ladies. Rameses is reputed to have fathered well over a hundred children.

Rameses took advantage of the relative peace of his rule by embarking upon a massive building program during which he oversaw the construction of a new capital, Per Rameses, in the Nile delta, and upgraded the ancient temple of Karnak, near Luxor. He also constructed the vast twin-temple complex of Abu Simbel, carved out of a mountainside in southern Egypt over a period of twenty years to celebrate his 'victory' at Kadesh, and to commemorate himself and his beloved Nefertari. He built a temple complex, the Ramesseum, also near Luxor, which incorporated several 17-metre (55-foot) high statues of himself, and included a writing school.

Rameses was idolised and imitated by later Egyptian kings, and his exploits lauded by leaders of foreign empires. But after his death the Egyptian empire gradually declined, succumbing in turn to the Persians, Alexander the Great and the Romans.

A note about dates: Dates in this era are disputed, and only approximate to within a few years, because witnesses and historians used various different systems to record events. To further confuse matters, at the accession of each new reign the Egyptian calendar reverted to Year 1.

431–404 BC

ATHENS AND SPARTA: 'IT'S WAR'

The fifth century BC was a golden age for ancient Greece, and in particular for its richest city-state Athens, with major advances in philosophy, mathematics, the arts, engineering and architecture. As Athens boomed the balance of power in the region shifted, setting Athens on a collision course with its hawkish cousin, Sparta. The Peloponnesian War can be described as a conflict between the two leading ideologies of the Hellenic ancient world—the democracy of Athens, with its reliance on trade and its strong navy, and the oligarchy of Sparta, with its agrarian base and dominant military might. The clash between these two ancient superpowers would last thirty years and change the course of western history.

THE EPIC CONFLICT BETWEEN ANCIENT GREECE'S TWO MOST POWERFUL CITY-STATES

The strongest are those who understand with perfect clarity what is terrible in life and what is sweet and then go out undeterred to confront danger.

PERICLES' FUNERAL ORATION

In the fifth century BC ancient Greece consisted of a group of warring city-states, the foremost being Athens, Sparta, Corinth and Thebes. Peace was an occasional interlude between periods of war. The Peloponnesian War was a series of battles fought in three stages between Athens and Sparta (joined by their respective allies) from 431 to 404 BC. Athens was the dominant member of a group of city-states known as the Delian League, while Sparta led an alliance known as the Peloponnesian League, named after the peninsula on which Sparta was located. Athens, the most glorious city in the ancient world, was a flourishing democracy of perhaps one hundred thousand people, where decisions were made by its male citizens in public assembly. Sparta was an agrarian oligarchy governed by a small, aristocratic elite. Whereas Athens' strength lay in its navy, Sparta depended on a well-trained and disciplined army. Its military qualities had become legendary, attributable in no small way

to the harsh and rigorous training young Spartan boys were subjected to when they left home at seven to live in barracks.

In 499 BC, though, the Greek city-states were united against a common enemy, the invading Persians. Eventually, they achieved victory over King Darius I at the Battle of Marathon in 490 BC. Darius' successor, Xerxes, invaded in 480 BC, but was driven out of the Aegean region by Athens and Sparta the following year. Following this victory, Athens became the pre-eminent state, forming an alliance with all the Mediterranean island states, many in Asia Minor, and most on the Greek mainland. Sparta, however, refused to join, preferring a policy of isolation and self-sufficient agriculture.

During this so-called 'Golden Age', Athens became the world centre of culture, a place where philosophy, literature and drama flourished. Famous buildings, including the Parthenon, were built, and many eminent personalities emerged, among them the philosophers Socrates and Plato, the historian and political analyst Thucydides and the playwright Aristophanes. Athens continued to lead wars against the Persians, but some states became restive and, disapproving of Athens' increasingly imperialist outlook, tried to leave the alliance. They were unsuccessful.

When Athens destroyed the Corinthian fleet in 460 BC, Sparta seized the opportunity to join with Thebes and other states—and together they defeated Athens in 457 BC in the Battle of Tanagra. Sparta returned to isolation while Athens rose again to achieve a series of victories, both on land and at sea. But just a decade later, in 446 BC, Sparta again allied with other states to drive Athens from its mainland conquests. Facing revolts from its overseas empire, Athens was forced to sue for peace and agreed to sign the Thirty Years Peace Treaty with Sparta. Soon, however, the treaty was threatened by friction between the member states. In 435 Sparta's ally

Pericles delivers the annual funeral oration for those killed in war against the backdrop of the newly built Parthenon.

Corinth attacked the island state of Corfu, which in turn sought help from Athens. The threat of Athens' fleet was enough to deter Corinth, but other battles and sieges ensued over the next few years. Athens attacked another Spartan ally, Megara, 40 kilometres (25 miles) west of Athens, in 432 BC. This was the last straw for Sparta, which declared that Athens had breached the terms of the Thirty Years Peace and resumed all-out hostilities. This was the start of what is known as the Peloponnesian War.

The battle lines are drawn

In the first phase of the war, Sparta invaded Attica, northeast of Athens in 431 BC, hoping to use the superior strength of its army to neutralise Athens' naval dominance. The Athenian leader, Pericles, determined to pursue a defensive strategy on land, while keeping his armies supplied with provisions and troops by sea. He cautioned the Athenian assembly not to become carried away with thoughts of expansion, but stated that the strength of Athens' navy gave reasonable expectation of a successful defence. Many, though, including Socrates, saw the looming war as an act of military madness, and probably doomed to failure.

Thucydides, who lived through the ensuing twenty-seven years of warfare and documented it meticulously, says of this period:

... The territory of Athens was being ravaged before the very eyes of the Athenians, a sight which the young men had never seen before and the old only in the Persian wars; and it was naturally thought a grievous insult, and the determination was universal, especially among the young men, to sally forth and stop it. Knots were formed in the streets and engaged in hot discussion; for if the proposed sally was warmly recommended, it was also in some cases opposed.

Oracles of the most various import were recited by the collectors, and found eager listeners in one or other of the disputants.

Assault on Athens

In 429 BC the Spartans quickly surrounded Athens, forcing its inhabitants to retreat behind the city walls. Plague soon broke out, causing a quarter of the population—including Pericles—to perish, and forcing the Spartans to retreat lest they also succumb. Thucydides also contracted the plague, but recovered. The following is an extract from his record of Pericles' famous oration on the occasion of the annual public funeral for the war-dead, in late 430 BC, in which he sets out the fundamentals of democracy:

... Our constitution does not copy the laws of neighbouring states; we are rather a pattern to others than imitators ourselves. Its administration favours the many instead of the few; this is why it is called a democracy. If we look to the laws, they afford equal justice to all in their private differences; if no social standing, advancement in public life falls to reputation for capacity, class considerations not being allowed to interfere with merit; nor again does poverty bar the way, if a man is able to serve the state, he is not hindered by the obscurity of his condition.

The Spartans then besieged another Athenian ally, the city-state of Plataea to the northwest. By 427 BC they had starved Plataea into submission, massacring the entire population and razing the city to the ground. Sparta also undertook annual attempts to invade Attica, but to no avail. Meanwhile Athens, undaunted by the loss of Pericles and the ravages of the plague, sent its navy on the offensive, wreaking havoc upon the Peloponnesian coast, destroying two naval fleets and blockading the Gulf of Corinth. Athens also quelled uprisings by Corcyra and the island of Lesbos.

Opportunity lost

Pericles' successor, the hawkish Cleon, reversed Pericles' more moderate defensive strategy by launching unsuccessful attacks on Sparta's allies, Boeotia and Thebes. Athens next turned its attention to Aetolia to the north, securing a rare victory. In 425 BC the usual pattern of attack and counter-attack continued, as Sparta attacked Attica while the Athenian fleet cruised along the Peloponnese coast. The Athenian general Demosthenes established a fort on the southwest Peloponnesian coast at Pylos while the Athenian fleet drove the Spartan ships ashore on the nearby island of Sphacteria. Outmanoeuvred, Sparta tried to sue for peace, offering its navy in return for Sphacteria, but Cleon demanded the return of all the lands Athens had relinquished at the end of the first Peloponnesian War in 446. Spartan king Agis demurred and the war continued, with Athens occupying Sphacteria and keeping the surviving Spartans as hostages. The next two years saw a series of battles, with both sides experiencing victories and defeats. In 422 the Spartan general Brasidas defeated Athens at Amphipolis in Macedonia to the far northeast, though he and Cleon were both killed in the fighting.

A truce and a new general

In 421 BC the Peloponnesian War entered its second stage. The overly optimistic Fifty Years Peace treaty was signed, with both sides agreeing to hand back the territories they had gained, and the Athenians returning the Sphacteria hostages to Sparta. But in 418 Sparta's allies, Argos, Mantinea and Elis, increasingly dissatisfied with the truce terms,

formed a breakaway group which Sparta tried unsuccessfully to prevent. This alliance, with the assistance of Athens (under the command of the brilliant yet reckless general Alcibiades), turned on Sparta but was defeated at Mantinea in the largest battle of the war, with some ten thousand troops on each side.

Sparta was again in control of the Peloponnesian League, and a period of relative peace followed. But in 415 Alcibiades (whose strategy invariably involved swift and aggressive action) persuaded the Athenian assembly that a threat by Spartan ally Syracuse, a city-state on the island of Sicily, to Athens' allies in Sicily offered an opportunity to conquer those areas of Sicily not already under Athenian control. Athens imported much of its grain from the island, and a total occupation would significantly increase its empire. This massive assault against Sicily launched the third and final phase of the Peloponnesian War.

Blockade and siege

Athens besieged the Syracuse position, building walls to surround its landward border. This strategic advantage was lost when, in 413 BC, a combined Corinthian and Spartan fleet won a convincing naval victory, breaking the blockade and persuading the Athenians to withdraw. However, on the night of the planned retreat, an eclipse of the moon was interpreted as an evil portent, causing the Athenians to postpone the operation until the next full moon. This was a crucial strategic error—in the ensuing weeks the Syracuse fleet destroyed what was left of Athens' navy, killing its leaders and forcing a complete surrender.

The home situation was just as dismal for Athens. Sparta had once again declared war on Athens in 414, and succeeded in causing rebellion among some Athenian allies. Even the

Their crushing defeat in the naval battle at Syracuse would prove the beginning of the end for the Athenians.

Persians came to Sparta's aid, providing funds as well as ships in return for recognition of their dominions in Asia Minor. Athens appeared to be doomed, and a coup in the city resulted in the suspension of democracy in favour of an opportunistic group known as the Four Hundred, who tried to sue for peace with Sparta. But, fortunately for Athens, it had preserved a fleet of a hundred ships and large reserves of currency specifically for use in a desperate situation such as the one it now faced. The fleet resumed operations in the Aegean Sea against the will of the Four Hundred, the troops disagreeing with the group's undemocratic structure. General Alcibiades had been branded a traitor, but nonetheless this charismatic soldier and politician retained a great deal of support. The Four Hundred were overthrown, democracy was restored and Alcibiades took charge of the Athenian fleet. From 411 to 408 BC Athens won a series of naval victories, causing Sparta to offer another truce. But the new Athenian leader Cleophon refused, and Sparta, under the command of Lysander and boosted by the Persians' support (which had taken a long time to arrive), defeated Athens at Ephesus in 406 BC.

Alcibiades, whose leadership was always controversial, was sacked as the Spartans blockaded the Athenian fleet in the harbour of Mytilene on Lesbos. Athens managed to assemble another fleet, which won an overwhelming victory, causing Sparta to offer peace yet again. Cleophon again declined, letting slip another gilt-edged opportunity to save the Athenian empire.

By 405 BC the endgame was near. Lysander took his fleet to the Hellespont (now known as the Dardanelles), a narrow channel connecting the Aegean and Black seas, and a vital Athenian trade route. The Athenians attempted to engage him in battle, but Lysander refused, playing a waiting game until one night, in the harbour of Aegospotami, when the Athenians had been lulled into a false sense of security and sent most of their troops on shore leave, he attacked. He completely destroyed the Athenian fleet, ending Athens' lengthy era of naval supremacy. Lysander followed up this victory by besieging Athens and, in the spring of 404, after a six-month blockade, starved it into unconditional surrender. Athens' defensive walls were completely destroyed and it lost all of its foreign territories. Sparta installed a puppet government known as the Thirty Tyrants, but this was overthrown by a popular uprising the following year and democracy was restored.

The legacy of Athens

Despite the war, Athenian artistic and intellectual life had continued apace. Sophocles pondered the human condition and produced his dramatic masterpieces *Oedipus Rex*, *Oedipus Colonus* and *Antigone* without ever mentioning the war. Aristophanes produced outrageous, hilarious and often obscene satirical plays lampooning war and its advocates, and extolling peace. Thucydides kept analysing, commenting and recording his superb contemporary history, giving us a vivid, comprehensive and meditative record of the war. Socrates, despite speaking against many of the manifestations of the war (and predicting Athens' defeat), nonetheless served heroically in several campaigns, and never stopped trying to convince anyone who would listen that the good of the soul is the supreme good, and that rigorous, sceptical debate and dialectic are the keys to intellectual advancement. His execution after the war in 399 BC for supposedly corrupting the morals of youth can be seen as symbolic of Athens' fall from grace.

Athens never regained its political power, and poverty became widespread in Greece as the draining economic effects of the long war became manifest. Although Greek cultural and artistic pre-eminence continued, its city-states proved unable to unite against common foes, and its declining political influence led to eventual occupation by Macedonia, and later Rome.

274 BC

RULER RENOUNCES BLOODY PAST FOR BUDDHIST PATH

The great Indian emperor Ashoka was born in 265 BC into the ancient Mauryan dynasty, and ruled over an empire that covered two-thirds of the Indian continent. As a young man he fought many battles to expand the empire, culminating in the Kalinga War. Remarkably, while Ashoka was victorious, he was haunted by the violence he had inflicted, and threw down his sword in shame, renouncing his path of aggression and suppression. The emperor then took up Buddhism and spent the rest of his life devoted to public works and the peaceful spread of the religion, and earned the name Ashoka the Great.

THE REMARKABLE REIGN OF EMPEROR ASHOKA

I have enforced the law against killing certain animals and many others, but the greatest progress of righteousness among men comes from the exhortation in favour of non-injury to life and abstention from killing living beings.

FROM ASHOKA'S EDICTS

The Emperor King Ashoka (304–232 BC), also known as *Devanampiya Piyadasi* ('Beloved-of-the-Gods') and Ashoka the Great, was the third monarch of the great Mauryan dynasty that had come to rule most of the Indian subcontinent. He ruthlessly conquered a vast domain that included present-day Afghanistan, Pakistan, Nepal, Iran (Persia) and most of India. British author and historian H. G. Wells wrote of him: 'In the history of the world there have been thousands of kings and emperors who called themselves "their highnesses", "their majesties" and "their exalted majesties" and so on. They shone for a brief moment, and as quickly disappeared. But Ashoka shines and shines brightly like a bright star, even unto this day.'

Conquest and expansion

In 262 BC, eight years after his accession, Ashoka sought to further expand his empire, and his armies attacked and conquered the Kalinga region, roughly corresponding to the modern east Indian state of Orissa. But in the wake of the bloody battle, contemplating the horrors he had unleashed, he experienced a spiritual epiphany that led to a complete turnabout in his outlook.

Ashoka spent the rest of his life applying pacifist and humanist principles of justice and virtue to his administration, and helped the fledgling religion of Buddhism to expand throughout India and nearby states. (Buddha died in about 480 BC.) In the nineteenth century a large number of Ashoka's edicts were discovered on rocks and pillars in India, Nepal, Afghanistan, Pakistan and Sri Lanka, giving us some clear insights into his philosophies, motivation and actions.

Ashoka's grandfather, Chandragupta, had established a large empire in northern India, which was further expanded by Ashoka's father, Bindusara. Little is known of Ashoka's early life, but upon Bindusara's death he embarked on a two-year war of succession that led to his ascent to the throne. On his accession, partly achieved by ruthless elimination of all potential opposition (including his stepbrothers), Ashoka found himself leader of a great empire which already stretched from northern India to the southern border of modern Karnataka state, eastward to Calcutta and Bangladesh and as far west as southeast Afghanistan.

However, he had even greater imperialist designs. He embarked upon a series of battles that extended his domain, and then set his sights on Kalinga, which had declared itself independent during the reign of Chandragupta and resisted several unsuccessful invasion attempts by Bindusara. Ashoka determined to regain control over the region, which was abundant in precious ores and rich farmlands, and was strategically situated on the busy Bay of Bengal trading route leading to the Krishna River valley, which held vast reserves of gold and precious stones. Ashoka's war against the king of Kalinga—the bloodiest in India's history—was successful, but at the cost of over one hundred thousand lives. Legend has it that, after the war, he ventured into the shattered streets of Kalinga and, seeing only smouldering buildings and countless corpses, cried 'What have I done?' In the aftermath, Ashoka's contemplations caused him to renounce his expansionist policy and determine to rule by compassion and education, rather than by conquering territories and repressing the masses.

Conversion to Buddhism

Another factor may have led Ashoka to Buddhism. According to legend, Mauryan princess Maharani Devi, the wife of Ashoka's brother, whom he had killed during the war of succession following the death of their father, fled with a maid in order to protect her unborn child. When eventually the exhausted princess collapsed under a tree, the maid ran to a nearby Buddhist monastery to seek help from a doctor or priest. Meanwhile Maharani Devi gave birth to male and female twins, Mahindra and Sanghamitra, who were brought up and educated at the monastery.

When Mahindra was about thirteen years old he met Ashoka, who expressed surprise that such a young boy was dressed as a sage. When he revealed that he was in fact Ashoka's nephew, Ashoka was overcome by remorse and compassion and allowed the twins and their mother to move into his palace. Mahindra, by now more a monk than a prince, advised Ashoka to embrace the Buddhist dharma and renounce war. *Dharma*—Law, or Truth—does not have a direct English equivalent, but may be roughly translated as referring to the inherent order and harmony in nature, and a life lived in accordance with that order. Mahindra and Sanghamitra were opposed to war so they asked Ashoka for permission to join the *sangha* (Buddhist monastic community), which he reluctantly approved. They went on to establish Buddhism in Sri Lanka. Henceforth Ashoka, who had been known as Chandashoka, 'Ashoka the Cruel', became known as Dharmashoka, 'Ashoka the Good'.

Ashoka, who had been born a Hindu, began to study Buddhism under the guidance of the great Brahmin Buddhist sages Radhaswami and Manjushri. For the rest of his reign he pursued *ahimsa* (the policy of non-violence that later found expression in Mahatma Gandhi's quest for India to gain independence from Britain). He freed his prisoners-of-war and returned control of their territory to their rightful rulers. He abolished the unnecessary hunting, slaughter, branding and mutilation of animals. Limited hunting was allowed for nutrition where necessary, but Ashoka promoted vegetarianism, and eventually adopted the practice wholeheartedly. All wildlife was protected under law—Ashoka was perhaps the first ruler in history to introduce animal conservation measures. He embarked upon a large public works program, building universities, irrigation and navigation canals, and free rest houses and hospitals for travellers and pilgrims. He abolished slavery and treated everyone as equal, regardless of religion, politics or caste.

Prisoners were released for one day per year. He abandoned the long-standing Mauryan policy of invading weaker kingdoms, instead favouring trade and negotiation.

The Edicts

Ashoka now began to formulate his Edicts, which are the earliest decipherable Indian written works. They are written on rocks, mountains and stone pillars, the last bearing testimony to the technological and artistic dexterity of ancient Indian civilisation. The pillars, between 12 and 15 metres (40 and 50 feet) high and weighing up to 50 tonnes, were excavated from quarries to the south of Varanasi. Some were transported hundreds of kilometres. Each pillar was originally capped by a headstone representing an animal such as a lion, bull or horse. Few headstones have survived, but the extant examples are recognised as artistic masterpieces. Both the headstones and the pillars have retained an extraordinary mirror-like sheen that has survived centuries of exposure to the elements.

Ashoka's Edicts fall into several categories. Some refer to the activities of the Buddhist *sangha*, and are addressed to local government officers or monks. The so-called Minor Edicts describe Ashoka's general commitment to Buddhism and to other philosophical issues,

Detail of a relief sculpture at the Great Stupa built by Emperor Ashoka at Sanchi.

while the Major Rock Edicts and the Pillar Edicts are more wide-ranging and comprehensive. In general they emphasise the importance of open-mindedness in regard to differing belief systems, and define social ethics as a respect for parents and teachers. They also highlight the necessity for harmonious relationships between family members, teachers and students, and employers and employees.

The following extract from Minor Edict 2 describes the kinds of harmonious relationships that should exist among all living creatures:

Father and mother should be respected and so should elders, kindness to living beings should be made strong and the truth should be spoken. In these ways, the Dharma should be promoted.

The Lion Capital of Ashoka has become an enduring symbol for India as its national emblem.

Likewise, a teacher should be honoured by his pupil and proper manners should be shown towards relations. This is an ancient rule that conduces to long life. Thus should one act ...

Kalinga Rock Edict 1 provides guidance on how to live one's life with wisdom, compassion and discipline:

... All men are my children. What I desire for my own children, and I desire their welfare and happiness both in this world and the next, that I desire for all men. You do not understand to what extent I desire this, and if some of you do understand, you do not understand the full extent of my desire. You must attend to this matter. While being completely law-abiding, some people are imprisoned, treated harshly and even killed without cause so that many people suffer. Therefore your aim should be to act with impartiality. It is because of these things—envy, anger, cruelty, hate, indifference, laziness or tiredness—that such a thing does not happen. Therefore your aim should be: 'May these things not be in me.' And the root of this is non-anger and patience. Those who are bored with the administration of justice will not be promoted; those who are not will move upwards and be promoted. Whoever among you understands this should say to his colleagues: 'See that you do your duty properly. Such are Piyadasi's instructions'.

Some Edicts were positioned in significant locations, such as Buddha's birthplace, while others were located in large population centres where they would be widely read. They appear to be written in Ashoka's own words rather than in the formal style of a royal proclamation, and their informal and personal tone provides a glimpse into the personality of this multi-faceted man. The style is at times repetitious and Ashoka often refers to his good works, although not necessarily in an egotistical way. The Edicts suggest a keen sensitivity and a concern that those who read of him in the decades and centuries to come would think of him as a sincere person and a good governor.

One of the Edicts in Afghanistan is written in both Greek and Aramaic, indicating that the Greek empire had expanded to this region, and that the Greek population within his realm converted to Buddhism. Most edicts are written in Brahmi, the root script from which all Indian and many southeast Asian languages evolved. In eastern India the edicts are written in Magadhi, which was probably the official language of Ashoka's court. In western India an early form of Sanskrit is used.

Ashoka's legacy

Ashoka was responsible for the first attempt to formulate government along Buddhist principles; he played a seminal part in helping Buddhism spread throughout India and abroad, and built the first major Buddhist monuments.

It is apparent that he considered his reforms part of his duties as a Buddhist. Nevertheless, he was not intolerant of other religions; rather, he encouraged everyone to practise their own religion with the same sincerity that he demonstrated in his own practice.

Ashoka ruled over his empire for only forty years, and within fifty years of his death the Mauryan Empire had ceased to exist. Nevertheless, legacies of his rule can be seen all over India today. The Ashoka Chakra, the 24-spoked Wheel of Dharma, can be seen in the centre of India's national flag, and the famous Lion Capital of Ashoka, the four sculpted lions standing proudly back to back that once adorned the top of the Ashoka Pillar at Sarnath, has since become the national emblem of India and can be seen today in the Sarnath Museum.

The Sarnath pillar also contains an Edict that sums up the theme of 'unity in diversity' that so perfectly captures the Indian attitude to its religiously disparate society: 'No one shall cause division in the order of monks'.

MASSIVE TOMB BUILT FOR CHINA'S FIRST EMPEROR

On 29 March 1974, in central China's Shaanxi province, three young farm workers were digging a well when they stumbled upon an ancient, cavernous passageway. To their amazement, they found themselves confronted by an unprecedented sight—rank after rank of life-sized, battle-ready terracotta soldiers. The site was secured and further excavations by archaeologists revealed more than eight thousand soldiers and a profusion of other astonishing objects. The farm workers had broken through the surrounds of the mausoleum of China's first emperor, Qin Shihuangdi, a megalomaniacal tyrant, obsessed with finding the elixir of life, whose battles and building works took place on a breathtaking scale, unsurpassed in the ancient world.

THE REIGN OF QIN SHIHUANGDI

I am Emperor, my descendants will be numerous. From the second generation to the ten thousandth, my line will not end.

QIN SHIHUANGDI

China's first emperor was born Zhao Zheng around 259 BC, the son of Zichu, a prince of the royal family of the Qin state. His mother was a former concubine of a rich merchant named Lu Buwei. He ascended the throne in 245 at the age of thirteen and ruled with the help of his mother and Lu Buwei until 238, when he rose to full power after a successful coup. He then executed his mother's lover, Lao Ai, who had joined the opposition, and exiled Lu Buwei.

Battle zone China

In the third century BC China consisted of a group of seven independent states that had been constantly warring for more than two hundred and fifty years. Zheng was born in Zhao state but his family, suffering persecution, fled to neighbouring Qin state. He began his conquest of the states in 228 BC by successfully invading Zhao with an army of 500,000 troops. (In comparison, at about the same time, Rome was fighting Carthage with a mere 6000 troops, while, in the early nineteenth century, Napoleon's army at its height numbered about 100,000.) He identified those Zhao responsible for his family's exile and tortured them before publicly killing them, often by dragging them behind a horse.

Zheng achieved loyalty with a mixture of reward and punishment; successful troops were awarded land, money, promotions and publicity. This had the effect of improving bravery, morale and recruitment rates. But failure was punishable by death. Success was measured by the numbers of enemy killed—calculated by the number of victims' heads which the returning armies carried as proof. The armies were divided into groups of ten; if just one member was killed, the other nine were required to obtain the head of an enemy, otherwise they would all be killed.

In 225 BC Zheng attacked Chu state deploying only 200,000 men, but suffered an almost complete rout, losing all but about 10,000 troops. Realising his error, he called upon one of his great generals, Wang Jian, who advised him to re-attack the following year with some 600,000 troops. This time the Chu, complacent and flushed with victory, were easily defeated, causing Yan state to pre-emptively surrender— or so it seemed. In fact, the capitulation was a ruse, and Yan emissaries tried unsuccessfully to assassinate Zheng. Enraged, Zheng invaded Yan and crushed it in a mere four weeks.

Heavy casualties and triumph for Zheng

By using espionage, bribery and ruthlessly effective military tactics, Zheng eliminated, one by one, the remaining six rival states. His defeat of Qi in 221 BC saw China united for the first time in its history, albeit at the cost of well over a million lives. Following these triumphs Zheng renamed himself Qin Shihuangdi (*shi*, the first; *huang*, august or great; *di*, son of heaven)—in other words, the first God-sent ruler of a unified China. *Qin* (pronounced 'chin') gave his name to the new integrated power.

But treason and treachery followed as rulers of the defeated states plotted their retribution. Recognising the threat they posed, Emperor Qin forced them to relocate to his own court, along with 120,000 aristocratic families, so he could keep an eye on them. He also imposed standardised systems of currency, law, measurement and language—which still exist to this day.

China's first emperor, Qin Shihuangdi, whose reign was both bloody and visionary.

Qin now embarked upon a huge capital works program. He organised the construction of a canal system that linked the Lijang and Xian Jiang rivers and used the canals to transport food and arms to his troops. He also decided to build a great wall—to join sections of wall built by previous provincial administrations—to keep out marauding Mongol 'barbarians' to the north. When completed, the wall measured over 4800 kilometres (3000 miles) and stretched from Mount Jeyshi in present-day North Korea to Linshao in western China. It was built with local materials: stone in some places, compacted earth and wood in others. It measured 6 metres (20 feet) high and up to 5 metres (16 feet) wide, with beacon platforms 8 metres (26 feet) high placed along its length within sight of each other to enable communication by smoke signal in daytime and by fire at night. It was the world's first communication highway, and it enabled messages to be sent from one end of the wall to the other in just a few hours. To construct the wall Qin conscripted up to 700,000 soldiers, peasants and criminals, each with a support staff of up to five who were responsible for providing food, building materials, horses, camels, carts and other essentials. Well over one million workers died during construction of the Great Wall of China, which progressed at an average rate of almost 1.6 kilometres (1 mile) per day for ten years. The bodies of many of the dead were used as filler within the walls.

Burning the books

To emphasise his status as the 'first' emperor, Qin ordered the burning of most traditional books of wisdom (with the exception of those on the topics of agriculture, medicine and divination). Qin became obsessed with the quest for eternal life, apparently believing that he would be able to retain power even after his death. He traversed his kingdom seeking the elixir of life, ingesting mercury-laced potions prepared by his numerous doctors in the belief that this poison, in combination with other substances, held the secret.

By 213 BC Qin suspected everyone of plotting against him, including his most loyal eunuchs, ministers, courtiers and priests (many of whom he ordered killed), and he surrounded himself with sycophants who fed his megalomania. When Confucian scholars warned him of genuine plots to overthrow or assassinate him, he ordered the live burial of 460 of them and banished the remainder to wall-building duties—a death sentence in itself. (When he was compared to Qin, Chairman Mao Zedong, leader of the People's Republic of China from 1943 to 1976, replied: 'He only buried 460 scholars alive; we have buried forty-six thousand scholars … You intellectuals revile us for being Qin Shihuangs. You are wrong. We have surpassed Qin Shihuang a hundredfold.')

A rule marked by suspicion and paranoia

Qin also killed most of the country's pre-eminent intellectuals and military officers. The populace grew ever more restive as Qin ignored the prevailing Confucian precept that good governors attract good portents and popular support. He became convinced that even the spirit world was against him; he was in control of his empire, but not of himself. He suffered hallucinations and came to believe that he would live forever (even though his body might die) and that, in any case, he could become lord of the underworld if he took sufficient resources with him. He ordered more and more additions to his mausoleum, including the terracotta warriors, who were intended to ensure that his power would last for ten thousand generations.

Qin had begun construction of his mausoleum in 220 BC, the year after he came to power, and just ten years before his death. It took an estimated 700,000 conscripts to build what is the largest pyramid on earth in terms of surface area. Its circumference is 1250 metres (three-quarters of a mile), its height 76 metres (250 feet). In comparison, the Great Pyramid at Giza in Egypt rises to 147 metres (almost 500 feet). The mausoleum is aligned to the north star, reflecting Qin's belief that his heaven-sent authority was the centre of the universe. It is surrounded by two perimeter walls that mark the limits of the inner and outer city.

Figures in terracotta

In between the walls of the pyramid, to the west of the sarcophagus, is a series of pits. One contains bronze horses (and the remains of real horses), chariots, the remains of various rare birds and animals, and pieces of gold, bronze and jade. Archaeologists have dubbed this area 'the zoo'. Nearby are eleven shallow graves containing the skeletons of prisoners bound hand and foot, and to the southeast ninety-one small pits house the 'royal stables', complete with bronze chariots, terracotta horses, the remains of real horses, and terracotta figures of grooms. The chariots feature paper-thin bronze umbrellas less than 0.2 centimetres (1/12 inch) thick to protect the drivers from the elements. Scientists today have no idea how the ancient metalworkers were able to manufacture such delicate and precise creations. No tools or technology capable of engineering such a feat have ever been discovered, although the technological methods they used to make many of the chariots' moving parts are still in use today. Another pit holds sixty-eight soldiers who are taller than the massed warriors: 188 centimetres (6 feet 2 inches) compared with 175 centimetres

(5 feet 8 inches). Archaeologists presume that this is the command centre for the highest-ranking warriors. Yet another pit contains some very unusual clay figures—acrobats, jugglers and other entertainers who are spinning, jumping or dancing.

To the northwest lies a palace, a miniature model of the empire that Qin created, complete with mountains and valleys, and lakes and rivers of mercury. The mausoleum is yet to be unearthed, but architects' plans describe how its ceiling is studded with pearls and other precious gems to emulate the pattern of stars in the sky. Whale oil lamps caused the 'stars' to shimmer and reflect in the mercury lake below. Concubines who had not borne children to Qin were interred next to him, to accompany him into the afterlife and perhaps provide him with heirs.

The smelting methods used to manufacture the arrows, arrowheads and trigger mechanisms were remarkably advanced. A similar crossbow design did not appear in Europe until some 1000 years later. The arrow shafts were made of iron doped with carbon in a blast furnace, indicating history's first use of steel. This technique next appeared in Scandinavia about 800 BC, a thousand years later, and in the rest of Europe about 300 years after that. The bronze tips of the arrows were coated in corrosion-proof chromium, a technique that did not appear in the West until the nineteenth century. These items, despite being buried for more than two thousand years, are still in perfect, untarnished condition. The precision and consistent proportions of the triangular arrow bolts indicate extremely advanced metallurgical techniques. The perfect consistency of the weapons' components meant that parts were interchangeable—a valuable strategic asset that allowed rapid running repairs in the heat of battle. Qin had created the world's first military–industrial complex.

Preparation for the afterlife

An army of terracotta warriors, each weighing about half a tonne, is contained in four pits to the east of the central tomb complex. They were transported, presumably by horse and cart, from the firing kilns several kilometres away. The torsos were constructed using coils of clay mixed with white quartz dust that were pressed together then forced into a mould. (Exactly the same technique is used to make terracotta today.) The limbs were constructed the same way and then attached to the body. The hands and feet, moulded separately, were inserted into holes in the limbs and secured with slip (wet clay). The bodies were then clad in handmade clay pieces fashioned to resemble the various soldiers' uniforms. Before the head was added, the bodies were slowly dried in a warm kiln then baked at 1000°C (1800°F) for five days. The heads were then fired before being loosely placed on the bodies; they are removable. The heads are as individual as the bodies are similar. Each was moulded and sculpted separately by artisans who created individual facial features and expressions, hairstyles and head gear. Some look serious and sombre; others appear amused, bewildered, startled or sad. The 'hair' on some of the soldiers was coloured with charcoal. After firing, some (perhaps all) of the soldiers were brightly painted.

The troops were then placed in formation, and the pit covered with pine logs. A layer of plaster powder was sprinkled on top, then a layer of woven hessian-type material. The plaster hardened as it gradually absorbed moisture. Finally, a layer of earth about 1.5 metres (5 feet) thick was placed over the matting, concealing the fruits of the world's first mass-production assembly line.

The actual mausoleum is protected by a series of booby traps comprising phalanxes of crossbows with bronze-tipped arrowheads, which are set up to be activated by tripwires and also by the opening of the entrance door. (This is one reason why the area remains for the present undisturbed; another is that we do not yet have the technology to prevent the paint from dissolving almost as soon as it comes into contact with air.) After Qin's burial, at his instruction, one of his trusted lieutenants sealed the door to the tomb from the outside, entombing all the workers who had built the mausoleum in order to keep its location secret.

The end of Qin

Qin died suddenly in 210, probably as a result of mercury poisoning, and was succeeded by

One of the terracotta regiments buried with Qin Shihuangdi which would help continue his domination in the afterlife.

his eighteenth son Huhai, who was not nearly as competent as his father. He was unable to prevent civil revolts and invasion by the other resurgent states, starting with the Zhao.

Three years later the Qin Empire collapsed, heralding the start of the Han Dynasty, which lasted four hundred years. The Han reintroduced the teachings of Confucianism from the earlier Zhou Dynasty, but preserved most of Qin's economic and political reforms. Thus Qin's work has carried on through the centuries and become an enduring feature of Chinese society. His widespread reforms had created the world's greatest nation-state. Giant projects like the Great Wall and the canal systems provided unprecedented security to the populace, particularly the peasant classes.

But in the process, the dynasty had become terminally fatigued.

Qin's historical legacy is mixed. He achieved greater power than Napoleon Bonaparte and controlled more territory than Alexander the Great. He commanded the biggest army in history. Some regard him as an imperialist megalomaniac who enslaved his people, brutally eliminated his opponents and imposed his views on the entire population. Others point to the efficiencies and economies of scale resulting from his standardisation of language, writing, weights, measurement and currency, and the newfound security experienced by most of the citizenry. The Chinese government has said that Qin's necropolis may remain forever unearthed. He has attained a kind of immortality after all.

30 BC

CLEOPATRA DEAD. SUICIDE ENDS EGYPTIAN DYNASTY

In 30 BC the last pharaoh of the ancient Egyptian Empire committed suicide—bitten by an asp that she had smuggled into her Roman-guarded prison. Cleopatra had a charismatic personality, was a born leader and an ambitious monarch, and one of the most dynamic rulers in the ancient world. Her reign was one of skilful opportunism, initially co-ruling with her father, then with her brothers, and later in alliance with the Roman juggernauts Julius Caesar and Mark Antony. When she and Antony pitted Egypt against the mighty Roman Empire, she set a course for one of the most dramatic downfalls in history.

THE DEATH OF EGYPT'S LAST PHARAOH

I will not be triumphed over.

CLEOPATRA VII

Cleopatra VII (69–30 BC) was the last of seven Ptolemaic Egyptian queens of the same name. She ruled from 51 to 30 BC and, with the assistance of Roman leaders Julius Caesar and, later, Mark Antony, extended the reach of the Egyptian Empire. But her downfall led to end of the Ptolemaic line, and marked the start of Roman rule over Egypt. The Ptolemaic line had been ruling Egypt since the brilliant military ruler Alexander the Great, king of Macedon, conquered the region almost three hundred years earlier, uniting Europe and Asia for the first time. Ptolemy, one of Alexander's generals, took control of Egypt after Alexander died.

Cleopatra was bright, politically astute and well educated; she was said to be the first Ptolemy to actually learn the Egyptian language (the Ptolemies' native language was Greek) and she was fluent in at least seven others. Cleopatra was also reputed to be a brilliant singer and orator, and very witty. Several contemporary accounts claim that she was not physically attractive in the conventional sense, but more than made up for it with her many other skills. There is no shortage of evidence that she was a superb and successful seductress.

An approach to Caesar

Cleopatra first ruled in association with her father, Ptolemy XII, who came to power in 80 BC. When he died in 51 BC, the eighteen-year-old Cleopatra shared the throne with her twelve-year-old brother Ptolemy XIII. The first three years of their reign were blighted by many problems, including economic difficulties, famine, drought (which prevented the River Nile from flooding and caused crops to fail) and political struggles—including civil war caused by Cleopatra's obvious intention to rule in her own right. When Ptolemy's supporters succeeded in ousting her from power in 48 BC, Cleopatra tried to muster support for a rebellion but eventually was forced to flee for her life to Rome, which at the time held a tenuous control over Egypt. She set her sights on Roman ruler Julius Caesar, determined to gain his favours by any means necessary to secure his alliance in her quest to wrest power back from her brother—even if it meant delivering to Rome full control over Egypt.

Greek historian Plutarch, writing over a hundred and fifty years later, describes how Cleopatra charmed Caesar with her beauty:

She took a small boat, and one only of her confidants, Apollodorus, the Sicilian, along with her, and in the dusk of the evening landed near the palace. She was at a loss how to get in undiscovered, till she thought of putting herself into the coverlet of a bed and lying at length, whilst Apollodorus tied up the bedding and carried it on his back through the gates to

Caesar's apartment. Caesar was first captivated by this proof of Cleopatra's bold wit, and was afterwards so overcome by the charm of her society that he made a reconciliation between her and her brother, on the condition that she should rule as his colleague in the kingdom.

An alliance is formed

Cleopatra's connection with Rome had first been forged through Roman leader Pompey, who had been appointed as her guardian when her father died. After Pompey was defeated by Caesar at Pharsalia (in northern Greece) in 48 BC, he fled to Egypt, where he was murdered at the behest of Ptolemy XIII—probably in an attempt to please Caesar and gain the support of Rome, to which Egypt was heavily indebted. This was a disastrous blunder, for when Caesar arrived in Egypt two days later and Ptolemy presented him with Pompey's pickled head, Caesar was enraged. Although they were political enemies, Pompey had been a high-ranking Roman consul, and the husband of Caesar's only daughter Julia, who had died while giving birth to their son.

As a result of the alliance between Cleopatra and Caesar, who was thirty-one years her senior, Cleopatra gained supreme power. Six months later Ptolemy XIII drowned in the Nile while trying to escape the combined forces of Cleopatra and Caesar. His youngest sister, Arsinoe IV, who had been proclaimed queen by the people of Alexandria, was captured and taken to Rome. Caesar was afraid that his affair with Cleopatra, by now an open secret, would further inflame Egyptian (and Roman) hostility. Knowing that it was an Egyptian tradition for royal siblings to marry each other, and that in former times pharaohs had commonly married their own daughters and sisters (an arrangement which Romans considered grotesque and degenerate), the lovers arranged for twenty-two-year-old Cleopatra to enter into a sham marriage of convenience with another, younger brother, Ptolemy XIV.

Death of Caesar

In 47 BC Cleopatra bore a son to Caesar, whom she named Ptolemy Caesarion. But, against Cleopatra's wishes, Caesar refused to appoint Caesarion as his heir, naming instead his grand-nephew Octavian—a decision which would, in time, rebound disastrously. Cleopatra and Caesarion went to live with Caesar in Rome in 46 BC, their open association causing a great scandal. There were whispers that Caesar intended to install himself as king of Rome with Cleopatra as his queen. After Caesar was murdered by his opponents in the Senate in 44 BC, Cleopatra and Caesarion fled back to Egypt. Soon afterwards her brother Ptolemy XIV died in mysterious circumstances—possibly poisoned—and Cleopatra set about regaining power, installing her toddler son as co-ruler.

By now the brilliant but debauched Roman general Mark Antony, having defeated Caesar's assassins Brutus and Cassius, ruled the eastern section of the empire of the Roman Republic. Concerned that Cleopatra might be making strategic alliances with his enemies, Mark Antony summoned her to Rome. She made a spectacular entrance—before working her magic on the married Antony just as she had on Caesar. She haughtily refused to meet him at his court; instead, she summoned him to her magnificent barge where he found her dressed as Venus (the goddess of love and beauty), reclining sumptuously on silken pillows and being fanned with gold-plated peacock feathers by young boys dressed as Cupid, her handmaidens dressed as

FOLLOWING PAGES: Ever the artful politician, Cleopatra summons Mark Antony to her barge.

mermaids with silver threads plaited through their hair. Plutarch chronicled the next stage of Cleopatra's seduction of Antony:

The following day, Antony invited her to supper, and was very desirous to outdo her as well in magnificence as contrivance; but he found he was altogether beaten in both, and was so well convinced of it that he was himself the first to jest and mock at his poverty of wit and his rustic awkwardness. She, perceiving that his raillery was broad and gross, and savoured more of the soldier than the courtier, rejoined in the same taste, and fell into it at once, without any sort of reluctance or reserve. For her actual beauty, it is said, was not in itself so remarkable that none could be compared with her, or that no one could see her without being struck by it, but the contact of her presence, if you lived with her, was irresistible; the attraction of her person, joining with the charm of her conversation, and the character that attended all she said or did, was something bewitching.

A new consort

Cleopatra and the besotted Antony soon returned to Egypt, spending the winter at Alexandria. In December 40 BC she bore him twins: Alexander Helios (Sun-god) and Cleopatra Selene (Moon-goddess). Cleopatra catered to Antony's every whim; at one feast she ordered her servants to cook twelve pigs at different times, so that one of them would be ready whenever he wanted it.

Shortly afterward Antony returned to Rome, correctly assuming that his political opponents would be taking advantage of his absence, and resumed married life with his wife Octavia Minor. But in 37 BC he returned to Egypt to rejoin Cleopatra and meet their children for the first time. They had another child, Ptolemy Philadelphus. Meanwhile, alarm was growing among Romans that Antony had abandoned his empire for a life of hedonism with an Egyptian. To make matters worse, Antony's co-ruler Octavian, grand-nephew of Caesar, was slandering Antony and boosting his own power base. Fearing Egypt's wealth and power, the Senate was intent upon gaining complete domination of the province (at this stage Rome was levying taxes on Egypt but did not hold full political control). Antony, however, still enamoured of his Egyptian lover, bestowed on Cleopatra huge areas of Cyprus, Lebanon and Syria, and appointed their children as monarchs of these and other countries. This was too much for Octavian and the Senate (and for Octavia Minor, who was furious that Antony had deserted her).

The end of a dynasty

Rome declared war on Egypt, eventually defeating Cleopatra and Antony's forces at the Battle of Actium in 31 BC. Believing that Cleopatra was dead, Antony committed suicide. Cleopatra fled to the luxurious mausoleum in Alexandria that she had constructed for herself and her treasures, where she remained under house arrest by Octavian's soldiers. Rather than face her inevitable fate, and perhaps preferring death to the humiliation of a Roman conquest, Cleopatra arranged for a venomous asp (a traditional symbol of Egyptian royalty) to be smuggled into her room in a basket of figs. One morning Octavian's soldiers found her dead; on her arm were two pinprick marks from the fangs of the asp. Caesarion was pronounced pharaoh by the Egyptians, but Octavian had him imprisoned, then strangled. (It is reputed that his name too closely resembled 'Caesar' and that Octavian, also known as Augustus Caesar, was advised that 'it was a bad thing to have too many Caesars'.)

Octavian declared himself Pharaoh of Egypt on 30 August, ending the Ptolemaic reign and the last Egyptian dynasty forever.

79 AD

POMPEII BURIED ALIVE

On 24 August AD 79, Mount Vesuvius unleashed its fury and erupted above the Bay of Naples. Residents and visitors in Pompeii looked up and watched a sinister cloud of ash billowing above the wealthy resort town. Nineteen hours after the eruption started the Roman towns of Pompeii, Herculaneum and Stabiae were destroyed, buried beneath tonnes of ash and volcanic rock along with all those who had not heeded the warning clouds and fled.

THE ERUPTION OF MOUNT VESUVIUS

A cloud ... shot up to a great height in the form of a very tall trunk, which spread itself out at the top into a sort of branches.

PLINY THE YOUNGER, WITNESS TO THE ERUPTION

Just before noon, towards the end of a hot August summer's day on the west coast of central Italy, the long-dormant volcano Mount Vesuvius burst into life with a deafening bang followed by the release of a tall, white cloud of smoke. The sky turned dark and the sun disappeared as dirt, mud and red-hot boulders were hurled into the air. Blown by the prevailing northwest wind, the debris began to rain down on the nearby city of Pompeii, which had a population of around twenty thousand people. Burning pumice stones followed by ash then rained down, and the air became poisoned with the acrid, deadly fumes of sulphur dioxide and hydrochloric acid. Those who survived the initial downpours and did not flee immediately were asphyxiated as they sought to escape—before being buried under a shroud of ash. After the poisonous gases came a rain of mud and damp ashes, which solidified as it cooled and preserved everything on which it fell.

Archaeologists uncover a forgotten city

We do not know how many people died, but the toll certainly measured in the thousands. Pompeii gradually faded from memory until 1748, when archaeologists began digging through layers of debris, unearthing human forms captured at the moment of death. After the

ashes had solidified around the bodies, all but the skeletons had decomposed. Archaeologists poured plaster of Paris into the moulds to produce perfect copies of amazingly intricate detail. Individual hairs, facial lines, fish scales, grains in loaves of bread and other such details of animal and vegetable matter were seen. The health, and even the profession of the victims, could be ascertained by study of the skeleton— young men with osteoarthritis caused by hard work were probably slaves, while skeletal indentations made by sharp objects indicate the body of a soldier, undoubtedly on leave.

The Pompeiians were obviously taken completely unaware by the disaster, even though the warning signs were well documented. We know from the reconstruction works in progress that Pompeii and the surrounding areas had experienced a devastating earthquake sixteen years earlier, in 63 AD, after a long period of seismic inactivity, and there had been lesser quakes in the intervening period. For example, in one house archaeologists discovered a baking oven that had incurred major cracking, been repaired and plastered over, and then damaged again. But there had not been a major eruption since about 1800 BC, which lulled the locals into a false sense of security. We now know that long periods of quietude followed by earthquakes are strong portents of an imminent, catastrophic volcanic eruption, as was the case with Krakatoa in 1883; but the Romans, though aware that Vesuvius was 'alive', knew nothing of this. Local citizens often took recreational strolls inside its crater. The Romans had so little experience of volcanic eruptions they did not even have a word for 'volcano' in their lexicon, much less 'eruption'.

The fateful day

On the morning of the explosion, bread was baking in ovens as donkeys, attached by harnesses to grain mills of interlocking stone wheels, plodded their circular route around the bakery yard. The central fish market was a hive of activity as the morning's catch was cleaned, scaled and sold. Shops and market stalls were in full swing and the numerous wine bars, or *thermopolia*, were serving luncheon snacks of fruit, fish, salads, nuts and hard-boiled eggs. Wine jars in the cellars bore the world's first-known advertising pun, Vesuvinum—a combination of 'Vesuvius' and the Latin for wine, *vinum*. Oil lanterns hung from the ceilings and bronze containers for drinks were set into the bar, coins lying alongside them in readiness for the drinkers' next order—a custom still evident today. Families were preparing lunch and the public heated baths, their fires lit earlier that morning, were starting to fill with customers wishing to perform ablutions or escape the heat of the day. At the Temple of Isis, priests were preparing to

Volcanic clouds billow ominously above the idyllic town of Pompeii and its unsuspecting inhabitants.

eat their lunch of eggs, fish, nuts and lentils. Street vendors were selling various products, including flatbread, pies, poultry and fish.

Workers were cleaning at the city's cultural venues such as the Odeon and the Great Theatre. The Odeon was a small, covered concert and poetry theatre that featured intricate carved figures 'holding up' the stone walls at the end of each row of the stone terraced seats; the Great Theatre was a large open-air amphitheatre that hosted plays, pantomimes and gladiatorial bouts. Cloth covers had been erected to provide shade for the spectators.

Although the Romans were often flippant in their artistic depiction of gods, religion was nonetheless deeply entrenched in their everyday life. The state-approved religion honoured Olympic gods and emperors, and many household shrines displayed religious art. Many Romans belonged to various mystery cults, worshipping exotic foreign gods or goddesses, such as the Egyptian fertility goddess Isis.

Pompeii's art works—high and low

Many of Pompeii's buildings featured superb wall frescoes and intricate mosaics on the floors and walls. Depictions of snakes representing domestic protector-gods were a common feature of the fresco art. One magnificent mosaic on the floor of the luxurious private house known as the House of the Faun consisted of about one and a half million stones measuring on average 4 millimetres across (less than a quarter of an inch). The mosaic depicted the Battle of Issus (333 BC) in which Alexander the Great (the Macedonian king and imperialist general much admired by the Romans) defeated the Persian king Darius III. Pompeii's library held thousands of books made of rolls of papyrus, a paper made from processed marsh reeds.

The Romans had a far more permissive attitude to sexual matters than we do, and the numerous brothels contained frescoes advertising and illustrating the cost and particular services available within for both men and women. Pompeii was a booming sea port, and crews of military and merchant ships availed themselves of its erotic services when they took recreational shore leave. The wage of even the lowest-paid prostitute was more than triple that of an unskilled labourer. Erotic art and frescoes were very widespread throughout the city, but much of what may appear pornographic to modern eyes was in fact fertility imagery, representing respectful supplication to various deities such as Priapus, always depicted with a very over-sized erect penis. Many household items, such as salt-shakers and lamps, also had sexual motifs.

Graffiti was widespread in Pompeii, covering many external and internal walls of both public and private buildings. In the red light district, comments such as 'I came here, screwed many women, then went home' and 'Atimetus got me pregnant' were scrawled on the walls. Some graffiti (and more permanent art works) cast aspersions on the poor quality of nearby business competitors' merchandise. Other popular graffiti subjects were businesses advertising daily specials, political slogans, election campaign material, and magic spells and invocations (the new heretical cult of Christianity had, as yet, few adherents). One city wall displayed the droll message 'I wonder, oh wall, that you have not fallen in ruins from supporting the stupidities of so many scribblers'.

Lives of luxury and plenty

An iron chest discovered in the house of Lucius Caecilius Jucundus, a banker, contained

132 wooden writing tablets covered in a thin layer of beeswax. Into the wax were carved such records as receipts and account details, signed by the banker and many of Pompeii's well-to-do citizens. One of Pompeii's most opulent buildings was a villa owned by the aristocratic Vetti brothers who made their fortune selling wine and other beverages. Situated in the centre of town, it featured a large, central, beautifully landscaped garden surrounded by a peristyle, or group of columns. Trees and herbs were arranged around stone tables, statues and mosaic pathways. In the house of another nobleman, Lucius Secundus, one wall featured a huge fresco showing lions hunting various kinds of prey, reflecting the popularity of African landscapes throughout the Roman Empire, which by this time stretched as far as northern Africa.

The house of Marcus Loreius Tiburtinus had a huge rear garden with water channels, magnificent landscaped beds of edible and ornamental plants, wooden lattice fences and an open-air dining room, or *triclinium*, with ornate fresco-covered walls. Some houses contained industrial workshops—fullers cleaned and dyed cloth, while mechanics' shops maintained and repaired chariots and carts. Warehouses held clay pots containing wine, grains, olive oil, vegetables and honey. Beekeeping was practised in and around Pompeii, and honey pots were labelled with the type of honey and its origin, for instance Corsican, thyme, or crystalline. Many Pompeiians adorned themselves with magnificent gold jewellery. The rich noblewoman Poppaea Sabina owned a magnificent, spiral upper-arm band in the shape of a snake, with intricately carved scales, eyes and other details.

At the nearby coastal town of Herculaneum (which would soon be buried by the lava flow rather than the pumice and ash that choked Pompeii), a festival to honour the memory of Augustus, Rome's first emperor, was under way as local fishermen sold the morning's catch.

Food, festivals and gatherings

Most food consumed at Pompeii came from the surrounding region. The Bay of Naples provided fish, crustaceans and other seafood, which were also farmed in ponds. Game such as pigs and deer were hunted in the nearby mountains, while the countryside contained fruit and vegetable market gardens, and cattle and poultry breeding farms. Vineyards flourished on many nearby farms and covered the hillsides on the outskirts of the city, while the foothills of Vesuvius, with its rich volcanic soil, produced wines of excellent quality. Grapes were pressed on farms and in the city itself.

Under Roman law, cemeteries had to be positioned outside the city walls. Pompeii's cemeteries were situated outside the Gate of Herculaneum and the Gate of Nuceria, and featured many impressive stone mausoleums holding the remains of the rich. Those who lived well died well, while the ashes of less wealthy citizens and slaves were buried in clay urns.

The Pompeii Forum was a large and important public meeting place, typical of those found in Rome and other cities throughout the empire. It was used for public meetings, court hearings, political rallies and markets. Pompeii's citizens enjoyed sports, both as participants and spectators. Inside the public gymnasium, or *palaestra*, men wrestled, boxed, jogged or lifted weights. Outside they participated in sports such as javelin and discus. Lessons were available, and competitions held. There were several public baths, including a complex comprising a 30-metre (100-foot) swimming pool with adjoining saunas, a ball court and a designated women-only area. The baths were a popular gathering place where people met friends, drank wine or sought sexual partners. The amphitheatre featured spectator sports including animal hunts, gladiator fights and chariot races. On the day of the explosion, sixty-three people died in the adjoining barracks, including two prisoners in their cells.

An eyewitness account

We have an excellent eyewitness account of the explosion, recorded twenty-five years later by the philosopher, administrator and poet Pliny the Younger, for the great Roman historian Tacitus. Pliny's uncle, Pliny the Elder, a naval commander who wrote the thirty-seven-volume *Natural History*—the longest scientific treatise in Latin that has survived from antiquity—was killed in the explosion, as he and his fleet attempted to assist fleeing citizens. Pliny was just seventeen years old at the time, and was stationed at Misenum, some 30 kilometres (18 miles) distant, so he had a grandstand view of the catastrophe. He was forced to flee for his life the next day as the deadly eruptions continued. The following extracts from his letters are from a translation made by William Melmoth in 1746.

Pliny describes the initial ash cloud and the upheavals that transformed the landscape:

And now cinders, which grew thicker and hotter the nearer he approached, fell into the ships, then pumice-stones too, with stones blackened, scorched, and cracked by fire, then the sea ebbed suddenly from under them, while the shore was blocked up by landslips from the mountains ...

He then describes the perilous situation confronting his uncle as he attempted to assist those escaping the conflagration:

The house now tottered under repeated and violent concussions, and seemed to rock to and fro as if torn from its foundations ... It was now day everywhere else, but there a deeper darkness prevailed than in the most obscure night; relieved, however, by many torches and diverse illuminations. They thought proper to go down upon the shore to observe from close at hand if they could possibly put out to sea, but they found the waves still run extremely high and contrary. There my uncle, having thrown himself down upon a disused sail, repeatedly called for, and drank, a draught of cold water; soon after, flames, and a strong smell of sulphur, which was the forerunner of them, dispersed the rest of the company in flight; him they only aroused. He raised himself up with the assistance of two of his slaves, but instantly fell; some unusually gross vapour, as I conjecture, having obstructed his breathing and blocked his windpipe, which was not only naturally weak and constricted, but chronically inflamed. When day dawned again (the third from that he last beheld) his body was found entire and uninjured, and still fully clothed as in life; its posture was that of a sleeping, rather than a dead man ...

Aftermath

The catastrophic eruption of Vesuvius lasted two days, extinguishing life, destroying buildings, homes and monuments, and leaving survivors vulnerable to looting and starvation.

The traumatised survivors chose not to rebuild Pompeii and it faded from memory until the mid eighteenth century, when archaeologists began their systematic excavation of the city and its splendours became known to the world once more.

RIGHT: Preserved beneath the ash at Pompeii is evidence of the town's rich and vibrant culture.

610 AD

A NEW PROPHET AND A NEW RELIGION

The prophet Muhammad (meaning 'praised' or 'glorified' in Arabic) was born in 570 AD in the desert town of Mecca, in present-day Saudi Arabia. According to tradition, he received a series of visions from the angel Gabriel, which he recorded and passed on to a small group of disciples. His revelations are found in the Qur'an, the sacred scripture that Muslims consider to be the final revelation of God. Together with the record of his acts and the 114 *suras* (verses) he composed, it forms a guidebook of divine and moral direction for humankind.

THE CALLING OF MUHAMMAD

[2:82] As for those who believe, and lead a righteous life,
they will be the dwellers of Paradise; they abide in it forever.

FROM MUHAMMAD'S 114 *SURAS*

At the time of Muhammad's birth the Arab world was made up of various warring states. Muhammad's parents died when he was very young; he was brought up by his grandfather, then by his uncle Abu Talib, whom he accompanied on business trips to Syria, where it is said he came into contact with the teachings of Nestorian Christian monks. The monks were part of the eastern tradition of Christianity advanced by Nestorius, Patriarch of Constantinople, in the fifth century. In 583 one of these monks, Bahira, predicted the twelve-year-old Muhammad's future as a prophet to Abu Talib after experiencing divine manifestations in his presence.

As a young man Muhammad entered the service of the rich widow Khadijah, a merchant who organised trade caravans. When she was forty years old and he twenty-five, she proposed and they were wed. Their happy marriage of twenty years produced three sons (who died during childbirth) and four daughters—including Fatima, who married Muhammad's adopted son Ali. This union produced Muhammad's only future bloodline.

Muhammad's retreat

Muhammad, despite being a respected and successful member of the community, found it difficult to accept the prevailing polytheism and superstition practised by some Arabs, and became attracted to the ideas spread by Jews and Christians. He would often retreat to a mountain cave outside Mecca to practise asceticism and meditation. One night in 610, at forty years of age, he dreamt he was gripped around the throat by a strange being who ordered him to read a cloth scroll covered in symbols. Upon awakening he felt that a book had been written in his heart, and saw in the distance an angel, later identified as Gabriel. Convinced he was going mad, he returned home and related his experience to Khadijah, who reassured him—and became his first disciple. More visions followed, which Muhammad related to a small but growing group of converts including Ali, his other son-in-law Uthman, and his future fathers-in-law, Abu Bakr and Umar (they later became the first four Muslim caliphs or leaders). After three years of regular visions, Gabriel ordered him to begin a public preaching career.

Muhammad delivered sermons on the evils of materialism, the wrath of God and the imminent Day of Judgment. His statements were largely scorned, not least because they endangered Mecca's religious—and hence economic—status quo. His followers (known as Muslims, 'those who give their souls to God') were persecuted although Muhammad himself, despite suffering constant insults and threats, was protected by his membership of the powerful merchant clan Banu Hashim.

Muhammmad's followers grow in number

As Muhammad's followers grew in number, they became a threat to Mecca's rulers, who depended for their livelihood upon the Ka'bah, a shrine made of granite that housed numerous statues representing over three hundred tribal gods. Muhammad now threatened to overthrow the shrine and rededicate it as an Islamic house of worship. His condemnation of traditional religion was a particular threat to his own tribe, the Quraysh, who profited by their guardianship of the Ka'bah, and thus had much to lose. They offered him entry into the inner circle of merchants, the kingship and a lucrative, prestigious marriage, but he refused.

In 619, the 'year of sorrows', both his wife Khadijah and his uncle (and leader of the Banu Hashim clan) Abu Talib died. The new clan leader was Abu Lahab, who was a sworn enemy of Muhammad and withdrew the clan's protection. Muhammad was now in great danger, since the removal of protection meant that, should he be murdered, retribution for his killing would not be required under law. However, he was able to find another guardian, Mut'im ibn Adi, and the protection of his clan Banu Nawfal.

Muhammad now experienced his most famous and intense vision, as Gabriel teleported him on the back of the winged horse Boraq from Mecca to Jerusalem (this event is referred to as the *isra*, meaning night journey), where he prayed in the ruins of a temple. He ascended to Heaven *(*the *mi'raj* or ascension), where he saw the throne of God and the prophets Moses and Jesus, and was told that he held similar exalted status. God then imparted to him the five daily prayers that are, to this day, the practical basis of Muslim religious observance.

Flight to Medina

In 622 Muhammad and his followers fled Mecca, an event described as the *hijra* or emigration, to Yathrib (soon renamed Medina, 'city of the prophet'), about 300 kilometres (186 miles) to the north, whose citizens had asked Muhammad to help mediate in their internal disputes. While his fame as a negotiator, judge and sage continued to grow, along with his group of followers, the Meccans still considered him a threat. Between 624 and 627, in a series of battles between the people of Medina and the Meccans, Muhammad displayed great political and military ability as he won significant victories over the Meccans. This helped to confirm the authenticity of his calling. In the first of these encounters at Badr, south of Medina, in March 624, just 313 Muslims defeated an army of 1000 Meccans. After the Muslims' victory in Medina in 627 over a combined Meccan–Jewish army at the Battle of the Ditch, a truce was called. Muhammad then sought the endorsement of Medina's thriving Jewish community, pointing out that he shared their monotheistic viewpoint and accepted the legitimate authority of all the biblical prophets, including Jesus. But the Jews, disagreeing with his interpretation of the scriptures, refused to be a party to the treaty—so the Muslims beheaded the men and enslaved the women and children.

In 629 Muhammad made the first *hajj* (or pilgrimage) to Mecca, a tradition still carried out annually by hundreds of thousands of pilgrims. He then created the *suras*, a series of precepts that are usually placed at the beginning of the Qur'an. The following year the Meccans broke

RIGHT: A sixteenth-century Persian painting showing Muhammad's ascent into heaven.

the truce, but by now Muhammad had an army of more than ten thousand followers. They conquered and captured Mecca, destroyed all the idols and pagan images in the Ka'bah and elsewhere, and either killed or expelled the Jews who were agitating against them. Muhammad held that the Jews had persecuted the exalted prophet Jesus and his mother but had in fact failed to kill him—a ghost had been crucified in his place.

A new faith takes hold

Muhammad had clearly defined the decrees of the new faith and now enjoyed increasing power. His religion had gradually become more Arabic in tone, and from this time became centred on Abraham, father of the Jews, and his son Ismael, precursor of the Arabs and believed to be the founder of the Ka'bah. From now on, Muslims would face Mecca when they prayed; previously they had directed themselves toward Jerusalem.

By 631 Muhammad's influence and support extended over most of the Arab world, thus ending what he called 'the age of ignorance'. In March 632, at the age of about sixty-two, he preached his final sermon to some two hundred thousand people at Mount Arafat, which was about 20 kilometres (12 miles) east of Mecca. On 8 June, at Medina, he died suddenly in the home of Aishah, the favourite of his nine wives and the daughter of Abu Bakr, one of his original followers. His body lies in a tomb at Al-Masjid n-Nabawiy ('The Mosque of the Prophet') at Medina, which was built next to his home and is venerated throughout Islam. Muslims believe that a prayer in this mosque is worth at least a thousand prayers in any other mosque, apart from the Ka'bah.

Muhammad proved to be a great military as well as religious leader, and led his followers to conquer Mecca.

Muhammad left as his successors his daughter Fatima—who had two sons—and his several wives, who included the daughters of his advisers, the caliphs Umar and Abu Bakr. Two separate factions emerged from this group, the Shiites and the Sunnis, setting in train a power dispute that is still evident today (notably in the sectarian bloodshed that blights modern Iraq). The minority Shiites held that future caliphs should be selected from the descendants of Fatima whereas the Sunnis recognised the lineage of the four caliphs.

Islam after Muhammad

Islam, which means 'surrender (to the will of God)' had already enjoyed a remarkably rapid expansion, which after Muhammad's death continued apace. Within a century Islam had spread its influence over large swathes of the Western world. After Muhammad's death, Sunni caliph Abu Bakr took only two or three years to consolidate Islam in Arabia by completing the task of uniting the numerous disparate tribes. After he died in 634 Muhammad's other father-in-law, Umar (an astute military commander), became caliph and conquered Jerusalem, Syria, Lebanon, Armenia, Egypt, much of North Africa, and most of Iraq and Persia (Iran). He was assassinated in 644, whereupon Muhammad's son-in-law Uthman took over, conquering Cyprus, the Caucasus, more holdings in North Africa and the rest of Persia.

Over the next fifty years Islam spread to the remainder of the Middle East, and to modern-day Pakistan, Uzbekistan, Kazakhstan and Tajikistan. Almost thirty years after the death of Mohammad, Ali (Mohammad's cousin as well as Fatima's husband) succeeded Uthman

after Uthman was killed in a civil war, but was himself assassinated in 661. His successor Muawiyah I, the governor of Syria, founded the Sunni Umayyad dynasty which ruled until 750, conquering Gibraltar, Catholic Spain and Portugal on the Iberian peninsula (with the help of the recently converted North African Moors), as far north as the Pyrenees mountains, the border between Spain and France.

This expansion of Islamic control continued more or less unchallenged until the French defeated the Muslim armies at the Battle of Tours in 732. Meanwhile the Shiites were fighting to secure various regions of Syria and Iraq against Sunni control. Shiite caliph Husain, a son of Fatima and Ali, was killed in Iraq at the Battle of Karbala in 680; his martyrdom is still mourned by modern Shiites.

Muhammad's teachings

The reasons for the extraordinarily rapid expansion of Islam are similar to the reasons that Muhammad's teachings were so vehemently opposed by the entrenched powers during his lifetime. He preached against the corrupt ruling hierarchies (which were based on class differences) in favour of the rights of the masses. He also spoke against many widespread Arab customs, including female infanticide, the vastly inferior status of women, and slavery. He abolished numerous tribal customs—which had led to endless conflicts— in favour of a single unifying Islamic law. He preached the virtues of modesty, fairness, respect, honesty, generosity of spirit, universal (rather than authoritarian) justice, and government based on merit rather than power, wealth or status.

THE MIDDLE AGES CHRONICLE

LEFT: In 1271 Marco Polo set sail from Venice on his twenty-four-year round trip to the court of Kublai Khan.

747–814

POPE CROWNS CHARLEMAGNE

On Christmas Day in 800, while Charlemagne, king of the Franks, knelt in prayer in Saint Peter's in Rome, Pope Leo III placed a crown on his bowed head. With this act Charlemagne was appointed the first modern Emperor of Romans. This account describes the rise of Charlemagne, who 'by sword and the cross' became the ruler of an area that now includes France, Switzerland, Belgium, the Netherlands, half of present-day Italy and Germany, and parts of Austria and Spain.

CHARLEMAGNE AND THE BIRTH OF THE HOLY ROMAN EMPIRE

To have another language is to possess a second soul.

CHARLEMAGNE

Charlemagne, known also as Charles the Great (742–814), was a formidable leader who unified western Europe through a combination of education, military force and the blessing of the Roman Catholic Church. He brought about wide-ranging political, religious and educational reforms that changed the history of Europe and more than doubled the size of the Frankish (roughly modern-day French) kingdom. The Frankish people were descended from the Germanic tribes who raided much of Europe from the third century onwards; they soon carved out a strong presence, gradually acquiring influence in Spain, Belgium, France, the Rhine regions and parts of Italy. One notable leader, Clovis, in 496, interspersed a career of conquest with his conversion to Catholicism. Almost three hundred years later, Charlemagne transformed Western Europe into a Christian empire that stretched from the west coast of France to Germany, the Low Countries (present-day Belgium, the Netherlands and Luxembourg), northern Spain and Italy. His court is renowned for its academic and artistic accomplishments, as well as its military achievements.

Early years

Charlemagne's birthplace is uncertain, but was probably in or near the town of Aachen (known by the French as Aix-La-Chapelle) near the border of Belgium, Germany and the Netherlands. His father Pépin III, unkindly known as Pépin the Short, and his grandfather Charles Martel were both rulers of the Frankish world. Martel had started the process of transforming Europe, operating from the standpoint that Christianity was not only the one true religion, but was also the most effective force for political unification and peace. He was largely responsible for stopping the spread of Islam into Europe. Pépin continued the process, as did the young Charles, who therefore inherited an established tradition by which a king's significance was gauged by his success at war. This required him to formulate a method of government that would be able to maintain power over an increasingly fragmented population.

Charlemagne and his forebears believed that the Catholic Church should be reformed and reorganised under the aegis of the pope. They assisted the popes of the day in their struggles against the temporal rulers of Rome, the Byzantines, receiving in return papal recognition of their right to rule, and support for their European military campaigns. This in turn assisted their rise to power as founders of what became known as the Carolingian (named for Charlemagne) dynasty. When Pépin died in 768, Charles and his brother Carloman each inherited half of the Frankish empire, following the tradition of the existing Merovingian dynasty. Three years later, when Carloman died, Charles took over the entire kingdom, inheriting great riches and a formidable army.

Christianity is enforced

Eighth century Western Europe was a largely heathen world, with many warring tribes and kingdoms. Charlemagne embarked upon a series of military operations, starting with the Saxons in northwest Germany. The Saxon wars lasted thirty-three years as Charlemagne rampaged across their lands, burning towns and massacring the inhabitants in persistent attempts to force Christianity on them. These campaigns marked one of the few occasions on which Charlemagne was not completely victorious; he actually defeated the Saxons several times, but did not maintain a strong enough occupying force to prevent them reverting to their previous beliefs and way of life.

Although Charlemagne generally respected the traditions and customs of the territories he conquered, providing his new subjects embraced Christianity, at times his resolute drive for domination spilled over into cold-bloodedness. His religious self-assurance led to his belief that ends, no matter how ruthless, generally justified the means. His nephews mysteriously disappeared while under his custody, and he deposed his cousin in order to conquer Bavaria. When his illegitimate son Pépin the Hunchback led a rebellion against him in 792, Charlemagne quashed the insurgency with great brutality. During one of the periodic Saxon rebellions, when they renounced Christianity and his authority (yet again), Charlemagne regarded it as heresy as well as treason, killing four thousand Saxons in one day in an attempt to discourage such uprisings in future. After Pope Gregory III approved and blessed his conquest of Byzantine Italy, he reneged on his promise to increase papal landholdings, deciding to keep Lombardy for himself.

Support for the pope

Charlemagne turned his attentions to Italy, where the papacy's sphere of influence had shrunk to only a small portion of land around Rome and was under continuous threat from the Lombards, a Germanic people who were at war with both Rome and Byzantium. In 773 Pope Hadrian I appealed to Charlemagne, who quickly defeated the Lombards. Charlemagne's second eldest legitimate son Carloman was granted the title King of the Lombards and took the name Pépin, while the pope regained power over northern Italy.

From Italy Charlemagne moved on to Spain, where he experienced partial success in annexing the northern area near the Pyrenees mountains, but failed in attempts to head south and conquer the Iberian peninsula. Southern Spain, controlled by the North African Moors, resisted several invasion attempts, and succeeded in maintaining its Islamic faith and control for several centuries to come. But Charlemagne was able to create a buffer between Africa and Europe; in 781 he created the kingdom of Aquitaine, which was ruled by his son Louis. The western Frankish empire was now largely peaceful, so Charlemagne headed north in a successful attempt to subdue the fiercely independent Bavarians of western Germany. This brought him up against the Avars, central Asian nomads who had occupied the lands around the river Danube and had their eye on further westward expansion. Charlemagne succeeded in looting and conquering their lands, and forcing them to convert to Christianity.

In 799 Pope Leo III, following a Roman insurrection against him, sought Charlemagne's protection. Although Leo was generally popular, members of the Roman nobility had attacked him during a procession, threatening to blind him and rip out his tongue. According to contemporary reports, the two leaders had arranged to have Pépin installed as king of Italy and Aquitaine. But on Christmas Day 800 at St Peter's Basilica in Rome, when the moment

On Christmas Day 800, Pope Leo III crowns Charlemagne Emperor of the Romans in Saint Peter's Basilica.

came, Leo placed the crown on Charlemagne's head instead, pronouncing him in traditional Roman terms *Imperator Romanorum* ('Emperor of the Romans'). This placed Charlemagne in an invidious position as it guaranteed the fervent opposition of the Romans—they looked very poorly on an attempt by an outsider to inherit the authority of the Caesars.

The Byzantine rulers of Italy already had a Christian leader in Constantinople and did not recognise papal authority, so Leo's actions were technically illegal and without authority. After his agreement to guard the pope, Charlemagne was not amused at this very public anointing and exposition of his role. But his irritation may have been feigned; although he had gone to Rome to restore the political equilibrium of Christianity, and despite the fact that Leo's actions had actually destabilised it, Charlemagne made the most of the situation, intending to restore unity by proposing marriage to the Byzantine Empress Irene. But the scheme was abandoned when Irene was deposed soon afterwards. Nonetheless, Charlemagne's armies continued to sweep through Europe, conquering many other tribes, including the Bretons on the western Frankish coast in modern Brittany, the Huns in western Asia, and the Danes.

Advances in education, art and architecture

The church and Charlemagne enjoyed a symbiotic relationship; they gave stability to each other's jurisdiction and quest for power. As each new area of Europe was conquered, Charlemagne murdered any leader who did not convert to Christianity and installed a new one, usually a high-ranking church official. Charlemagne employed church leaders as educators who used the Bible to teach morality in the numerous educational institutions he established. This was an important factor in aiding Charlemagne's genuine aim to improve the education of the people at a time when, other than members of the clergy, very few people were educated.

Another beneficial consequence of this policy was that Charlemagne was provided with ever-increasing numbers of educated people who proved very useful in assisting his administration. Although himself virtually illiterate (despite being fluent in Latin and able to speak some Greek), he standardised western European language by reviving Greek and making the study of Latin compulsory in all his institutions. He founded the Palace School in his home town, Aix-La-Chapelle. Many of the scholars brought to teach there were foreigners, including Italians, Spaniards and Irish who together developed a new style of script known as Carolingian minuscule, characterised by simple, rounded letters, which made it easier to learn, read and write.

Charlemagne attended the school, studying Latin, Greek, grammar, rhetoric, dialectics and astronomy. He tried to learn to write, but was not very successful, being a very late starter—although he was very articulate and eloquent in speech. His sons and daughters attended academic classes, as well as studying the traditional Frankish pursuits of riding and hunting for boys and cloth-making for girls. The education systems were very similar to those followed by classical Greek and Roman scholars. A teacher would read a text then explain it. The class then discussed the material, applying analytical, logical and disciplined reasoning.

Charlemagne introduced standard trading laws across his kingdom and stabilised coinage, regulating the amounts of silver and gold contained in each denomination. Since the fifth century, coins had been minted by many different manufacturers—with the result that their actual value varied greatly. Money was now publicly guaranteed and controlled by one source, rather than many.

Charlemagne also had a significant influence on art and architecture, restoring ancient Roman traditions. He commissioned impressive chapels for monasteries, providing large spaces where the masses could worship. The early constructions were mostly made of wood because it was a familiar material to the nomadic people of the time. But the need for defence and durability caused a return to stone construction, resulting in the resurrection of the Roman style of churches, monuments, gardens and arches. Aesthetic adornments, such as mosaics, gilding, marble statuary, ivory carvings and paintings, were other architectural features of the period. Precious gems, gold, silver, frescoes, terracotta, and plaster were also incorporated into the designs of churches, monuments and other buildings.

Honouring past achievements

Charlemagne attempted to honour traditional Frankish customs while responding resourcefully to new social forces. Intellectual and artistic stirrings were occurring throughout all of Latin Christendom. There was a growing desire to re-establish contact with the Classical past, which was seen as a fundamental requirement for the revitalisation of Christian society. Charlemagne possessed the personal qualities to successfully confront such a challenge. He was the supreme warrior chief, with an imposing physical presence and charisma, and possessed a remarkable constitution. Renowned for his personal courage and iron will, he loved action and physical pursuits of all kinds—fighting, travelling, hunting and swimming—but he was also a popular court companion, generous with

gifts and skilful at establishing and maintaining friendships. He married five times, owned several concubines and sired at least eighteen children, whose interests he oversaw conscientiously. These traits commanded respect, loyalty and affection. He was a natural leader, capable of making and acting on informed decisions and proficient at persuading others to assist him.

New threats from the sea

Although Charlemagne's armies were virtually invincible on land, the same could not be said for his navy. Vikings were attacking from the north while Spanish Muslims harried him from the south. Finding it difficult to repel advances on so many fronts simultaneously, in 811 Charlemagne began a concerted but unsuccessful military and diplomatic campaign to persuade Byzantine Emperor Michael I in Constantinople to recognise his Roman holdings. He planned to divide his empire among his three legitimate sons in the traditional way, but two of them, Charles (the eldest) and Pépin, died before him. In 813 he arranged for his son Louis, king of Aquitaine, to succeed him. He tried to confirm his religious primacy by holding the ceremony in Germany (as far as possible from Italy, the centre of Christian rule), and did not ask the pope to perform and legitimise the accession, as would have been expected.

When Charlemagne died in 814 Louis inherited a festering and complex (indeed byzantine) series of rivalries that, without Charlemagne's strong guidance and charisma, he was unable to negotiate. Nor was he able to effectively retain control over the many disparate tribes that had united under his father. It turned out that the empire's strength had rested not on its institutions and systems, but in its leader. Upon Louis' death in 840, his three sons inherited various separate parts of

the kingdom, but the lack of effective leadership they (and, in turn, their sons) displayed, led to the fragmentation of the previously united kingdom and its overthrow by the Frankish nobility in 880.

Charlemagne's legacy and a new empire

Nonetheless, Charlemagne's legacy lasted for centuries. The ambition to increase his empire was driven (and tempered) by his unswerving devotion and his desire to spread the Christian religion and use it as a source of peace and unity. His legislative system, constitution and governmental practices were used as the model by the French Capetian dynasty that ruled from 987 to 1328. His Carolingian empire eventually provided the model for the Holy Roman

LEFT: The oldest cathedral in northern Europe, at Aachen (Aix-la-Chapelle) in Germany, was built by Charlemagne in 792.

Empire, which was highly influential around the world until its dissolution in 1806. He revolutionised European cultural and spiritual life, and the relationship between politics and religion. He left behind thriving libraries, cathedrals and monasteries, and introduced schools and universities, which researched and taught many disciplines, including architecture, visual arts and history. He set up systems whereby eminent scholars educated the clergy, who in turn set up schools. He was extraordinarily persistent, compassionate in his actions (with a few exceptions that he deemed necessary in order to eliminate entrenched harmful practices), and perhaps wiser than any other ruler of his era.

In January 813, aged 72, Charlemagne contracted pleurisy and died a week later in the forty-seventh year of his reign. He was buried in Aachen Cathedral. His body was exhumed in 1215 on the orders of Frederick II and placed inside a gold and silver casket.

1043–1099

VALENCIA VANQUISHED

The popular hero of the chivalric age of Spain, El Cid, famously laid siege to Valencia and established a kingdom. He was given the title of *seid* or *cid* (lord, chief) by the Moors and that of *campeador* (champion) by his admiring countrymen. One legend has it that after El Cid died, his wife strapped his body to his horse and sent it back into battle, believing that his demoralised troops were about to be defeated. The troops, thinking that their leader was riding to fight beside them, rallied. The opposing army was so afraid of what looked to be an invincible fighter that they retreated to their boats. While the truth of his death is less dramatic, the story of El Cid is nevertheless spectacular.

THE CONQUEST OF A KINGDOM AND THE LEGEND OF EL CID

Ride, Cid, most noble Campeador, for never yet did knight
Ride forth upon an hour whose aspect was so bright.

VERSE I 14 FROM *EL CANTAR DE MIO CID*
(THE POEM OF THE CID)

Rodrigo Díaz de Vivar, the national hero of Spain, was one of the most complex military leaders of the Middle Ages. At various times he led armies on behalf of both the Christians and the Muslim Moors, who were fighting for control of Spain and the Iberian peninsula. Both groups—as well as warring with each other—were deeply divided within themselves. This led to a constantly shifting series of alliances between kingdoms, which often made it difficult to tell who was fighting whom.

Rodrigo's sobriquet 'El Cid', which he acquired during his lifetime, is a combination of the Spanish *el* (the) and the Arabic *cid* (lord), which seems appropriate since, alternately, he served both Christian Spain and the Moors. Sometimes the epithet *campeador*, a Latin word that roughly translates as 'master of military arts', is added to his name, further reflecting the multicultural nature of his exploits. His reputation has contradictory aspects—he was known for his diplomatic skills, his courage and his innate fairness, but also for being a duplicitous, opportunistic, cunning and ruthless man.

Beginning of a legend

El Cid was born about 1043 in the village of Bivar in northern Spain. His parents were minor nobility—his father Diego Laínez Díaz was an administrator in the Royal Court and a soldier. The young Rodrigo trained in knightly and military arts at the court of Prince Sancho, the eldest son of the reigning King Ferdinand I of Castile and Léon, and distinguished himself as a formidable soldier, winning the respect of his peers and mentors. When Ferdinand died in 1065 he was given command of Sancho's army.

Before he died, King Ferdinand allocated different areas of his kingdom to each of his three sons. His second (and favourite) son Alfonso was given the kingdom of Léon (a substantial area to the north) and the recently conquered Moorish kingdom of Toledo. García, his youngest son, was granted Portugal, Seville and the western province of Galicia. Sancho, despite being his first-born, was granted the smaller areas of Castile and Saragossa. (His two daughters, Urraca and Elvira, were granted power over all the monasteries in the kingdom, on condition that they did not marry or bear any offspring, thus creating new heirs.) Sancho was displeased with this arrangement, and told Ferdinand that he refused its terms on the grounds that it was unfair to him, the eldest son. But the old king refused to waver. Furthermore, he told the sons that they would be disinherited unless they deferred to Rodrigo, effectively placing him *in loco parentis*, even though he was roughly the same age as the brothers.

Sancho appointed Rodrigo as commander of his army and determinedly went about increasing his territory. In 1067 Rodrigo led Sancho's Castilian armies in a successful campaign against the Moorish city of Saragossa in northeastern Spain, extracting a promise of loyalty and immediate payment of the first annual tribute (tax) instalment. A contemporary Jewish chronicler attributed the success of the operation exclusively to Rodrigo, dubbing him *Cidi*, or 'my Lord'.

War between the brothers escalates

After Ferdinand's widow died in 1067 Sancho abandoned his adherence to his father's

The Castilian military leader Rodrigo Díaz, or El Cid, is one of the most celebrated knights in history.

allocation of territory and, by 1068, Castile was at war with Léon, which was ruled by his brother Alfonso. El Cid (as he was increasingly known) defeated Alfonso's army at the brief war of Llantada Plain on 19 July 1068 but Alfonso, reneging on an agreement that the loser would surrender and throw in his lot with the victor, fled south. He mustered his forces and successfully attacked the Moorish state of Badajoz, extracting a promise of future tributes even greater than those the state was already paying to the third brother, García. Inevitably, the war between the three brothers escalated; Sancho pretended to side with García against Alfonso, all the while awaiting his opportunity to annex García's domains of Portugal and Galicia.

It is not known whether El Cid tried to mediate in these internecine battles, as he had promised Ferdinand, but in 1071 Sancho and Alfonso defeated and captured García and split up his lands between them. Songs of the period say that that it was El Cid himself who captured García and delivered him to his brothers; perhaps he saw this as a way of ending the civil war that was destabilising Christian Spain. In any case, he stayed faithful to the eldest brother, Sancho, who escalated his war against Alfonso now that García was, to all intents and purposes, out of the picture.

Several border skirmishes led to the battle of Golpejera in which El Cid played a crucial role in Sancho's victory. During the battle Sancho was heard to comment that *he* was worth a thousand men—and Rodrigo another hundred. El Cid's humble reply was that he was only equal to a single man, and the rest was up to God. Alfonso was taken prisoner, perhaps by El Cid, and exiled to Toledo. Sancho declared himself King of Léon, which made him ruler of the largest kingdom in Spain. But Urraca, who,

some historians believe, held an incestuous infatuation for her brother Alfonso, organised a rebellion against the new king. While Sancho was waiting to visit Urraca's castle at Zamora an assassin murdered him. El Cid gave chase but the perpetrator escaped into Zamora where he was given refuge. Alfonso crowned himself King of Léon, Castile and Galicia and sought El Cid's support. El Cid agreed, but not before forcing Alfonso to declare before his subjects that he had had nothing to do with his brother's murder.

Despite this public humiliation, Alfonso honoured El Cid by arranging for him to marry his niece, Ximena Díaz. This had the effect of demonstrating the high esteem in which El Cid was held by the king, and was also designed to help heal the schism between Castile and Léon, though it did little to dispel the ongoing suspicion and mistrust between two strong individuals. Ximena bore El Cid two daughters, Cristina and Maria, and a son, Diego Rodríguez.

Intrigues at Alfonso's court and a new protector

Despite his marriage, El Cid's status at Alfonso's court was shaky. His enemies whispered to Alfonso that he was an unrepentant secret supporter of the Castilians who resented being ruled by the king of Léon, and they reminded him of the humiliation El Cid had subjected him to after Sancho's death. El Cid, for his part, disapproved of the influence of the nobility over Alfonso, and probably resented losing the position of Ensign (or Commander) of the Royal Armies that he held under Sancho. His inclination to humiliate powerful leaders probably contributed to his impending exile.

Alfonso exiled El Cid in 1081 after he invaded Alfonso's Moorish kingdom of Toledo. After several unsuccessful attempts to heal the rift, El Cid aligned himself with Moktadir, the Muslim king of Saragossa—whom he had helped defeat in 1067. The king jumped at the chance to employ the services of such a successful Christian warrior and El Cid served him, and his successor Motamid II, for the next ten years. This experience no doubt gave him an insight into the byzantine and ever-changing intricacies of Christian–Muslim and Spanish–Arabic politics, which would hold him in good stead in his future exploits.

In 1082 El Cid routed Moktadir's enemy, the Moorish king of Lérida, and his Christian allies, including the King of Barcelona. Two years later, despite being vastly outnumbered, he conquered an army that was led by the Christian king Sancho Ramírez of Aragón. His appreciative Muslim masters rewarded him greatly for these victories.

El Cid sets his sights on Valencia

But in 1086 Alfonso swallowed his pride and requested El Cid's assistance—his forces had been almost completely annihilated by the invading Berber Muslim Almoravids from Morocco. El Cid spent a short time at Alfonso's court in 1087 until, under the influence of El Cid's opponents, old animosities surfaced and Alfonso imprisoned his wife and children and banished El Cid to Saragossa. El Cid took no part in the war that was raging as the Almoravids threatened the very existence of Christian Spain. After a period as a mercenary, offering his skills to whoever would hire him, he decided to attempt an invasion of the prosperous Moorish kingdom of Valencia, ruled at the time by a Muslim–Christian coalition.

El Cid had no problem raising an army —many were keen to serve under such a successful and renowned warrior. They invaded the kingdoms of Deria and Lérida, capturing two castles and appropriating a cave full of treasure belonging to the lord of Lérida. With his forces boosted by the enemies of the vanquished Lérida, and new recruits attracted by the handsome wages he was now able to offer, El Cid set off for Valencia. Al-Kadir, the faint-hearted and indecisive ruler of Valencia, agreed to restore the tribute he had been paying to El Cid before his second banishment. But trouble loomed in the form of Berenguer, the powerful Count of Barcelona, who had been captured by El Cid in an earlier battle. Berenguer had formed a partnership with the Moorish lord of Lérida, and had tried to enlist the support of Alfonso. Much to the surprise of almost everyone, Alfonso refused. Nonetheless, El Cid's forces were so outnumbered as to make the prospect of victory, even for such an excellent leader as El Cid, very remote. El Cid's troops left Valencia and set up camp in a nearby valley, fortifying its three entrances with wooden bulwarks. Berenguer and El Cid exchanged a series of letters, accusing each other of treason and cowardice.

Meanwhile El Cid had allowed several of his men to desert, carrying the disinformation that he was preparing to make his escape through one of the passes leading into the valley. This had the desired result. Berenguer split his forces into three, one guarding each of the entrances to the valley. A chaotic night battle followed, during which El Cid was wounded. The men blundered back and forth in the darkness but, despite El Cid's incapacitation, his troops were able to hold sway. They captured Berenguer and five thousand troops with the loss of very few of their own. This latest stunning victory led to the leaders of east and southeast Moorish Spain voluntarily offering to install El Cid as their warlord, with the payment of huge tributes

Fourteenth century manuscript illumination from the Chronicles of Spain *showing El Cid in battle.*

in return for his future protection. Eventually Berenguer was ransomed and in 1096 his son Ramón was married to El Cid's daughter Maria as insurance against future discord.

A complex network of alliances

El Cid's influence in Valencia grew, but his huge domain, with its many complex and uneasy alliances, was proving increasingly difficult to control. The Almoravid Berbers had renewed their attacks from the south and there was an ever-present danger that El Cid's Moorish vassals would request aid, or simply change their allegiance. He played a delicate balancing act, striving not to offend or overpower either Moors or Christians, and balancing mercy and justice to such a successful degree that even Alfonso, impressed by his triumphs, ceased his attacks on the Moors and sought treaties. The Berbers continued their attacks in ever-increasing numbers and, even though Alfonso and El Cid were to some extent united again, captured large tracts of land in Alfonso's Moorish fiefdom of Granada and Andalusia to the south.

The threat of a total Muslim conquest of Spain loomed large, and only El Cid stood in its way. From his base in Valencia he began to negotiate with Christian princes, encouraging them to enter into treaties with Muslim lords to unite against the common foe. Alfonso, although still mistrustful of El Cid, eventually succumbed to the reality of his popularity and power and reinstated him to his court. But it was El Cid who was seen as the true leader, and Alfonso's influence gradually waned.

In 1092 El Cid journeyed north to Saragossa to plan the renewal of his assaults on the Almoravids, but in his absence their leader, Yusuf, stormed northward, capturing several Christian strongholds along the way, including Granada. When news reached El Cid he returned and began to raise an army to reconquer the city he had so recently ruled. After a complicated series of battles and sieges lasting almost two years, Valencia succumbed to El Cid on 15 June 1094. Although he nominally ruled in the name of Alfonso, he was now effectively the king of Valencia. He sent for his wife and children to join him and they took up residence in the palace. Christian knights and Muslim warriors from all over Spain flocked to his banner and soon he commanded a force of some eight thousand Christians and twenty-five thousand Muslims.

But there still remained the matter of Yusuf. In late 1094 the Almoravid leader amassed a force of some 180,000 under the stewardship of his nephew Mohammed and ordered them to crush El Cid forever. But at the Battle of Cuarte near Valencia in December, the Christian forces led by El Cid defeated the Almoravids using unconventional tactics. They cut a path through the massed opposition troops with a force of heavily armoured, mounted knights, then swiftly turned around, trampling the chaotically disorganised Berbers underfoot. In 1096 Valencia's nine mosques were converted into Christian churches under the bishopric of French priest Jerome, and an uneasy peace ensued for nearly three years until, in 1097, Yusuf's army returned to southern Spain. El Cid remained in Valencia waiting for an attack that never came. His son Diego, however, was slain by Yusuf's troops and El Cid was inconsolable for months afterwards. In 1098 he attacked and besieged the Moorish forces at the castle of Murvideo, south of Valencia, and by the middle of the year the starving Moors had collapsed and El Cid was again triumphant. He had avenged the death of his son and showed yet again that

Valencia was invincible so long as he was alive to rule over it.

El Cid died unexpectedly at Valencia on 10 July 1099. His wife Ximena succeeded him but was able to rule for barely three years, even with the aid of Alfonso, who at last realised that he was largely helpless without the assistance of his famous knight. Valencia was soon besieged by the Almoravids, and Alfonso decided that it was impossible to defend unless he maintained a huge army there. He evacuated then burned the city. On 5 May 1102 the Almoravids finally succeeded in occupying Valencia, which remained in Muslim hands until 1238. El Cid's body was taken to Castile, where it was buried in the San Pedro de Cardeña, a monastery near Burgos.

Most of the lands won by El Cid also returned to Muslim rule and, without El Cid, Alfonso was unable to make any further inroads against the Moors. El Cid's remarkable legacy was recorded in numerous songs and poems and, although there were many more wars between Muslim and Christian to come, Spain gradually evolved into a cultural melting pot of East and West, a process started by El Cid.

1162–1227

BARBARIAN HORDES STORM THROUGH ASIA

The Mongol Empire under Genghis Khan and his children was the largest contiguous empire in history—in terms of square kilometres conquered the empire was four times larger than the empire of Alexander the Great—and extended from Korea in the east to Poland in the west, and from the Russian Arctic in the north to Vietnam in the south. Genghis Khan came to power by uniting many of the nomadic tribes of northeast Asia. His disciplined army grew to include Tartars and Turkish warriors and a multitude of religions as he conquered civilisations across Asia and Eurasia, making him one of the greatest tacticians of all time.

GENGHIS KHAN AND THE RISE OF THE MONGOL EMPIRE

My greatest good fortune was to chase and defeat my enemy, conquer his lands and people, and share his riches.

GENGHIS KHAN

Few details are known of Genghis Khan's early life. Born in Mongolia in about 1162, the son of Yesukai, the *khan* (leader) of the local Yakka clan, he was named Temujin. When he was thirteen years old his father was poisoned by the rival Taidjut clan, whose khan, Targutai, claimed all the Yakka territory. Temujin inherited his father's leadership, in the Mongol tradition, but most of his clan members refused to be ruled by a mere boy and defected to other clans. Temujin's enemies attacked his weakened clan and the young khan was forced to become a fugitive, continually fleeing from one refuge to another on the fringes of the Gobi Desert with his few remaining loyal clan members. Temujin managed to win a series of tribal battles and regain some territory for his clan. He formed an alliance with Toghrul Khan of the Kerait tribe, an erstwhile ally of his father, and together they fought more successful campaigns. During times of peace, Temujin worked on organising his tribe into a ruthlessly effective fighting force that would go on to create the largest empire the world had ever known.

By 1206 he had succeeded in uniting or overcoming six major tribes and numerous smaller ones, and at a council of Mongol chiefs was recognised as khan of the united tribes. It was at this point that he took the new title of Genghis Khan.

A belief in his own divinity

Genghis had an unshakeable belief in his own divinity, and assumed that all states were already subject to his rule, even before being conquered. As long as foreign rulers accepted this simple and, to him, self-evident reality, everyone was happy. As his empire grew, his power and fame led many (such as the northern Chinese) to believe that he must indeed possess a divine power. He rewarded loyalty and bravery among his subjects, and furthered his aims by various means, including blackmail; for instance, his bodyguards were often the sons of his senior officers, effectively making them hostages. He was good at delegating, leaving large tracts of territory under the aegis of trusted officers as he expanded the empire elsewhere. He was physically fit well into his sixties, remaining simple in tastes and habits, retaining the elements of his inherited nomadic life and avoiding the trappings of luxury. He was famous for his self-discipline, never indulging in anger or losing his temper. He was as accepting of the peoples he conquered as he was of his own; he rewarded merit and talent without prejudice, bestowing power and privilege where he saw it being most effective for his ends. Possibly a Shamanist or a Tengrist in his religious beliefs, he employed Christians, Buddhists, Muslims and Chinese Confucians.

His tolerance, however, ended with those who opposed or betrayed him. No matter whether the miscreant was a close friend or family member, he ruthlessly murdered all opponents. He took insults personally, as well as seeing them as blasphemy against Heaven. He saw it as his divine duty to stamp out opposition at whatever cost, and believed that any opposition to him demanded immediate and total retribution. He saw opponents as inferior beings, by dint of the fact that they did not perceive his obvious divine greatness. He was something of a hedonist as well. Fourteenth-century Arabic historian Rashid al-Din Hamadani quotes Genghis as saying, during a debate with his warriors over man's greatest happiness:

Man's greatest good fortune is to chase and defeat his enemy, seize all his possessions, leave his married women weeping and wailing ... use the bodies of his women as nightshirts and supports, gazing upon and kissing their rosy breasts, sucking their lips which are as sweet as the berries of their breasts.

But Genghis was never accused of unnecessary cruelty for its own sake, or sadistic impulses. While he did not often display tolerance and forgiveness towards his opponents, neither did he indulge in ideological, gratuitous brutality. Though illiterate, he quickly discovered the advantages of writing and an efficient bureaucracy, charging his officers with making records and conducting administration in his absence. This quality is all the more impressive considering that he was the first Mongol to embrace such concepts, and that his only mentors and teachers were his conquered former enemies.

The Chinese, and the emperors who ruled them, regarded nomadic peoples such as the Mongols as barbarians. They had no cities; nor did they produce fine architecture, beautiful arts, crafts or even furniture. They could make a living only by moving across the land with the seasons. They did, however, possess animal-tending skills, and together with their ability to clothe and shelter themselves they were able to survive their harsh environment. And they had weapons. They also had a spoken language that gave expression to historical traditions, songs and legends, but had not invented a method of writing. They had rules of behaviour to help them govern themselves, but were nonetheless often at war with neighbouring tribes. The defining proof of their perceived inferiority was their lack of a currency. The Chinese had money, and this alone was enough to make them consider the Mongols primitive and brutish beyond redemption.

Organisation and equipment of the army

The organisation of Genghis Khan's army was based on the decimal system, similar to that used by the ancient Romans, the Chinese and other Asian nomadic tribes. The groups ranged in size from divisions of ten thousand, regiments of one thousand squadrons of five hundred, companies of one hundred and squads of ten. This allowed flexibility of deployment but

With an unwavering belief in his own divinity, Genghis Khan meted out punishment to those who threatened his rule.

Genghis' brilliant organisational skills allowed him to develop this long-proven structure to new heights of efficiency. After periods of war the troops returned to their home pastures to herd horses and cattle, always returning to their particular squads whenever hostilities broke out. This military arrangement was also used in times of peace—the leader of ten men became the leader of ten tents, and so on. Genghis maintained a personal army of bodyguards numbering ten thousand.

Genghis set great store on the principle that commanders and subordinates should serve each other with unquestioning loyalty and obedience. There was a complete prohibition against troops transferring from one unit to another, punishable by death. He instituted a system of relay runners to carry his orders to the commanders at the front. Looting of vanquished states was forbidden until he gave permission, at which time the commanders and troops had equal rights. The exception was that beautiful women must be handed over to Genghis.

The Mongol battle dress comprised a helmet with an upper section made of metal and a lower section (which hung over the ears and neck) of buffalo leather. The body was protected by leather armour several layers thick, with separate pieces for the arms and legs. Next to the skin was a vest of raw silk, so tightly woven that it would not rip when hit by an arrow. This allowed army surgeons to remove an arrow from a man's body by pulling it out using the silk.

The troops, mounted on small, leather-armoured horses, each carried a variety of weapons and tools including two bows, light and heavy arrows (for combat at long range and close quarters), three quivers, and a lance with a curved hook behind the point, which was used to pull an enemy off his horse. Commanders carried a curved sabre. Each soldier also carried an axe,

a horsehair lasso, a cooking pot, a grindstone for sharpening lances and arrowheads, and a horsewhip. A leather bag was used to carry reserve supplies of water, and to keep weapons and clothing dry during river crossings.

Most food was obtained from the land, but the soldiers also carried emergency supplies of dried milk curd, which was dissolved in water as required until it had the consistency of syrup. Troops also drank mare's milk, and occasionally carved a slice of flesh from the rump of a living horse (a practice that apparently was not fatal). In times of extreme need the soldier would cut his horse's jugular vein, suck out some blood, then reclose the wound with stitching.

Military tactics: ingenious and ruthless

Mongol boys were taught riding and archery from a young age and could hit targets at a distance of more than 200 metres (around 650 feet), even while on horseback. Every soldier had at least one reserve horse, enabling the armies to travel large distances quickly. A favourite tactic was to retreat as soon as the enemy attacked or stood its ground, luring it into an awkward strategic position from which it could be surrounded and massacred. The mass slaughter of defeated victims was a necessary strategy because the Mongols were usually numerically inferior to their opponents and Genghis simply could not supply enough personnel to maintain an occupying force while his armies continued their expansive campaigns; he could not risk insurgencies by defeated enemies.

Genghis learned siege techniques from the Chinese, whose mercenary soldiers he welcomed and employed for the information they could provide. He once offered to end a siege at the city of Hsian if its leader gave him thousands of cats and pigeons. The commander complied, hoping and expecting that Genghis would then go away. Instead, Genghis attached a small flaming torch to each animal, then released them. The cats rushed back to their homes, squeezing through gaps in the wooden walls, while the pigeons returned to their nests. The city burned to the ground.

Various ploys were used to create the illusion that the army was much bigger than it appeared. In one such ploy, the troops would advance along a very broad shallow front. Realistic fake armies of man-sized puppets on horseback were constructed. Then, at night, each soldier would light several torches, placing them some distance from each other to give the impression that each torch represented one soldier. Spies, often disguised as merchants or traders, would spread false rumours ahead of advancing armies, implying they were much larger than in actuality; they also provided Genghis with accurate information about the strength and position of the enemy.

Scientists measure an emperor's legacy

In March 2003 the *American Journal of Genetics* published a remarkable report by twenty-three geneticists who had been studying DNA from about two thousand Eurasian men. They found that, despite the enormous area under study, which stretched from the Caspian Sea to the Pacific coast of east China, more than a hundred of the men, or about 8 per cent, contained the same DNA. This meant that people from the sixteen disparate groups studied had a single common male ancestor. Extrapolating this to the rest of the population in the region gives a total of some 16 million descendants.

They were studying the Y chromosome, and although everyone has their own unique DNA

pattern, enough characteristics survive through the generations to allow researchers to group us in family trees. The DNA information also allows a reasonably accurate estimate of when the common ancestor existed. The team allowed thirty years between generations, dating the common ancestor about one thousand years ago. But if we allow a more realistic twenty-five years between generations, the date becomes 850 years ago—exactly the period of Genghis Khan's rule.

When the researchers superimposed a map of the area they were studying over a thirteenth-century map of Genghis' empire, the fit was perfect. This proved that the common ancestor was either Genghis or one of his immediate ancestors—in any case we know that Genghis was responsible for dispersing the DNA signature across central Asia and north China between 1209 and his death in 1227. Part of the spoils of war were the most beautiful of the vanquished women, and Genghis, though not a libertine as such, was anything but celibate. Furthermore, he was able to display authority and generosity at the same time by allocating women as rewards to his most loyal and senior offspring and officers. He had access to hundreds of women during his forty-year period of empire-building.

The achievements of Genghis Khan

In 1995 the *Washington Post* dubbed Genghis Khan 'the most important man of the last 1000 years', on the grounds that for the first time 'a single species fully exerted its will upon the earth'. Most people in 1200 were unaware of any other continents or even

FOLLOWING PAGES: Genghis Khan's army continues its wave of conquest, capturing yet another town.

other societies or countries. Though Asians traded with the eastern reaches of the fading Byzantine Empire, they knew almost nothing of the European lands to the west. With the exception of a few Viking explorers, Europeans were unaware of America's existence. Genghis Khan's legacy was to unite East and West into one realm, absorbing (and transforming) what we now know as China, Russia, Tibet, Afghanistan, the eastern part of Iran, Syria, Turkey, Ukraine, Hungary and Poland. He facilitated the spread of Islam and Christianity from the Middle East to the Pacific Ocean. He established new trading routes, and reopened old ones, such as the Silk Road, whose use had been severely limited by the rise of Islam in the seventh century. Genghis had no argument with any religion or its adherents; his sole ambition was earthly power and as long as a group accepted his rule and heavenly authority—and there were of course very strong practical reasons for doing so—he was mostly tolerant of beliefs and the devotional practices of others.

When Genghis Khan died in 1227, his empire stretched from the Pacific Ocean to Poland. His sons and grandsons continued to expand it, and by the time Marco Polo arrived in 1274, Genghis Khan's grandson Kublai Khan had extended it to include all of China as well as Turkestan, the rest of Persia (modern-day Iran) and the area covered by the former Soviet Union. Caravans and couriers traversed his entire empire in peace, allowing the free flow of ideas and merchandise between East and West. Numerous Chinese inventions found their way to Europe, including gunpowder, movable print type, noodles, tea, and paper made from wood pulp.

Just how Genghis Khan died has long been a matter of dispute. Some stories have him falling from his horse while being chased through Egypt, whereas others say he was killed in battle with the Tanguts of western China. There is no reliable record of where Genghis Khan's body was buried. China and Mongolia, each determined to be the true heir of his tradition, have conflicting stories about his death. The Chinese emphasise the glorious trappings at his funeral, while Mongolians hold that in accordance with tradition his corpse was transported across the Gobi Desert to a secret, unmarked resting place in Mongolia.

c. 1295

MARCO POLO DISCOVERS WONDERS IN THE EAST

Marco Polo is undoubtably the most famous Western medieval traveller along the Silk Road—exceeding all other travellers in his determination, his writing and his influence. His journey through Asia lasted twenty-four years, taking him further than any other traveller from Europe, beyond Mongolia to China. He became a confidant of Kublai Khan, travelled the whole of China and returned to Venice to tell the tale with the publication of *The Travels of Marco Polo*.

MARCO POLO'S EPIC ACCOUNT OF HIS TRAVELS ALONG THE SILK ROAD

This province, called Tebet, is of very great extent.
The people, as I have told you, have a language of their own,
and they are Idolaters, and they border on Manzi and sundry
other regions. Moreover, they are very great thieves...

FROM *THE TRAVELS OF MARCO POLO*

Marco Polo was a Venetian trader and adventurer who travelled to China and the Far East in the thirteenth century—at a time when very few Europeans knew that China even existed. He made his famous journey with his father Niccolo and uncle Maffeo, who had some years earlier journeyed to the court of Kublai Khan. The travellers ate the food that was common to the regions through which they passed. Along the Tigris River south of Baghdad they ate quail, salted fish, olives and meat fried in coriander, and tasted spices such as cinnamon and saffron. Along the Silk Road, they delighted in quinces, apples, apricots, persimmons, pomegranates and wild garlic. In India they ate mangoes and in Cathay (China) they learned how to smoke fish.

After Marco returned to Venice he was imprisoned by the enemy state of Genoa, where he dictated tales of his adventures to a fellow inmate, producing a book known variously as *Description of the World*, *Travels of Marco Polo* and *Il Milione* ('The Millions', because he used the word so often to convey the vast scale of what he observed). His book, a mixture of direct observation, history and hearsay, created a sensation when it appeared. So alien was most of what he described that many readers believed the entire journey was a wild and fanciful fabrication.

There had been virtually no overland contact between Europe and Asia until the Mongol warlord Genghis Khan conquered the vast lands that lay between China and Poland, almost a century before Marco Polo's expedition. East–West trade had been carried out since that time, but as it was conducted in relays few had direct knowledge of other places on what was known as the Silk Road. Polo travelled along parts of the Silk Road on his way eastward, but often diverged from it for various reasons, including local wars.

Niccolo and Maffeo Polo's first journey to the East

Marco Polo was born in Venice in 1254. Little is known about his early life, but his family had been successfully trading with the Middle East for a long time, amassing substantial wealth. When Marco was six years old his father Niccolo and uncle Maffeo went to Constantinople on business. When unrest broke out there in about 1261, the Polos decided to sell their property holdings and convert their capital into precious stones. They set off for modern-day Bulgaria where they commenced trading with Berkhe Khan, ruler of the western regions of the Mongol Empire. They managed to double their wealth, but when war blocked the path of their return to Venice they decided to head east to China carrying messages and gifts for Kublai Khan from Berkhe and other leaders. At the time Kublai, grandson of the great conqueror Genghis Khan, ruled over an empire that encompassed Mongolia, modern-day Korea, China, North Vietnam, Tibet, northern India, the Balkans, the Caucasus, Persia (Iran), Turkey, Poland, southern Russia, and everywhere in between.

The travellers arrived at Kublai Khan's magnificent summer palace at Shangdu on the vast Mongolian Plain in 1265. (Shangdu was the model for Xanadu, celebrated in Samuel Taylor Coleridge's poem 'Kubla Khan', published in 1816.) They were very well received, and when they departed for the return journey they were given Kublai's ambassadorial protection. The Mongols had recently come into contact with Islam and Christianity, and were interested in learning more about these religions, so Kublai gave them a letter addressed to the pope in which he requested one hundred educated priests and some oil from the Holy Sepulchre lamp in Jerusalem.

In 1269, when the brothers arrived back in Venice, they found that Marco's mother had recently died. When, in 1271, they decided to return to China, the young Marco accompanied them. Pope Gregory X gave them his credentials, along with gifts including precious gems, and the requested holy oil. He also assigned two friars to accompany them, authorising them to ordain

priests, consecrate bishops and grant absolution, but they fled soon after the expedition began.

Marco's epic journey begins

The travellers began their journey in a fast galley supplied by the Christian king of Armenia. They arrived on the Levantine coast of the Mediterranean, then set out across Syria toward Iran. As they neared the Caspian Sea, Marco reported a strange and wonderful black oil seeping from the ground, which the locals burned for light and heat. At Kerman in Persia, at the crossroads of the great east–west trading routes, they saw vast warehouses containing spices from India, incense from Oman and India, metalwork from Damascus, and porcelain and silk from China. Soon they passed across one of the most inhospitable places on earth, the Dasht-e Kavir, the great salt desert in central Iran. Marco reported that swallowing even a small mouthful of the salt would make a person violently ill for days.

Leaving the edge of the known European world, they headed through the mountains of Afghanistan, exposed to the burning heat of the sun during the day and freezing cold at night, and under constant threat of bandit attack. Amazed at the height of the mountains, they were even more amazed when, after several weeks' travel, they started to ascend even higher. The locals claimed that it was the highest place in the world, and they were not far wrong; this mountain range was the Hindu Kush and just to the south was K2, the second-highest peak in the world. To the north lay the Pamirs, lofty mountains completely unknown to Europeans until Marco reported them (they would not be explored for another six hundred years). As they descended to the foothills of the Tibetan plateau they joined the Silk Road, passing through a number of cities more than a thousand years old. Eventually they reached the Gobi Desert in Mongolia, a trackless wasteland that took them thirty days to cross. After a journey of almost four years they were now in China. The twenty-year-old Marco Polo would remain there for about fifteen years.

Marco is presented to Kublai Khan

In Shangdu, Niccolo and Maffeo renewed their acquaintance with Kublai Khan, whom they had first met at his court in Shangdu in 1266. The return of the Venetians was celebrated with much 'mirth and merry-making'. They presented the papal gifts—along with the young Marco, to whom Kublai took an instant shine—and were 'well served and attended to in all their needs'. Marco turned out to be the best gift of all; he would soon make known to the world the power and the glory of the great Khan. Although he did not speak Chinese, Marco, apparently an excellent linguist, could speak several other languages, including Turkish, Farsi (Persian) and perhaps Mongolian. He soon learned the languages of other places where Kublai sent him on various diplomatic and exploratory missions. Marco 'learnt in a short time and adopted the manners of the Tartars, and acquired a proficiency in four different languages, which he became qualified to read and write'.

Kublai loved hearing stories of the various far-flung reaches of his empire, so he sent the trusted Marco on numerous information-gathering assignments. He went to Yunnan in southwest China, where he reported on 'snakes and great serpents of such vast size as to strike fear into those who see them, and so hideous that the very account of them must excite the wonder of those to hear it ... some of them are ten paces in length ... the bigger ones are about

ten palms in girth. They have two forelegs near the head, but for feet nothing but a claw like the claw of a hawk or that of a lion. The head is very big, and the eyes are bigger than a great loaf of bread. The mouth is large enough to swallow a man whole, and is garnished with great pointed teeth.

Marco was also amazed to discover that in many places corpses were burned rather than buried, as cremation, once popular in Venice and Europe in general, had died out about eight hundred years earlier.

He was also amazed to observe coal—'stones that burn like logs'—as it was not used in Venice with its temperate Mediterranean climate. (He had obviously never been to England where coal was just as commonplace as in China.) He also exposed the myth that salamander lizards were fireproof and lived in fire, a misunderstanding caused by the fact that they often scurried out from under the bark of logs when they were placed on a fire. He gleefully reported that a 'salamander is not a beast as commonly believed' but a type of rock. Asbestos was unknown in the west, and he reported that a gift of fireproof cloth had been sent as a present to the pope. Strangely, Marco made no mention of tea, which was very commonly used in China and did not appear in the west for another two hundred and fifty years. Perhaps he did not like it. Not so strangely, he made no mention of gunpowder or its obvious value for warfare. Since he was in prison in Genoa, which was at war with Venice over control of the lucrative Mediterranean trade routes at the time he wrote his book, he doubtless did not wish to reveal the existence of such a valuable weapon to the enemy.

Marco's travels took him to Myanmar (Burma) and other places in the distant south, far from Mongolia. He may have been entrusted with administrative duties, for example the collection of taxes and revenues from trade in goods such as salt and iron. It is not known what Marco's father and uncle were doing during this time; however, Marco was certainly making himself at home. But, ultimately, he was not at home, and gradually his desire to return to Venice grew. Unfortunately, Kublai Khan was so enamoured of him that, for a long time, he refused to allow the Polos to leave and, without his consent and support, the long and

The epic journey of Marco Polo opened up the world for the map makers of medieval Europe.

hazardous journey would not have been possible. But, eventually, in 1291, an opportunity arose when the ruler of Persia, a grand-nephew of Kublai, lost his wife and wished to marry a woman from the same tribe. He asked Kublai for help and an appropriate girl was chosen. Pointing out their excellent knowledge of the lands between China and Persia, the Polos succeeded in being chosen for the task of escorting and protecting the bride-to-be on her journey, after which they would be permitted to return to Venice.

Return to Venice

From the southern Chinese port of Zaitun (Quanzhou), they travelled in a fleet of fourteen large junks via Vietnam, the Straits of Malacca and Sumatra, where bad weather forced them to remain for five months. With no option but to camp among cannibals on the Sumatran coast, they protected themselves by constructing a fortress surrounded by pointed sticks and guard towers. They eventually continued their voyage across the Bay of Bengal and through the strait

A sample of some of the wondrous beasts that Marco Polo's published story included for spellbound European audiences.

between India and Sri Lanka, where they made landfall. Marco was fascinated by the variety of high-quality gems—rubies, sapphires, amethysts, topazes, garnets and pearls. At the city of Chennai in India he was amazed at how long pearl divers could hold their breath as they collected oysters from a depth of more than 20 metres (66 feet), as they still do today. The party continued its voyage via the coast, ending their journey at the port of Hormuz in Persia. From there they travelled overland to Trebizond on the Black Sea, where they delivered the bride before continuing overland to Venice. When they arrived in 1295 they caused a sensation when they cut open the seams of their bizarre oriental clothes to reveal that the linings were stuffed with gems.

Soon afterwards, in 1297, Polo was imprisoned in Genoa after being captured during a sea battle in the Mediterranean. He dictated his story to Rustichello, one of his fellow prisoners-of-war and a popular writer of romances. Marco was released after the war ended in the summer of 1299, returning home to Venice to live with his father and uncle, who had bought a mansion with their profits. In 1300 he married the noblewoman Donata Badoer, who bore him three children. He died in his home on January 1324 at the age of 69, and as he lay dying he is reported to have said: 'I didn't tell half of what I saw, because no one would have believed me'. Marco Polo was buried in Venice in the Convent of San Lorenzo.

His descriptions of China and its riches inspired Christopher Columbus to try to reach it by sea, travelling westward in 1492. He owned a heavily annotated copy of Polo's book. Marco Polo's epic journey also greatly assisted the development of European cartography and helped make possible the accuracy of the famous Fra Mauro map (created around 1450), one of medieval Europe's most detailed maps of the known world and seen by many as an improvement upon the map that Polo had brought home from Cathay (China).

1297

SURREY'S MEN SLAIN AT STIRLING BRIDGE

On 11 September 1297, William Wallace and an army of Scottish nationalists faced off against his English foe the Earl of Surrey at Stirling Bridge. During the battle English forces gathered on the southern side of the narrow Stirling Bridge, which could only be crossed two by two. This tactical blunder led to the slaughter of 5000 English troops. It was a huge psychological as well as military victory for the nationalists, and their leader William Wallace was subsequently made Guardian of Scotland. Wallace went on to lead the Scots in their battles against the English until his defeat ten months later at the Battle of Falkirk.

WILLIAM WALLACE AND THE FIGHT FOR SCOTTISH INDEPENDENCE

I'm William Wallace, and the rest of you will be spared.
Go back to England and tell them ... Scotland is free!

WILLIAM WALLACE AT THE BATTLE OF STIRLING BRIDGE

Sir William Wallace, also known as Brave Heart, was one of Scotland's greatest heroes. A fearless knight and landowner, he led the Scottish resistance through a long, and ultimately successful, fight to free Scotland from English rule. For such a revered hero, his origins are shrouded in mystery and controversy. Probably born in the town of Ellerslie in Ayrshire, he was the landless younger son of a minor nobleman who, without patronage, privilege or inherited power, rose to become the political and military leader of his country. At the time, Scotland's fortunes were at their lowest ebb; the Scots were suffering under England's rule and their independence had been virtually obliterated.

Wallace is regarded as the greatest hero of the Scottish Wars of Independence, which raged from 1296 to 1357 and ended in the Treaty of Berwick, which guaranteed Scotland's status as an independent nation. In 1297 his vastly outnumbered troops won a stunning victory at Stirling Bridge in central Scotland against an English army led by John de Warenne, Earl of Surrey—only to suffer a crushing defeat at the Battle of Falkirk the following year. Wallace then disappeared as abruptly as he had emerged,

reappearing in 1305 when he was captured by the British and judicially murdered.

A power vacuum is created

Wallace was born into an era of relative stability and peace. Scotland was ruled by King Alexander III, who had successfully repelled English claims to sovereignty. But when, in 1286, Alexander fell off his horse and died without heirs (apart from Margaret, his four-year-old granddaughter), a series of contenders to the throne came forward. From this time onwards, Scotland's natural leaders—earls, barons, landowners and priests—began continually betraying their countrymen to the English, in return for the retention of their own assets and status. The English king Edward I took advantage of the power vacuum by arranging for Margaret to marry his son Edward, agreeing that Scotland would remain an independent state. The Scottish lords set up a provisional government to rule until Margaret came of age, but Margaret died in 1290 at the age of seven. The claimants to the throne invited Edward to arbitrate, and he installed John Balliol as ruler on 17 November 1292 on the condition that

Scotland recognise Edward as Lord Paramount of Scotland. The Scottish reluctantly agreed, presumably because they reasoned that, under the circumstances, they would be easy pickings for the English if they refused, and because a civil war between the various claimants (who included Robert the Bruce, who much later became king of an independent Scotland) loomed as a real possibility.

The English king proceeded to make life difficult for the new King John, undermining his reign and embarking on a series of 'divide and conquer' deals with Scottish nobles to establish English authority over various areas of their domain. By March 1296 John had had enough and renounced his homage to Edward, who responded by sacking the border town of Berwick-on-Tweed and massacring most of its residents, even if those who surrendered or fled. In April he defeated the Scots at the Battle of Dunbar in the town of Lothian; in July he forced John to abdicate. Many Scottish nobles were imprisoned, and the remaining 1800 or so were forced to pay taxes to the English. As a final insult, Edward purloined the Scottish coronation stone, known as the Stone of Destiny, from its location at Scone Palace, and took it to London. Scotland's subjugation was almost complete; the time was ripe for a saviour to arise to unite the oppressed, alienated populace against the common enemy. The stage was set for William Wallace.

The art of warfare

In the late thirteenth century, war was not a matter of technology or science, but mostly of raw strength in hand-to-hand combat, individual courage and adroitness in the use of the weapons of the day—the dirk (a long, straight dagger), the broadsword, battleaxe and spear. The longbow had only just been invented and, as one of the first weapons capable of killing at a distance, it was frowned upon under the international rules of war. Soon enough it would transform warfare, as did the introduction of guns and gunpowder a century later. But the wars between England and Scotland were fought at close hand by relatively small numbers of men in bloody combat. The successful war hero would have to possess military expertise, extreme moral and physical courage, and a spiritual commitment to duty. Wallace displayed all these traits, along with a fierce desire to defend and protect the interests of his beloved Scotland when many others were all too willing to compromise their country and countrymen for their own self-interest.

The town of Stirling was of great strategic importance, buttressed on the south by one of the most unassailable castles in the British Isles, and situated on a high peak overlooking the plain of the vast river Forth. It was the gateway to the highlands, and formed a natural barrier that effectively prevented the wild Highlanders from swarming over the Lowlands at will. The crucial point of the gateway was the narrow wooden bridge that spanned the Forth just above the town. This bridge was critical in any conflict against invaders from the south; all the lands north of the bridge still remained in Scottish hands, apart from Dundee which was holding out against an English siege. English commander John de Warenne, Earl of Surrey, decided to send reinforcements to Dundee to finish off the resistance, but to do so he would need to cross the heavily defended Stirling Bridge. He led a large army through the centre of the country, planning to seize the bridge before pouring north into the Highlands. The stakes were high—if the English won, Wallace would be reduced to a mere political leader. If Wallace won, he would be in a strong position to expel the English and take over as leader of all

Scotland, which had never before stood up to the might of an English army. It is highly significant that the common people, the lesser gentry and the peasantry were prepared to rally under the Wallace banner. It is also a tribute to the leadership abilities of the youthful Wallace that he was able to persuade them to risk everything against the experienced warrior Warenne, and the most battle-hardened army in Europe.

The stage is set at Stirling Bridge

The English contingent comprised around one thousand cavalry and fifty thousand troops drawn from England, Wales and Ireland. Eight thousand reinforcements were also heading north. This intimidating force included veterans of campaigns in the Holy Land, France, Wales and earlier Scottish battles. It was heavily armed and had never known defeat. The Scots, on the other hand, had performed poorly at Dunbar, where they demonstrated lack of discipline and poor tactics, as the English were well aware. Furthermore, the Scottish gentry were generally lying low, ignoring the young nonentity. Cowed by the recent successes of the English, they were no doubt fearful of the consequences if, as they expected, the English were victorious. Nor would they be likely to serve under an untitled leader, even if he won. In addition, many of the Scottish leaders were in Flanders, assisting Edward in a simultaneous campaign against France. Yet, despite these seeming obstacles, Wallace was able to tap into the indomitable spirit of his countrymen, who had been enduring the contempt and brutality of the English for seven years and hence had little to lose if they risked their lives to rid themselves of English tyranny.

At Stirling Bridge the Forth was about 30 metres (100 feet) across, slow-moving but very deep; there was no other way to cross the river. At the north end of the bridge a causeway

Sir WILLIAM WALLACE,
GENERAL and GOVERNOR of SCOTLAND

An etching of the Scottish patriot and national hero, Sir William Wallace.

traversed a wide, low-lying area of swampy marsh. The bridge was barely wide enough for two horsemen to ride shoulder to shoulder; the causeway not much wider. The marsh was too soft to allow horses to operate at all. The English gave the Scots the chance to submit, which was common medieval practice. On 10 September 1297 Warenne sent his herald to Wallace to demand his surrender, which was not forthcoming. That evening Warenne ordered his troops to be ready to cross the bridge at dawn the next day. Accordingly, at daybreak, about five thousand foot soldiers, including a Welsh archery contingent, crossed the bridge; but the exhausted Earl was still asleep, and no further commands were issued. Confused and lacking support, they re-crossed the bridge. It was a moment of high farce, and a harbinger of the tactical failures to follow. Once Warenne finally arose, he held a parade to confer knighthood on a number of his troops, many of whom would be dead by day's end. Still the Earl dithered, and failed to issue orders to advance. Across the river in the distance he could see the summer sun glinting on the Scottish spears, and it must have occurred to him that the Scottish position looked invincible. They were positioned in the foothills of Abbey Craig, a sheer cliff which of itself would have halted his advance soon after he had breached the northern bridgehead. He would have noticed that the surrounding bog

William Wallace rallies his men and leads the charge against the English at the Battle of Stirling Bridge.

would not only have hindered his armoured troops: it would have been impossible for his mounted cavalry to traverse. The Scots had the opportunity to retreat into the foothills if necessary, but once Warenne had crossed the bridge, retreat would have been impossible in the face of his own advancing forces.

Tension mounts as tactics are argued

But his army was fired up for battle, and as time passed the soldiers' frustration grew. Warenne sent two Dominican friars over the bridge and causeway to offer terms for surrender, but Wallace sent them back with the message that he was inviting Warenne to attack as soon as possible, and that they were more than prepared for the fray. Unnerved, Warenne called a conference of war to discuss the matter. One participant was Scottish nobleman Sir Richard Lundie, who had betrayed the Scots earlier that year at the battle of Irvine by surrendering without a fight (along with all the other Scottish gentry). Lundie was very familiar with Stirling and its surrounds, and cautioned that to advance would be suicidal. He pointed out that progress across the narrow bridge would be very slow, and that once they reached the northern bank of the Forth they would be surrounded, with no chance of retreat. He requested command of a group of five hundred knights and foot soldiers who would ford the river at a nearby shallow point he knew of, and mount a rearguard attack. In that case, it would be the Scots who were constricted by the inability to escape, and Warenne's troops would be able to cross the bridge safely.

The war council descended into confused disarray as the two cases were loudly argued—until the English Treasurer, Hugh de Cressingham, had his say. He was a physically repulsive man, grossly obese and pompous, and

hated by the English almost as much as by the Scots. Having exchanged priestly garments for chain mail, he became a grotesque figure who surely attracted the contempt of the professional soldiers in his charge. He shouted down the tumult and, ever mindful of his duty to the royal coffers, reminded Warenne how much the war had cost already, and suggested that they advance without further ado. The Earl was irritated by this interruption, and by the substance of the argument, considering it a minor irrelevance when so much was at stake. But in the end, tired of the inconclusive arguing, he issued the command to cross the bridge. At the front was Sir Marmaduke de Thweng, who rode ahead of the troops with a small contingent of knights. Their task was to secure the northern end of the causeway in order to protect the advancing troops behind. Cressingham followed just behind, along with various other nobles and flag-bearers. The Scots resisted the temptation to rush headlong into battle as they had done at the Battle of Dunbar, rather maintaining their positions in the foothills. They held their nerve as more and more English troops reached the northern bank and spread out over the marshes.

This was Wallace's great advantage—he could choose against what odds he would fight. At about eleven o'clock he made the prearranged signal of a single horn blast and the Scots poured forth *en masse* with spine-chilling war cries, wielding their comparatively few swords and spears as they swarmed down the mountain and into the midst of the English troops. The men on the right flank cut a swathe through the less manoeuvrable English cavalry and succeeded in taking the northern bridgehead, thus cutting off all chance of retreat. Panic reigned as the fleeing English came up against their fellows still trying to advance across the bridge; many fell or jumped into the river where they drowned, weighed down by their armour. The main mass of the Scottish forces ran headlong into the midst of the English forces, spears levelled. Their lack of armour or heavy weapons proved an advantage as the unwieldy Englishmen struggled in the marshy ground. The English infantry, disoriented and unfamiliar with the territory, were reduced to a confused rabble as the Scots stabbed and hacked their way through the lines. Thweng was one of the few to stay in control; he charged and managed to scatter the Scots who were guarding the causeway, but the English advance had halted and all around him wholesale slaughter was occurring. With screams of 'On them! On them!' the Scots killed virtually all the English troops who had crossed the bridge, including about three hundred Welsh archers and five thousand infantrymen. A bare few managed to strip off their armour and swim back across the river, including Thweng. Scottish losses were very few.

Wallace's changing fortunes

Warenne ordered a hasty retreat, leading the remnants of his army hastily southwards. The Scots followed and harried them for a long way, stealing their pack animals and killing stragglers. Then, in October, Wallace invaded northern England, ravaging the counties of Northumberland and Cumberland (for reasons that are not clear, as it seems there was little strategic benefit in doing so). When he returned to Scotland in December he was knighted and proclaimed Guardian of the Kingdom, ruling in the name of John Balliol. But many nobles resented him, and King Edward, after returning from his Flemish campaign, invaded Scotland on 3 July 1278. On 22 July, with a much bigger army than Warenne had deployed, his troops routed Wallace's forces at Stirling in the Battle of Falkirk, ruining Wallace's military reputation.

Nothing is known of Wallace's activities for the next four years. Although the Scottish nobles surrendered to Edward in 1304, the English continued to pursue Wallace unremittingly. On 5 August 1305, he was arrested near Glasgow and taken to London, where he was illegally condemned as a traitor to the king even though, as he correctly pointed out, he had never sworn allegiance to Edward. Following a travesty of a 'trial', he was publicly hanged, cut loose before his strangulation was complete, disembowelled while still alive, decapitated then quartered by four horses, one tied to each of his limbs. His preserved head was placed on a pike on top of London Bridge.

The violent and pitiless nature of his death, and the ongoing agitation of the Scots for freedom from English rule, ensured a legendary status for this warrior hero, whose exploits have been celebrated across the centuries in poetry and song.

1440

NEW MACHINE PROMISES INFORMATION REVOLUTION

In 1440 in the German city of Mainz, Johannes Gutenberg printed the world's first mass-produced book using movable type, a special press and oil-based inks—the Bible. The invention was to cause shockwaves across Europe as books, and therefore ideas, became accessible to people outside Church institutions or the highest levels of the aristocracy, leading to a new information era.

JOHANNES GUTENBERG AND THE INVENTION OF THE PRINTING PRESS

We should note the force, effect and consequences of inventions ... which were unknown to the ancients, namely, printing, gunpowder and the compass. For these three have changed the appearance and state of the whole world ... no empire, no sect, and no star seems to have exerted greater power and influence in human affairs than these mechanical discoveries.

FRANCIS BACON, *NOVUM ORGANUM*, 1620

It is easy to appreciate how the compass revolutionised navigation and gunpowder transformed warfare, but the changes wrought by the printing press extend into almost every field of human activity, even into consciousness itself. Communications theorists often refer to the last five hundred years as the Gutenberg Age. The explosion in knowledge and social change that flowed on from the availability of inexpensive, mass-produced books was unprecedented in human history. Not until recent decades, with the rise of television and then the internet, has human civilisation been so greatly affected by a new communication medium.

The term 'Dark Ages' was coined by Petrarch, Europe's most renowned fourteenth-century scholar. He saw himself as living in an age where learning was such a rare and precious thing that the few books in existence shone like lights 'surrounded by gloom and darkness'. Like many scholars, he spent much of his life wandering across Europe searching for small, scattered text collections and tattered manuscripts, in order to reproduce them.

Armies of scribes

Copying by hand meant that armies of scribes—almost invariably monks—had to spend their time preserving knowledge, instead of extending it through writing new books. Equipped with only quills and inkpots, their years were consumed by the tedious, seemingly never-ending task of copying, and they frequently changed the text as carelessness or opinion interfered with their work. It was even harder to accurately reproduce more challenging technical information, such as maps, tables, diagrams and sketches of natural phenomena. Knowledge was constantly being lost as manuscripts went missing or were destroyed by accidents of history. The Renaissance (or 'rebirth') is the name later given to one of several revivals of learning that occurred after the Dark Ages. This great revival, an effective transition from the medieval to the modern world, was given impetus by Gutenberg's printing press.

Following the ravages of the bubonic plague (the Black Death), which killed about a third of the population of Europe, the late fourteenth century was a time of growing prosperity. Many new churches and noble estates were built, and copies of the Bible were hard to find. Scribes could not meet the demand, and many people were experimenting with ways to produce books more quickly. The first to make the breakthrough and print an entire book was a secretive, determined man named Johannes Gutenberg. Ironically, if it weren't for his court records, we would know almost nothing about him at all, because he kept his work secret for decades, fearing that it would be stolen and copied.

Gutenberg's 'secret' breakthrough

Little is known about Gutenberg's life. In about 1398 he was born to a family of coin makers and goldsmiths in Mainz, Germany, and the precision metalwork skills he learned at home were at the heart of his innovation. Printing itself had been invented by the Chinese centuries earlier—text was carved into wooden blocks that were covered in ink and then pressed onto paper. Carving out enough pages for a whole book was not much faster than hand copying, however, and few woodworkers had the level of skill needed to make letters the same size and keep them perfectly aligned. Moreover, wood is too soft to maintain its shape if pressed repeatedly. Gutenberg's breakthrough was movable metal type. Drawing on his experience as a goldsmith Gutenberg created individual letters made of metal that were arranged on a frame, coated with a black, oil-based non-running ink that he invented, then placed into a modified wine press. Gutenberg's letters were made from a combination of tin, lead and a crystalline solid called antimony. His lettered plates were durable and could be used for hundreds of printings, resulting in the production of books on a scale that had never before been achieved. His new method was several hundred times faster than

hand copying, and few major improvements were made on it until the nineteenth century, when the introduction of steam power enabled automation of the printing process.

Gutenberg also split his letters, which were designed in the round, cursive handwriting style of the time, into upper and lower case and included punctuation such as commas and semi-colons. All his letters were precisely the same height and individually hand cast, and his screw-type press was designed to transfer the text evenly onto paper (and occasionally the more expensive vellum). Gutenberg took almost a year to create a total of some 270 characters for his new Bible. He was also the first European to use durable oil-based inks in preference to the more common water-based inks

Gutenberg loses a lifetime's work

With the aid of about twenty men in his workshop, Gutenberg completed a Bible in 1455. He made 180 copies in the first year—the same time it took a monastery to produce a single copy. By this time, however, Johann Fust, the financier who had bankrolled Gutenberg's years of experimentation, lost patience with waiting for a return on his investment. Fust successfully sued Gutenberg, seized everything in the workshop, and went on to make a fortune printing Bibles and prayer guides. It had taken Gutenberg his entire life to accumulate the tools in his workshop and construct his famous press, and now it had been taken away from him. Gutenberg's fame did not spread far in his lifetime, but he did receive a pension for his achievements from the town authorities, along with 2000 litres (440 gallons) of wine. A friend later gave him a press, and he spent his last days as a humble bookseller, dying in 1468 of natural causes.

His invention, however, was an idea whose time had definitely come. By 1500 practically every European city had a printer's workshop, and over twenty million books had been printed. Like the Gutenberg Bible, three-quarters of those books were in Latin, the language of religion and academia, but, by the end of the century, publishers were already reaching out to the masses of Europe by publishing books in languages that people actually spoke. While most early printed books were reproductions of old texts—Bibles, works by Greek and Roman authors, and so on—vernacular books emerged to cater to popular tastes, and the idea of reading for pleasure took hold. Illustrated travel guides, popular histories, collections of ballads and short stories, books on astrology, etiquette, mythical animals, costumes, playing chess and so on, were soon inundating the market.

The spread of books and the rise of literacy

As books became readily available, more people had the chance to become literate, and were willing to pay for books. These factors fed into each other, constantly expanding the market for books, the number of readers, and the range of titles—and this process has never really stopped. At the dawn of the Gutenberg Age, literacy was rarely found beyond the university towns and monasteries. But soon literacy spread to the nobility and wealthier merchants, then to skilled tradesmen and small shopkeepers and other members of what we could call the middle class. In many households it was the women who first learned to read, and it became a common pastime for women to read aloud to their families during the long winter nights. Until universal primary school education was introduced in the nineteenth century, many of Europe's poor could not afford schooling and

thus remained illiterate, but even the poor were served by chapbooks—small pamphlets with illustrations, song lyrics, descriptions of newsworthy events, and the like.

Besides reading for pleasure, there was a great desire for practical knowledge. The first centuries of printing saw an incredible number of publications aimed at those who wanted to learn how to play an instrument, give a sermon, run a farm, balance accounts, brew beer, identify plants, and so on. Students who had previously been forced to learn their crafts orally were now in the novel position of being able to outshine their teachers, assuming they could get their hands on these books.

What little knowledge of the workings of nature did exist was often located in ancient texts or practical crafts, and printers collected and published such information in a genre known as *libri secretorum*, or 'books of secrets'. These were eclectic collections of everything from medical prescriptions and technical formulas, to recipes, parlour tricks and jokes. Advances in chemistry, for instance, owe a great deal to the publication of guides to dying fabrics—but this information was mixed with advice on how to breed multicoloured horses, create men out of clay, or get chickens to lay eggs the size of human heads. The later development of the scientific method by Francis Bacon, with its emphasis on observation and experiment, was spurred by the need to separate the useful 'secrets' from the claptrap. This ensured an ever-faster accumulation of discoveries that could be applied to the creation of new technology—another process that shows no sign of stopping.

Impact on the Church

Yet it would be a mistake to think that the shift from a medieval to a modern world was at all smooth or straightforward. Vernacular Bibles allowed many more people to read the Bible for themselves, and controversies erupted over the accuracy of Bible translations, the role of priests as interpreters of divine truth, and pretty much every other aspect of Catholic teaching and practice.

A key issue was the role of indulgences, documents promising forgiveness for sins that could be bought from licensed church authorities, usually professional pardoners. Indulgences had long existed, but it was not until the advent of printing that they could be easily mass produced, and Gutenberg himself

Johannes Gutenberg inspects a page proof from his miraculous printing press.

Sanct Johannes.   CXLI

die künig auff erden/vnd die obersten/vñ
die reychen/vnd die Hauptleütte/vnd die
gewaltigen/vnd alle knecht vnd alle frey
en/verborgen sich inn den klüfften vnnd
felsen an den bergen/vñ sprachen zů den
bergen vnd felsen/Fallet auff vns/vñ ver
berget vns vor dem angesicht deß/der auf
dem stůl sitzt/vnd vor dem zorn deß Lam=
mes/Dañ es ist komen der groß tag seines
zorns/vnd wer kan bestehn.

a Diß sind allerlay plagen/so mit auff zhůr vnd zwi=
tracht sich land vñ leüt verendern biß an jüngste tag.

Von dem geschlecht Juda/zwelff tau= B
sent versigelt. Von dem geschlecht Rube/
zwelff tausent versigelt. Von dem geschle
chte Gad/zwelff tausent versigelt. Von
dem geschlecht Aser/zwelff tausent versi=
gelt.   Von dem geschlecht Nephthali/
zwelf tausent versigelt. Von dē geschlecht
Manasse/zwelff tausent versigelt. Vō dē
geschlecht Simeon/zwelff tausent versi=
gelt. Von dem geschlecht Leui/zwelff tau
sent versigelt. Vō dē geschlecht Jsaschar/
zwelff tausent versigelt. Vō dē geschlecht
Zabulō/zwelff tausent versigelt. Vō dē ge
schlecht Joseph/zwelff tausent versigelt.
Vō dē geschlecht Ben Jamin/zwelff tau
sent versigelt.   Darnach sahe ich/Vnd
sihe/Ain grosse schar/wölch niemāt zelen
kunt/auß alle haide vñ völckern/vñ spra
che/vor dē stůl stehēd vñ vor dē Lāb: ange

Das VII. Capitel.

a   VND darnach sahe ich vier Engel
stehn auff den vier ecken der er=
den/die hielten die vier wind der
erden/auf dz kain wind vber die erde blie=
se/noch vber das meer/noch vber ainige
baum. Vnd sahe ᵃ ainen andern Engel
auff steygen von der Sonnen auffgang/

A page from a 1535 edition of Martin Luther's bestseller, a German-language Bible.

was printing them long before he finished his Bible. Pious Christians were scandalised to see pardoners hawking their wares for profit, promising, for example, that for a few coins, dead relatives could be released from hell even if they had committed murder. In 1517 Martin Luther, a German professor of theology, became so outraged by this and other clerical abuses that he nailed an indignant protest—the 95 Theses—to a church door. Within a few days, several printers were selling copies of this document, and within fifteen days of its appearance it had reached every part of Germany.

Pope Leo X ordered Luther to renounce his views, but his defiance remained and grew more radical, leading to his denunciation as a heretic. Many had defied the popes in the past, but they had always lost because heretical ideas had travelled too slowly to escape church repression. Within a couple of years, however, Luther was a bestselling author, and he had literally armies of supporters. Similar movements emerged in other countries, especially England and Switzerland, and a split developed between the Catholic kingdoms of the south and the followers of new, Protestant creeds in the lands to the north.

The printed word fuels nationalism

Another source of tension was nationalism itself, which was also fired by printed material in a number of ways. Maps in Gutenberg's time were rare, very basic, and filled with errors, and the ones that were any good were among the most prized state secrets. Ships' crews frequently had to rely on accounts from other mariners. But map making flourished as printing presses spread, and ships' captains were invited to send corrections to Europe's cartographers. A century after Gutenberg, Mercator created a very modern world map, one that took into account the curvature of the earth and thus allowed accurate navigation at sea. And now that political atlases were widely available, people began to see themselves as members of states, where previously they had tended to identify themselves with their local region and their place in the social ladder.

This shift in consciousness accompanied the emergence of vernacular literature, which destroyed the Latin monopoly on educated thought. Now the Bible, current affairs, philosophy and a thousand other topics could be read in people's own national language, which was frequently the dialect of national capitals. This development was encouraged by national governments, hoping to extend their power, and added another dimension to the religious strife. In 1549, for instance, the English prayer book, *The Book of Common Prayer*, was created and imposed across the kingdom, replacing Latin as the language of worship. It was wildly unpopular in some areas of the countryside, and helped fuel a rebellion in Cornwall, where a minority language held sway. The English-language Bible was also a prime factor in accelerating the religious Reformation promoted by King Henry VIII. The masses could now read the word of God for themselves, rather than depend on the translations provided by clergymen who could speak Latin. In another seismic shift, the Pope's authority gradually lessened as people came to realise that the Bible attributed holy authority to God alone, not his human servants.

1453

CONSTANTINOPLE FALLS

In 1453 Constantinople, the centre of the thousand-year-old Roman–Byzantine Empire, was defeated by the Ottoman Empire under the leadership of Mehmed II. This event marked the end of the Middle Ages, and contrasted an emerging Muslim power with a decaying and ancient Christian empire. During a siege campaign that was defined by over a month of constant bombardment, the city was finally taken, Emperor Constantine XI was killed, as were many of his Genoese and Venetian supporters and many of his townspeople. Mehmed established an empire which ultimately would extend from the Euphrates to the Danube.

THE END OF THE BYZANTINE EMPIRE AND THE RISE OF THE OTTOMANS

Surely, Constantinople will be conquered; how blessed the commander who will conquer it, and how blessed his army.

PROPHECY OF MUHAMMAD

On 29 May 1453, twenty-year-old Sultan Mehmed II triumphantly rode his white horse down the avenue that ran through the centre of Constantinople and watched as the Islamic soldiers of his victorious Turkish Ottoman army sacked the city that had been the capital of the Roman Empire throughout the Middle Ages. According to Nicolo Barbaro, a witness from the city-state of Venice, blood flowed through the streets like water following a downpour and corpses floated out to sea like melons along a river. Tursun Beg, an Ottoman administrator, wrote that the soldiers 'took silver and gold vessels, precious stones, and all sorts of valuable goods and fabrics from the imperial palace and houses of the rich. In this fashion many people were delivered from poverty and made rich.'

Mehmed rode on to the Cathedral of Holy Wisdom, or Hagia Sophia, the leading church of eastern Christendom and the seat of the Ecumenical Patriarch. It had been built nine hundred years earlier by Byzantine emperor Justinian, and boasted the largest dome in Europe. Mehmed dismounted and, as a gesture of humility before God, poured a handful of dirt over his turban. The Greeks had long considered the shrine a symbol of heaven on earth, and the temporal throne of the Christian God, but now the cathedral was being re-consecrated as the Aya Sofya mosque. Hundreds of Greeks who had taken refuge inside were rounded up and slaughtered. But when the Sultan saw one of his soldiers hacking at the marble floor he stopped him, saying 'Be satisfied with the booty and the captives; the buildings of the city belong to me'. Watched over by golden mosaics of Jesus Christ, the Virgin Mary, Greek Orthodox saints and Byzantine emperors, he offered a prayer of thanks to Allah, begging for his eternal blessing and protection.

A magnificent walled city

Constantinople (now Istanbul) had been the centre of the Christian world in the east, largely because of its strategic location on a triangular peninsula on the geographic boundary of Europe and Asia. On its north was a scimitar-shaped harbour six kilometres long and a kilometre wide, known as the Golden Horn because the setting sun bathed its waters in a golden light.

Constantinople was founded by the Greeks in about the seventh century BC. In 324 BC the

Roman emperor Constantine the Great declared it to be 'New Rome' and for the next thousand years it served as the eastern capital of the Roman Empire. It was the largest and most advanced city in Europe. In 1203 the French knight-crusader Geoffrey de Villehardouin wrote that his fellow crusaders were filled with wonder 'when they saw these high walls and these rich towers by which it was completely enclosed and those rich palaces and those lofty churches of which there were so many that no one could believe it unless he had seen it with his own eyes'. The walls, built in the fifth century AD, were indeed magnificent, stretching from the Golden Horn to the Sea of Marmara and completely enclosing the city, which was fortified by moats, parapets and one hundred and ninety-two towers. They were essential to the security of Constantinople.

But in 1204 the city was finally sacked, not by enemies but by so-called friends—fellow Christians of the fourth crusade, backed by Constantinople's commercial enemy, the seafaring state of Venice. The Byzantine Empire regained power in 1261 but in the following period the city endured continual attacks from Muslim enemies and civil wars between rival emperors. Constantinople's Greek population dwindled from four hundred thousand to about fifty thousand. They still proudly referred to themselves as Romans, in commemoration of the Roman Empire's first Christian emperor Constantine (272–337), after whom the city was named. But by 1453, Constantine XI's kingdom had dwindled to the city, a few islands, and part of the Peloponnese in southern Greece. The powerful seafaring states of Venice and Genoa had taken over all the commerce in the region and Constantinople was surrounded by foes on all sides. It was ripe for the picking.

The Ottoman threat

Mehmed's father Murad II was a man of peace and scholarship. A friend of Constantinople, he led a contemplative life, but Mehmed was ambitious, conceited and trusted no one. Constantine was well aware of the imminent threat he posed so in January 1453 he enlisted the help of Genoese nobleman Giovanni Giustiniani—an expert in defending walled cities—and his seven hundred well-armed troops. He persuaded the ever-bickering Genoese and Venetians within the city to unite under his command against the common enemy. But the Turks had a formidable new weapon on their side—an awesome bronze cannon designed by Hungarian engineer Urban, who had initially offered his assistance to Constantine in return for the funds needed to build the behemoth. But Constantine could not even afford his asking salary, let alone the construction funds, so Urban approached Mehmed, who granted him four times his asking wage and all the other necessary finance. The cannon's barrel was over 8 metres (26 feet) in length, with a bore of 60 centimetres (23 inches). Stuffed with more than 50 kilograms (110 pounds) of gunpowder, it could propel a 250-kilogram (550-pound) stone cannonball over a distance greater than a kilometre (over half a mile).

On 2 April 1453, Mehmed and his troops set up camp outside the city and began their barrage. Constantine had installed a huge chain boom across the harbour entrance, guarded by his strongest galleys. Over the next few days, the Turks tried but failed to breach the harbour boom, but did succeed in demolishing a small section of the wall. Urban's cannon was yet to arrive so Mehmed decided to postpone his

RIGHT: Sultan Mehmed II, victor at Constantinople in 1453 and the greatest ruler of the Ottoman Empire.

attack for a few days. He was well aware that the siege would be a daunting task, despite his far larger army of eighty thousand men. The weakest section of the city wall was the Golden Horn, where the shore was dotted with warehouses and wharves. Mehmed decided he could breach it once he gained control of the harbour, so he put his fleet of several hundred vessels under the command of Suleiman Baltoghlu, the governor of nearby Gallipoli. But until Baltoghlu secured the harbour, Mehmed would have to concentrate his attack on the heavily fortified landward walls. Inside the surrounding moat, a series of walls ranged from the relatively low Mesoteichion wall to walls as high as 18 metres (60 feet), with towers interspersed along their length. Mehmed concentrated his attack on the Mesoteichion wall, the weakest part of the walls.

The battle escalates

On the second night of the attack Constantine oversaw repairs to the section of the wall that the Turks had destroyed that day. All able-bodied citizens—women, men and children—participated in filling the breach with wood and stones, and by morning the repairs were passable, if not perfect. While Mehmed waited for Urban's cannon, he ordered his soldiers to fill in the moat—no small task as it ranged in depth from about 8 to 50 metres (26 to 164 feet), and could be flooded from tanks within the city. For several days the Turks worked with bundles of sticks, barrels and tree trunks, rushing the moat under a barrage of stones, arrows and walnut-sized bullets, then scurrying back to their trenches. The defenders retaliated using mechanical engines and catapults to release boulders and darts—as well as Greek fire, an incendiary substance that burned on water as well as land.

By 12 April Mehmed's reinforcements, including Urban's cannon and fifty smaller cannon, had arrived. The monster weapon had been manufactured at Adrianople, the Turkish capital, then hauled over 240 kilometres (800 miles) on a wooden raft, by thirty carts drawn by sixty bulls, and assisted by four hundred men. The gun took so long to reload that it could be fired only seven times a day. The defenders tried to reduce its impact by hanging sheets of leather and bales of wool over the walls, but this proved ineffectual. The cannon was unpredictable—after each deafening blast and discharge of pungent smoke it would recoil violently, often toppling off its wooden platform. To prevent it splitting or melting, oil was immediately poured down the barrel. Unfortunately for Urban, its inventor, it backfired early in the siege, killing him.

Meanwhile Baltoghlu, having received reinforcements, launched another attack against the harbour boom. His fleet now consisted of six two-masted triremes (with three tiers of oarsmen), ten biremes, almost a hundred other galleys and longboats, and numerous smaller craft. Constantinople's sailing fleet consisted of twenty-six large battleships, of which ten were anchored outside the chain boom to guard the 400-metre (1300-feet) wide harbour entrance. Despite being vastly outnumbered, Constanine's forces were able to force Baltoghlu to retreat by using the height advantage of their battleships to send down a hail of javelins, arrows and large rocks projected by catapults.

Mehmed decided to concentrate on a land attack. On the night of 18 April, having succeeded in filling in the moat, he launched an attack on an ageing section of the wall. Waves of Turks swarmed toward the city under a hail of weaponry but were eventually repelled. Once again Mehmed had been thwarted—he had lost over two hundred men, the heavily armoured defenders had lost none.

An eclipse recalls a fearful prophecy

The battle raged for another five weeks—after which several harbingers of imminent doom appeared. On 24 May there was a lunar eclipse, recalling a prophecy that Constantinople would fall under a waning moon. The next day, in a plea to the Lord, it was decided to remove the city's holiest statue from the church of Hagia Sophia and parade it through the streets on the shoulders of the faithful. Every citizen—including every soldier (except for a skeleton crew who remained on the walls)—joined the sombre parade. Suddenly, to everyone's horror, the icon tumbled off its stand. It took several minutes to restore its position, at which time a massive thunderstorm struck. The streets became raging torrents and several children were swept to their death as the populace fled for shelter. The next day the city was enveloped in a dense fog, which was unheard of at that time of year. That night an ominous, unnatural glow illumined the Church of the Hagia Sophia. It was noticed by the Turks in their camps and alarmed the troops—until the muezzins, whose responsibilities included leading the daily prayers to Allah, convinced them that it was an omen that the true light of God would soon shine from the church. Constantinople's counsellors begged Constantine to order the evacuation of the city, but he refused. The dispirited Turks also seemed no closer to achieving their aim, and had heard rumours that Christian reinforcements were on their way from Venice.

On 5 May Mehmed offered to spare the city if its inhabitants surrendered, but Constantine refused. For one thing, he could not afford the enormous annual tribute Mehmed demanded.

He sent back a compromise offer—he would hand over all his personal riches, but not the city. But Mehmed replied that the citizens must surrender and convert to Islam, or be killed. Thus the negotiations broke down. The next night, by torchlight, the Turks amassed materials to fill the moat, in preparation for a final, massive attack. On 27 May all the cannon were focused on the Mesoteichion, by now unstable from the constant bombardments. Urban's cannon blasted holes in the wall three times, and each time the wall was repaired. Mehmed promised all his troops that they would be given the run of the city for three days, free to plunder and rape to their hearts' content. Morale soared.

That night ten thousand torches blazed as the Turkish troops set about filling the moat and gathering weapons. The exhausted defenders made no attempt to stop them; many knelt and prayed. At midnight all work abruptly stopped; Mehmed had ordered that there would be a day of rest and religious observance before the final offensive. Shortly after 1 am on 29 May, a fanfare of drums and trumpets announced that the onslaught was about to begin. The Turks began bombarding the Mesoteichion wall, but were repelled by Giustiniani and his men.

Simultaneous attacks commenced on the sea wall, which faced the Golden Horn, but once again the defenders were able to repel the invaders. Mehmed's battle plan was to allow the Christians no relief, to wear down the resistance of the tired, hungry defenders by sheer force of numbers. Wave after wave of his troops advanced, with the dead immediately replaced by others. It was a high-priced strategy in terms of casualties, but Mehmed was taking advantage of his great numerical superiority. He positioned armed troops behind the front lines whose job was to kill anyone who hesitated or retreated. Ottoman troops surged over the moat and through the breaches created by the cannon. They grappled with the defenders on the outer wall and swarmed up ladders placed against parts of the wall that were still intact. Just before dawn Giustiniani, who had been leading his troops from the Mesoteichion for more than six hours, was wounded. Constantine pleaded with him to stay at his post, but to no avail; his injuries had incapacitated him. He and his bodyguards fled to the harbour and boarded a Genoese ship. Once his soldiers realised that their leader was gone they lost heart and the

The siege of Constantinople, which lasted for just over a month, ended the 1000-year-old Byzantine Empire.

defence faltered. The demoralised Genoese and many others fled. A group of soldiers led by a giant Turk named Hasan managed to climb to the top of the outer wall. Hasan was killed, but the followers succeeded in swarming over the wall, then through the damaged inner wall and into the city.

Meanwhile about fifty Turks had broken in through a small gate further up the hill. It had not been properly bolted and yielded to their pressure. They were the first invaders to enter the city; fortunately for them, they had not been noticed in the fierce battles for the walls, otherwise they would have been easily overpowered and killed. But it was too late—they had mounted the turret over the gate and raised the Ottoman flag above it. Their emboldened comrades yelled the news that the city was taken and the defenders retreated as more and more of the invaders flooded through the walls, smashing them as the Christians withdrew. Constantine

tried to lead by example, leaping into the fray and fighting bravely as a common soldier, but to no avail. He was killed after throwing away his royal regalia and charging defiantly into a mass of advancing Turks.

End of an empire

The locals began rushing to their houses in a vain attempt to save their families. The Venetians and Genoese who had escaped the slaughter fled for the safety of their ships. The commanders of the fleets hacked away the boom protecting the harbour and, their vessels packed with refugees who had managed to swim to the ships, sailed away, along with a bare few of the emperor's ships. They were the lucky few who avoided the terrible fate that awaited the Christian survivors now at the mercy of the rampaging Turks. The Byzantine Empire, which had survived for over a thousand years, was no more.

THE NEW WORLD JOURNAL

LEFT: A defiant Henry VIII presents his second wife, Anne Boleyn, to the English court, in 1533.

1519

NAVIGATOR CIRCLES THE WORLD

Perhaps the greatest journey in the age of discovery was Ferdinand Magellan's circumnavigation of the world. On 20 September 1519, after convincing the Spanish king to fund the expedition, the Portuguese explorer Magellan set sail from Spain with five ships to find a westward route to the Spice Islands. By November he had reached South America, and the following year he rounded the Strait of Magellan and entered the Pacific Ocean, arriving in the Philippines in March 1521. Although Magellan did not make it home—dying in battle in the Philippines—he did circumnavigate the globe by passing the easternmost point he had visited on an earlier voyage. On 6 September the last remaining ship, in his fleet, the *Victoria*, loaded with spices, arrived in Seville under the leadership of Sebastián del Cano and history was made.

MAGELLAN'S VOYAGE AND THE AGE OF DISCOVERY

Most versed in nautical charts, he knew better than any other the true art of navigation.

ANTONIO PIGAFETTA, WRITING ABOUT FERDINAND MAGELLAN

The expedition of Portuguese explorer, sailor and navigator Ferdinand Magellan (c. 1480–1521) completed the first circumnavigation of the world. Magellan was the son of Rui de Magalhães and Alda de Mesquita, members of the Portuguese nobility. He spent his childhood in the northern state of Minho, and at the age of eleven was enrolled in the Royal School for Pages where he studied etiquette, music, fencing, dancing, astronomy, cartography and navigation. These subjects reflected Portugal's status as a great seafaring nation—since the 1430s the Portuguese had been colonising the west coast of Africa, setting up trading centres and proving that humans could actually live in the tropics (previously regarded by Europeans as uninhabitable).

By the time Magellan entered page school, his countryman Bartholomew Diaz had travelled south, rounded the Cape of Good Hope at the southern tip of Africa and, sailing in a northeasterly direction, discovered an ocean route to India and the Far East. This was significant because the overland trade routes across Europe and into western Asia were controlled by middlemen in the Middle East, making goods far more expensive. By the time such goods as silk, porcelain and spices reached Europe their price was a hundred times greater than the cost at the source.

During Magellan's first year at school the Genoese navigator Christopher Columbus, sailing under the flag of Portugal's bitter naval and trade rival Spain, reached the islands of the New World in the Caribbean. A few years later Portuguese explorer Vasco da Gama sailed around Africa to India and then to the Molucca Islands (known as the Spice Islands), at the southern tip of Malaya. When da Gama returned home, he brought such riches of spices, silk, emeralds and pearls that overnight Portugal was transformed from one of the poorest to one of the richest countries in Europe. Magellan started dreaming of leading his own expedition ship to the east, but obstacles were put in his way. For some reason the supervisor of the page school, Duke Manuel, brother-in-law of Portuguese King John II, took an enduring dislike to Magellan. A page needed royal patronage in order to gain employment at sea, and his hopes faded further when the king was assassinated in 1495 and Manuel ascended to the throne. For the next nine years Manuel thwarted all Magellan's attempts to go to sea on one of the many ships that sailed from the port of Lisbon to the Spice Islands.

Magellan joins his first expedition to the East

In 1504 Magellan saw his opportunity. Manuel ordered Admiral Francisco Almeida to India with the largest fleet ever to leave Portugal— twenty-two small, highly manoeuvrable caravels and some two thousand men. Magellan took leave from his inconsequential job at court, concealing his reason for doing so, and signed up as a common sailor on one of the caravels. Almeida's mission was to destroy the Arab trading centres on the east coast of Africa and the west coast of India, in order to gain control of the lucrative commerce routes. The armada spent eighteen months in the Indian Ocean, attacking numerous African ports, setting up sieges and blockades, and driving the occupants—those who survived their massacres—into the inland jungles. Magellan proved to be an excellent sailor and soldier, and was promoted to captain of a barge equipped with six cannon. He and his small crew sank over two hundred Arab craft and Magellan was rewarded with another promotion, to captain of a segment of the fleet. In early 1509 the armada was involved in one of history's bloodiest sea battles off the Malabar Coast of south India, eventually taking over all the trading ports in the region. Magellan was seriously wounded and spent five months in hospital.

The fleet then sailed to Malacca on the southwest of the Malay Peninsula, where Magellan was again wounded in a skirmish with the local sultan, from whom he acquired a thirteen-year-old slave named Black Henry, who would remain with him from that point on. Magellan captured a Malaccan caravel and embarked upon a journey to the Philippines. He displayed his honesty by reporting back that he had found some islands, but did not claim them because they belonged to Spain. (This was based on the Treaty of Tordesillas, brokered by the pope and signed by the kings of Spain and Portugal, under which the non-Christian world was divided by an imaginary line from pole to pole. Lands to the west of it belonged to Spain; to the east, Portugal.) Magellan's naval superiors, infuriated, sent him home to be punished by King Manuel, who was only too happy to comply. Magellan was demoted, put on half pay and sent as a soldier to North Africa, where the Portuguese were at war with the Moors. He was wounded in action by a spear to the right knee, leaving him lame for life. He was also accused of treason for supposedly trading with the Moors, and sent home. The charges were eventually dropped but Magellan's star had waned to the extent that he saw no future for himself in Portugal. He requested command of a caravel and when Manuel refused asked permission to seek another master. Manuel replied, 'Serve whom you will, Clubfoot, it is a matter of indifference to me.'

Magellan seeks patronage to fulfil his dream

Magellan hatched his plan to reach the East by travelling west from Europe, believing that he could find El Paso, a passage through the Americas to the Far East. He had no chance of receiving Portuguese royal patronage for such an expedition, but fortunately made the acquaintance of two wealthy and powerful Spanish brothers, Duarte and Diogo Barbosa. They arranged his marriage to Diogo's wealthy daughter Beatriz, then introduced him to King Charles I of Spain, better known as Charles V, emperor of the Holy Roman Empire. The king, delighted to be told that Magellan had not

RIGHT: Theodor de Bry's sixteenth-century allegorical rendering of Magellan's incredible voyage.

 ERDINANDVS *Magallanus à Rege Portugalliæ offensus, Carolum V. Imperatorem adit, atq; illi demonstrat Moluccas Insulas Castellanorum iuris esse: sperare se, nauigatione ad Occidentem facta, fretum inuenturum in Occidentali India, per quod in mare Australe penetraret, & inde ad Moluccas insulas peruenire posset: Ea autem via minoribus sumtibus, & minore difficultate, aromata, aliasq; Orientis merces inuehi possé. Carolus ex eorum sententia qui rerum Indicarum Concilio præerant, illi naues instruit quibus eum præficit. Is Hispali soluens, post longam nauigationem tandem fretum inuenit centum decem leucas in longitudinem patens, binas in latitudinem, interdum plures, cui, ab Inuentoris nomine, Magallanici cognomen inditum.*

attacked his holdings in the Philippines, gave him five tall, square-rigged sailing ships, fully equipped with captains, crew and supplies. Magellan chose the 110-tonne caravel *Trinidad* as his flagship, and one of his countrymen, John Serrano, and three Spaniards to captain the carracks *San Antonio, Victoria, Concepcion* and *Santiago*. At the last minute he also received a passenger, Venetian nobleman Antonio Pigafetta, who was actually a spy sent by the rulers of Venice to report on any new trade routes to the East discovered by the expedition. Pigafetta did us a favour by keeping a detailed diary, the only surviving account of the journey.

The fleet, with about two hundred and seventy men, set off on 20 September 1519, sailing south down the coast of west Africa, then crossing the Atlantic to South America. In January Magellan thought he had discovered El Paso, but it turned out to be the estuary of the Rio de la Plata, the dividing line between present-day Uruguay and Argentina. Disappointed but not discouraged, they headed south and soon found themselves in the icy, stormy waters near the Antarctic. On 31 March they anchored in a bay that Magellan named St Julian, not far from the Falkland Islands, to sit out the southern winter—but unrest was growing among the crew. Food was running low, largely because about one-third of the provisions had been stolen by secret agents of King Manuel before they set sail. In addition, the Spanish crewmembers, who resented being under the command of a Portuguese captain, began to hatch plans for a mutiny. They had already tried to take control of the expedition in the Atlantic by murdering Magellan, who got wind of the plot and saved his life by agreeing to follow their sailing orders for a while. But he was still in a highly fraught position. Pigafetta's diary describes what then took place:

On the night of 1–2 April, (Spanish captain) Cartagena boarded the San Antonio *and forced her ship's company to acknowledge them as their leader. By dawn the Spaniards had seized three ships, leaving Magellan in charge of just the* Trinidad *and the* Santiago. *But Magellan was equal to the task of restoring his power. He sent some of his men to the* Victoria *to announce that they wished to join the turncoats, but once aboard they pulled out concealed weapons and recaptured the ship. Magellan then covered the harbour entrance with the three ships he now controlled, leading the outnumbered rebels to surrender. Cartagena was court-martialled then left to die on an uninhabited island; another Spanish captain, Mendoza, died in the fighting while the third, Quesada, was executed. The latter two were strung up and left hanging on the* Trinidad *as a warning to the rest of the crew that Magellan was in control.*

Magellan had thwarted the mutiny, but still faced the bitterly cold winter ahead. The crew constructed wooden huts while the mutineers were forced to clean the ships' hulls, in chains and often up to their waist in freezing water. They would not be unchained until the start of summer when the journey resumed.

The discovery of El Paso— and a vast ocean

When the ice floes eventually started melting, the fleet set southward once again. The wonderful day came on 21 October 1520 when they finally discovered El Paso, the winding, mountain-edged waterway across the southernmost tip of South America that we now know as the Strait of Magellan. By the time they reached the western end of the passage on 27 November, the fleet had been reduced to three ships. The *Santiago* had been wrecked on a sandbar, while the *San*

Antonio had mutinied, deserted, and headed back across the Atlantic for Spain. Now that they had traversed El Paso, Magellan was certain that they would soon reach the Spice Islands—but the world turned out to be much larger and the journey ahead much longer than anyone had imagined. Finding himself at the edge of a large, peaceful sea, Magellan wrote: 'we are about to stand into an ocean where no ship has ever sailed before. May the ocean be always as calm and benevolent as it is today. In this hope I name it *El Mar Pacifico* (Pacific Ocean).'

On 25 January they found a small island where they were able to stock up on water and food. They set sail after a week but soon the food ran out again, and Magellan knew that they would all die unless they could find land within two days. On 6 March they had the good fortune to come across the island of Guam. They were attacked by natives in a flotilla of canoes, waving spears and clubs and bearing oval shields. Magellan fired the cannon on them, causing them to retreat into the jungle, and the crews feasted for a few hours on the food they found in the natives' huts before resuming their voyage with stolen food. Nine days later they discovered a series of wooded islands where they rested for a few days and replenished their supplies. On 28 March they were approached by eight natives in a large canoe. Magellan's young slave Black Henry hailed them in Malay, the language of his native Malacca. They replied in the same language and Magellan realised that they had finally reached the Philippines—the very islands that he had approached from the opposite direction in 1511. The first circumnavigation of the world was complete.

Fatal encounter in the Pacific

Magellan befriended Columbu, the rajah of the island where his ships were anchored. He and many of his people soon converted to Christianity, but the rajah told Magellan of some islands nearby where the locals refused to convert. Magellan, like all Spanish explorers, was commissioned to bring souls to God, and decided that they must be punished. A group of his men were sent to attack the island of Mactan. They destroyed the villages and killed the warriors, but the Mactan's leader stood firm. On 26 April 1521, Magellan led a force of some sixty men onto Mactan, where they were met by an opposing force of about three thousand. Too late Magellan realised that he had been led into a trap, and he ordered a retreat. Most of his men escaped back to their boats, but Magellan and about twelve of his men were left stranded. The Spaniards who had escaped refused to come to the aid of their Portuguese captain, and he was stabbed to death. In the words of Pigafetta:

The natives continued to pursue us, and picking up the same spear four or six times, hurled it at us again and again. Recognising the captain, so many turned upon him that they knocked his helmet off his head twice, but he always stood firmly like a good knight, together with some others. Thus did we fight for more than one hour, refusing to retire any farther. An Indian hurled a bamboo spear into the captain's face, but the latter immediately killed him with his lance, which he left in the Indian's body. Then, trying to lay hand on sword, he could draw it out but halfway, because he had been wounded in the arm with a bamboo spear. When the natives saw that, they all hurled themselves upon him. One of them wounded him on the left leg with a large cutlass, which resembles a scimitar, only being larger. That caused the captain to fall face downward, when immediately they rushed upon him with iron and bamboo spears and cutlasses, until they killed our mirror, our light, our comfort, and our true guide.

The *Victoria* limps home

Magellan's remaining men accepted an invitation to a feast by the rajah of Cebu, who got them thoroughly drunk and killed most of them. Juan Carvalho took command and ordered the burning of the *Concepcion*, along with all Magellan's records, in the hope that evidence of their treachery would be destroyed. The *Trinidad* and *Victoria* set sail, running amok around the southwest Pacific for four months, plundering and attacking ships and harbours. On 8 November they reached the Spice Islands

Magellan is killed on the Philippine island of Mactan, after getting involved in a local dispute.

and were welcomed by the king of Tidor, who invited them to stay and trade. In February 1522 they set off for the long return voyage, stocking up (according to Pigafetta's record) with 'many bahars of cloves, plumage of the terrestrial bird of paradise, roots of ginger dried in jars … very many quintals of pepper … sandalwood, white gold … robes of silk …' The *Trinidad* headed east for the Spanish port of Panama, but was captured by a Portuguese fleet in the Pacific, and all on board were hanged as pirates. The *Victoria* headed west for Spain on 13 February and, after a gruelling voyage during which many of the men died of starvation and scurvy, finally arrived at San Lucar harbour in Spain on 6 September 1522.

Of the two hundred and seventy men who had set out, only eighteen returned alive. The *Victoria* had sailed more than 64,000 kilometres (around 34,000 nautical miles) around the world, more than half of which had never been traversed by Europeans.

1519–21

MONTEZUMA WELCOMES 'GOD' CORTÉS

After Christopher Columbus discovered the New World in 1492, stories of wealthy empires and fabulous riches encouraged many Europeans to travel across the Atlantic Ocean in search of their fortune. Spaniard Hernán Cortés was one of these thousands of adventurers, and perhaps the luckiest. By an amazing stroke of coincidence, he was mistaken for a god by the Aztec occupants of Central America, leading to his conquest of Tenochtitlán, the Aztec capital, in 1521 and the eventual Spanish occupation of much of South America and the Caribbean. The treasures plundered by Cortés and succeeding Spanish *conquistadors* (conquerors) and brought back to Europe were so great that the fragile economy of sixteenth-century Europe almost collapsed, while the lives of the people of the New World were changed forever, and great civilisations, such as the Aztecs, were destroyed.

THE SPANISH DEFEAT OF THE AZTECS

Among these temples there is one which far surpasses all the rest, whose grandeur of architectural details no human tongue is able to describe; for within its precincts, surrounded by a lofty wall, there is room enough for a town of five hundred families.

HERNÁN CORTÉS' SECOND LETTER TO CHARLES V

Cortés was born in 1485 in the Spanish town of Medellin, to a family of 'little wealth but much honour', according to his secretary. At the age of fourteen he commenced studying law and classics at Salamanca, in western Spain. He left before graduating and joined the Spanish navy as a clerk. In 1504 he travelled to the island of Hispaniola, a recently conquered Spanish colony in the Caribbean, where he worked as a farmer and trained as a soldier before joining the army of Diego Velázquez, participating in the conquest of Cuba in 1511; he was subsequently appointed mayor of the Cuban city of Santiago. By 1518 Velázquez was governor of Cuba and Cortés one of his most trusted allies. He originally commissioned Cortés to explore the Mexican coast, but changed his mind, perhaps fearing that the ambitious Cortés would assume governorship of the mainland. But Cortés, mutinously, decided to go anyway, setting off with his mutinous fleet of some eleven ships, six hundred men, sixteen horses (unknown in the Americas at the time), numerous steel swords and shields, and about twenty guns, including a bronze cannon. The fleet made landfall on the Yucatan Peninsula, far from the centre of the Aztec empire, and proceeded to sack the Mayan town of Tabasco. Cortés had heard many tales of fabulous riches further to the west, and determined to claim and plunder the territory in the name of Spain and Christianity.

An astonishing civilisation

The fierce Aztecs ruled an empire encompassing most of Central America where they had created an astonishing civilisation. On an island in the middle of Lake Texcoco, in modern-day Mexico City, stood a beautiful and opulent city with a population of some 250,000, making it one of the largest in the world. Tenochtitlán was just one of several such Aztec cities. Its two-storey royal palace contained hundreds of rooms, a three-thousand-seat hall, and walls covered with paintings, stone and wood carvings and solid-gold panels. It was surrounded by gardens with ponds and fountains, and a large zoo where its ruler Montezuma kept exotic birds and animals.

The Aztecs practised human sacrifice as part of their religion, often using captured soldiers from nearby states. Their need for a constant, daily supply of human hearts to offer to the sun-god Huitzilopochtli made them very unpopular with their neighbours—a situation which Cortés would use to good advantage. Montezuma, who lived in an opulent palace in the centre of Tenochtitlán, enjoyed god-like status and ruled a vast army.

The Aztecs believed that, Quetzalcoatl ('Feathered Serpent'), a god who opposed human sacrifice, would one day return to punish them in what they called a '1-Reed year' on their calendar. These occurred every fifty-two years, and it so happened that 1519 was a 1-Reed year, and that Cortés made his appearance at the coastal town of Vera Cruz on 22 April, the very day predicted by the prophecy. Furthermore, Quetzalcoatl was always depicted with dark clothes, a white face and a feather in his cap—just like a conquistador in uniform. There had been other recent portents of evil for the Aztec world. A blazing comet crossed the skies; temples were hit by lightning, causing many to burst into flames; Tenochtitlán was hit by several unprecedented floods; and some said they had seen the water in Lake Texcoco boil.

When Montezuma's envoys met Cortés, they were overcome with both reverence and terror. It would not do to harm one of their most revered deities, but, on the other hand, if the newcomers with their terrible weapons were hostile, the Aztec empire was in grave danger. They presented Cortés with gifts including twenty women and a huge, solid-gold disc of the sun, the size of a cartwheel. One of the women was Doña Marina, who would learn Spanish and go on to accompany Cortés as adviser and translator in his future exploits. She also became his mistress and bore him a son.

Montezuma hoped that the strange intruders would be impressed, take their gifts and leave the Aztecs alone, but the ploy merely reinforced Cortés' determination to complete his terrible ambitions. He destroyed all but one of his boats, offering his troops a last chance to return to Spain, but none took up the offer. In any case,

retreat or escape was now impossible for the Spanish contingent—it would be death or glory. Cortés wrote to Spanish King Charles V: 'I intend to advance and see him [Montezuma] wherever he might be found and bring him either dead or in chains if he will not submit to your Majesty's crown'. He correctly predicted that victory, and booty, would prevent him being punished for his mutiny against Velázquez.

An invasion, a massacre and a farewell to Montezuma

Cortés' army began the trek to Tenochtitlán, receiving support from tribes who had suffered at the hands of the Aztecs. En route, they invaded the powerful state of Tlaxcala and gave the Indians their first sight of the awesome power of European weaponry. Though outnumbered by at least fifty to one, the Spaniards quickly won an overwhelming victory. The vanquished Tlaxcalans agreed to join his cause against the hated Aztecs. Cortés marched onwards to the city of Cholula, where Montezuma's agents tried to poison him. Cortés responded by massacring the city's entire population as a brutal demonstration of power before continuing onwards to Tenochtitlán. Montezuma's spies had told him of the Tlaxcalan alliance; so, rather than fight such a formidable force, he invited the Spaniards to cross the narrow protective causeways that led to Tenochtitlán. Upon meeting Montezuma, Cortés feigned friendship, but soon made him a hostage in a bid to protect his position, surrounded as he was by a quarter of a million furious Aztecs.

At the beginning of 1520 Cortés received word that a Spanish force was on its way from Cuba with a royal contract to imprison him and confiscate his bounty. He and most of his troops headed off to the coast, leaving Tenochtitlán in the hands of just eighty of his men. Cortés managed to defeat his would-be gaolers, and persuaded most of them to switch allegiance and join his cause in the battle for Tenochtitlán. But when Cortés returned, he discovered that there had been an uprising, and that his countrymen and his hostage Montezuma were under siege.

The greatly outnumbered Cortés convinced Montezuma to address the furious mob from a tower in an effort to placate them, but they stoned him to death. On 30 June 1520, Cortés tried to escape with his men under the cover of darkness. He got away, but about two-thirds of

The Aztec capital of Tenochtitlán, where Montezuma welcomed Cortés, was larger than any European city in the 1500s.

his men were killed, and many others wounded. Some drowned as they swam across Lake Texcoco, weighed down by the gold that they had pillaged from Montezuma's palace. The dead Spaniards were offered as sacrifice, and their skulls and those of their horses were displayed on the enormous skull-rack in Tenochtitlán's main square. The remaining troops were pursued by hordes of Aztecs but, on reaching the other end of the causeway, the Spanish turned around, attacked and somehow emerged victorious. This awful night became known as *La Noche Triste*.

The Spaniards had another, invisible ally: they had inadvertently infected the city's population with smallpox, which rapidly decimated the population and severely weakened the Aztec military force. Montezuma's successor, his brother Cuitlahuac, died of the disease after reigning for just 80 days.

Return to Tenochtitlan

Cortés, after reaching the safety of the coast, rounded up a 75,000-strong army of Cuban mercenaries, Tlaxcalan volunteers and more new arrivals from Spain. On 28 April 1521 he returned to Tenochtitlán with 86 horsemen, 118 crossbowmen and musketeers, 700 swordsmen, his new native army and 18 cannons. They were confronted by troops who no longer believed in the divinity of the interlopers. The Aztecs' primitive weapons included wooden swords edged with razor-sharp obsidian, wooden clubs known as *macanas*, lances and axes. Some used bows, but their arrows were unable to penetrate the Spanish steel coats of armour.

Cortés and his brigands swarmed to the edge of the causeways and began their attack and siege on Tenochtitlán. The troops were split into three sections. Cortés' deputy, Pedro de Alvarado, took 30 horses, 18 bowmen, 150 Spanish infantrymen and 25,000 Tlaxcalans

along the northwest causeway. Cristóbal de Sandoval led 30 horses, 18 bowmen, 150 infantry and 25,000 Tlaxcalans down the southwest causeway. Gonzalo de Sandoval advanced along the southeast causeway with 24 cavalry, 4 musketeers, 13 bowmen, 150 infantry and 30,000 foot soldiers, while Cortés commanded 13 recently constructed brigantines which contained the remaining Spanish musketeers and archers. He left one causeway free hoping that the Aztecs would escape, rather than fight to the death, but few took this option. The Spanish first destroyed the city's fresh water supply; the Aztecs responded by showering them with the arms, legs and heads of the Spaniards they had captured and sacrificed. The defenders hoped to demoralise the Christian Spaniards, knowing how appalled they were by the practice of human sacrifice, and screamed 'Bad men, your blood appease our gods and will be drunk by our snakes'. This psychological ploy would be used, unsuccessfully, for the duration of the siege. When the brigantines entered the lake from the river, the Aztecs attacked them with more than five hundred canoes but were repelled by Spanish gunfire. The Aztecs managed to slow the progress of the ships, and of the advancing causeway troops they were supporting, by driving wooden stakes into the bottom of the shallow lake. Many tried to swim out to the ships and surprise them, but this was rarely successful. Meanwhile, famine increased as the besieged city was unable to import foodstuffs from the surrounding countryside.

Defence of the causeways descends into slaughter

By 9 June the Spaniards had made some progress along the causeways; Alvarado in particular had advanced 400 metres (1300 feet). Their progress was slowed by the Aztecs' destruction of the wooden bridges on the walkways, which they were forced to painstakingly repair time and again as the defenders destroyed by night what they had constructed by day. As the troops reached the edge of the city, they destroyed every house and used the material to repair the gaps in the bridges. The ships prowled the lake, smashing every canoe they could find, and stringing up the captured Aztec warriors from their masts. The Aztecs were not used to this style of battle—their custom was to capture prisoners from enemy states in a form of limited, ritualistic warfare with neighbouring, loosely allied states, then offer them up as sacrifices— but they soon learned. They gleefully sacrificed all their prisoners, accompanied by the ominous pounding of a gigantic drum which the invaders learned to hate, knowing that their comrades' living hearts were being ripped out by priests encrusted in Spanish blood. Conquistador and diarist Bernard Díaz del Castillo wrote this gruesome eyewitness account:

We saw them put plumes on many of them, and then they made them dance with a sort of fan in front of Huitzilopochtli. Then, after they had danced, the priests laid them on their backs on some narrow stones of sacrifice and, cutting open their chests, drew out their palpitating hearts which they offered to the idols before them. Then they kicked the bodies down the steps, and the Indian butchers who were waiting below cut off their arms and legs and flayed their faces, which they afterwards prepared like glove leather, with their beards on, and kept for their drunken festivals. Then they ate their flesh with a sauce of peppers and tomatoes.

Siege of the city

At one point Cortés was almost captured after he advanced too far past the nearest opening in the causeway. He was ambushed by Aztecs, who killed many of his men and drove him to the edge of a 20-metre (65-foot) gap. But his life was saved by a comrade who severed the arm of an Aztec chief who was hauling Cortés towards a canoe. The Aztecs bombarded Cortés with Spanish heads as they cursed him and taunted him with the claim that they had killed Doña Marina. But Cortés and the invaders, having crossed the causeways and invaded the city, were gradually destroying Tenochtitlán, forcing its ever-decreasing defence forces into a small area near the city centre. Many of the starving Aztecs were little more than skin and bone, but they fought to the death nonetheless. Many were also dying of starvation and disease, particularly smallpox to which they had no resistance— unlike the Spaniards.

Cortés' three columns burned everything in their path as they advanced toward the marketplace in the city centre. When they smashed the gigantic holy pyramid of Huitzilopochtli, they found at its apex a mountain of clotted human blood, whipped corpses and heads, some the identifiable remains of their recently slain comrades. The carnage became enormous as the Aztec defiance wilted. On some days the Spaniards captured and massacred over ten thousand prisoners; at this point even the resolute, hard-hearted Cortés lost his stomach for the slaughter, and began trying to persuade King Cuauhtémoc (who had ascended the throne after the death of Cuitlahuac from smallpox) to surrender. But the Aztec king threatened to kill any of his countrymen who retreated, or dared to advocate peace. Not until the city was almost completely controlled by the Spanish was the king captured as he tried to escape in a canoe. The Spaniards tortured him until he revealed the location of the gold and other riches that they had gathered before they fled on *La Noche*

CONQVISTA DE MEXICO POR CORTES. Aº 7

Triste. Cortés led the final attack on 13 August 1521, and the Spanish victory was complete.

After the carnage

Within forty years of Cortés' conquest of Tenochtitlán, Spain had plundered over 100 tonnes of gold—more than double the amount previously held in the whole of Europe. They also pillaged some 7000 tonnes of silver, and other riches in the form of precious stones,

LEFT: Slaughter on the causeway—the Aztecs were no match for the sophistication of the Spanish weaponry.

artefacts, woods, spices, food (including chocolate) and animal skins. Within eighty years, three-quarters of the Aztec population had died of smallpox and other imported diseases. It would be another three hundred years before Mexico regained its independence from Spain.

Meanwhile, Cortés was appointed governor of 'New Spain', as the region was now called. Christian churches replaced Aztec temples and, in 1540, a new Spanish viceroy was appointed and Cortés returned to Spain. He died, poor and in debt, at Castilleja de la Cuesta, near the town of Seville, on 2 December 1547.

1533

COURTESAN CATCHES THE KING

In 1527 a young woman at the English court, Anne Boleyn, caught the eye of the sovereign, King Henry VIII. When she refused to become his mistress Henry determined to seek an annulment of his marriage to Catherine of Aragon. The pope in Rome, however, refused this request—leading to a stalemate as both Henry and Anne refused to compromise their positions, and setting in motion the end of Catholicism in England.

HENRY MARRIES ANNE BOLEYN—THE END OF CATHOLICISM IN ENGLAND

In this world I will confess myself to be the king's true wife,
and in the next they will know how unreasonably I am afflicted.

CATHERINE OF ARAGON, 1532

The tumultuous reign of English king Henry VIII (1491–1547) is notable for Henry's succession of wives and the separation of England from the Roman Catholic Church. When Henry ascended the throne he became the second monarch of the Tudor line, which began with the ascension of his father Henry VII in August 1484 and ended with the death of Elizabeth I in March 1603. Henry married six times, but it was his pursuit of and subsequent marriage to his second wife, Anne Boleyn, that would lead to the establishment of the Church of England and mark the beginning of the end of papal power in England.

Henry was the second son of Henry VII and, after the death of his elder brother Arthur in 1502, knew that he would one day be king. In his youth he was a keen student of a wide variety of learning, particularly the explosion of new, empirical knowledge that was beginning to appear across Europe. In addition to intellectual pursuits, he also became well versed in the various physical accomplishments expected of a nobleman, and by the time he ascended the throne in 1509 he was an accomplished athlete, jouster, hunter and dancer. He was very popular with the masses and

widely admired for his excellent physique and appearance: he was 182 centimetres (6 feet) in height (unusually tall for the time), powerfully built and very handsome.

The young king marries Catherine of Aragon

On 11 June 1509, soon after his accession, Henry married his brother Arthur's widow, Catherine of Aragon. She proved unable to provide him with a male heir, suffering several stillbirths and infant deaths. Her only living child, Mary, born in 1516, would go on to reign from 1553 to 1558. While there was no legal hindrance to a female monarch, the fragile and treacherous nature of royal politics in Europe meant that a king was far preferable in terms of providing future stability. Contemporary wisdom held that a woman was too weak to rule alone, and would need to marry into another royal family, thus risking instability or war as the new king exercised his right to rule.

Henry eventually tired of Catherine and embarked upon a series of unconcealed affairs with ladies of his court—which Catherine, by and large, endured with a stoic and gracious understanding. In about 1526 his attention was taken by Anne Boleyn, one of his wife's maids of honour. Henry had had an affair with Anne's elder sister, Mary, in 1520. Anne, daughter of aristocrat and successful diplomat Sir Thomas Boleyn, had spent much of her youth in France, eventually serving as a maid of honour for several years at the French royal court of Francis I, as her sister had done. She returned to England in 1522, taking up residence at Henry's court. The manners and style she had acquired in France did not go unnoticed, and she quickly gained a reputation as a most accomplished and intelligent courtier. She had received an excellent, wide-ranging education in the Netherlands and France, was fluent in French and Latin, and soon attracted numerous young suitors. She became secretly engaged to Henry Percy, son of the Earl of Northumberland and a famous debaucher, but when Henry discovered this he ordered archbishop of York Cardinal Wolsey to prevent the marriage. Henry had effectively delegated to Wolsey the power to rule England, freeing the king to concentrate on more hedonistic pursuits.

The pursuit of Anne Boleyn

Henry became completely besotted with Anne, but she refused all his advances. Previous mistresses had rapidly succumbed to Henry's charms, but Anne was made of sterner stuff. Henry's usual practice was to discard and marry off his mistresses when he tired of them and Anne was determined to avoid that fate. Although Henry pursued her fervently, she kept him at arm's length, telling him she would not be seduced as an unmarried woman. She knew of Henry's disaffection with Catherine, and no doubt saw an opportunity to take advantage of his passion and to become queen. Anne's brother and her sister Mary were renowned for their

promiscuity, and her mother's reputation was also suspect. King Francis had mentioned to the Duke of Norfolk 'how little virtuously Anne had always lived'. Her refusal to submit to Henry's advances, therefore, was almost certainly the result of calculating ambition rather than an inherent sense of morality.

There was still the matter of Henry's marriage to Catherine, and his need for a divorce. The Book of Leviticus warns that a man who marries his brother's wife (as Henry had) will be punished with childlessness and Henry, despite having received permission from Pope Julius II for the marriage, suspected that Catherine's failure to produce a son might indeed have been that punishment. In addition, the leader of the French embassy, Gabriel de Grammont, Bishop of Tharbes, had told Henry that, even though the pope had permitted his marriage to Catherine, he was not sure that it was legitimate under canon law. From now on Henry wanted to do everything according to the precepts of church law.

A request for an annulment

On 22 June 1527 he told Catherine that he had sent an envoy to Rome to ask Pope Clement VII for an annulment. This was the beginning of what became known as 'the Great Matter'; it would dominate the court—and English domestic and foreign policy—for the next decade. Catherine and Henry continued to keep up appearances, dining together in public and maintaining courteous relations. Cardinal Wolsey's spies (at Henry's behest, and bribed by money, gifts and sex) were keeping Catherine under surveillance and scrutinising all her letters before they were sent. But as the pope had been recently imprisoned by Catherine's nephew and ruler of the Holy Roman Empire, King Charles V, Henry and Wolsey soon realised that he would

Official portrait of Henry VIII around the time of Anne's execution.

probably be unwilling—or unable—to agree to an annulment. Henry thus put Wolsey in charge of facilitating the divorce. Wolsey, who was jealous of Anne's increasing influence, nonetheless had no choice but to comply. Anne would soon gain her revenge against Wolsey for disallowing her earlier marriage to the Earl of Northumberland.

Anne continued to play hard to get. When Henry became too ardent, she would retreat to her family home until Henry begged her to return to him. The Vatican archives contain seventeen letters from Henry to Anne dating from 1527 to 1529. In one he says: 'Hence shall my heart be dedicate to you alone, greatly desirous that so my body could be as well ... Written by the hand of the servant who in heart, body and will is, Your loyal and most ensured servant, H.' In another letter he ends with: 'wishing myself, specially an evening, in my sweetheart's arms, whose pretty dukkys [breasts] I trust shortly to kiss'. (We know that Anne somehow resisted these passionate beseechings, because other letters, according to a 1530 report by the Spanish ambassador, provide proof. And in 1531 Henry, who did not hide his affairs from Catherine, swore to her that he had not committed adultery with Anne.)

In 1528 the pope, wishing to play for time, sent his envoy Cardinal Lorenzo Campeggio to England to hear Henry's arguments for annulment, and to try to broker a reconciliation between Henry and Catherine. By now the Great Matter had led to the formation of three factions in a fierce power struggle among the nobility, and in the court and the houses of Parliament. One bloc comprised followers of Cardinal Wolsey and supported Henry, another secretly supported Catherine but wanted to get rid of Wolsey, while a third faction, which would soon become the most powerful, supported Anne and also wanted an end to Wolsey's influence. The last group attracted many who had long sought a way to end Wolsey's monopoly of power; they saw Anne as the key.

Stormy negotiations

Campeggio quickly realised that the king and queen were irreconcilable, so he suggested that Catherine enter a convent, which would clear the way for Henry to remarry. Catherine refused outright, and Campeggio reported to Clement that Henry 'sees nothing, he thinks of nothing but Anne; he cannot do without her for an hour. He is constantly kissing her and treating her as if she were his wife.'

On 31 May 1529 the English church leaders, led by co-judges Wolsey and Campeggio, convened to consider Henry's case for annulment. Catherine refused to recognise the court and made a dramatic exit. The case went ahead anyway, but after weeks of inconclusive discussion Campeggio announced on 23 July that the case must now adjourn to Rome. Henry stormed off in fury, and blamed Wolsey for his failure to stage-manage the proceedings more effectively. Wolsey was demoted, stripped of his government office and property, and exiled to Yorkshire. Henceforth his influence would decline until his death on 29 November 1530 as he was travelling from Yorkshire to London to face charges of treason—which would undoubtedly have led to a death sentence.

Stalemate—and an execution

The next few years were marked by stalemate, as Henry and the pope both dithered. Henry could not see a way to annulment, while Clement's hands were tied by his reluctance to offend Henry or Charles V. Henry exiled Catherine to remote Kimbolton Castle in Cambridgeshire. (For the rest of her life, Catherine of Aragon referred to herself as Henry's only true common law wife. She died from cancer, alone and still in exile, in January 1536.)

Meanwhile Lord Chancellor Thomas More told Henry that he would not support the divorce, but did support Henry in his persecution of Lutheran heretics. In 1530 he refused to sign a letter asking the pope for an annulment. In 1531 he requested Henry to permit his resignation after being forced to sign an oath declaring the monarch 'the Supreme Head of the English Church', but Henry declined. However, in 1532 More was allowed to relinquish office after claiming illness. After refusing to attend Anne's coronation in 1533, he was found guilty of high treason and beheaded.

The English public loved Catherine as much as they hated Anne. After Catherine's exile and, as Henry and Anne's relationship became increasingly public, citizens in London rioted to show their disapproval of the union. Anne became known as 'the great whore' and Henry's urgency to sort out the annulment situation increased. He realised how much he had depended on Wolsey to run the ship of state as he found himself barely capable of organising the daily affairs of the court, let alone the religious, political and romantic storms that raged all around. Anne's position was unchanged; until she had a ring on her finger and a crown on her head, her bed was off limits to the king.

Henry was becoming increasingly paranoid and megalomaniac, when an ally appeared in the form of Thomas Cromwell—an urbane, well-travelled banker, parliamentarian and former servant of Wolsey. Henry appointed him to the Privy Council and he quickly became as indispensable to Henry as Wolsey had been. In Italy Cromwell had become familiar with the writings of Machiavelli, whose pragmatic, often brutal ideas about politics and the supremacy of the state he began putting into practice. One of his closest friends was a minor cleric, Thomas Cranmer, whom Henry appointed Archbishop of Canterbury. Cranmer advised Henry that God is the only authority, and that no human, not even the pope, could replace His word. This, of course, was music to Henry's ears. In August 1532 he appointed Anne to the high nobility, meaning that any child she bore would qualify for accession to the throne. In January 1533 he married her, very recently pregnant, in a secret ceremony which Cranmer and Cromwell pronounced legal under both clerical and common law. Anne Boleyn had achieved her ambition. The pope responded by excommunicating Henry from the Catholic Church, but by now papal authority in England was so diminished that nobody in power took any notice.

Anne becomes queen

Henry now resumed his sexual affairs but Anne, unlike Catherine, did not turn a blind eye. Henry brusquely reminded her that she owed her position to him, and should 'shut her eyes and endure as her betters had done', or he would send her back whence she came. Still unpopular among the general citizenry, Anne's only hope was to deliver a male heir but, unfortunately for her, she gave birth to Elizabeth on 7 September 1533. She became increasingly miserable and demanding, as the carousing Henry became ever more autocratic and preoccupied with his religious and political machinations.

By October 1535 Henry was involved with Jane Seymour, one of Anne's ladies-in-waiting. Unlike Anne she was demure, tactful and submissive—traits Henry had come to admire in a woman. He now wanted to be rid of Anne as much as he had wanted to have her in the first place. Following a miscarriage in early 1536, he alleged that she had seduced him into marriage by using witchcraft. Jane started using Anne's delaying tactics, refusing Henry's lavish gift in March of a purse of gold sovereigns, on the grounds that she was unmarried. Their affair continued, but in secret. By now Catherine was dead, opening the way for Charles V of Spain to form a strategic alliance with England. He still refused to recognise Anne as the legitimate queen, but let it be known that he would approve a new wife. Henry decided to eliminate Anne, and ordered Cromwell to produce evidence of crimes that would enable him to sentence her to death. Cromwell duly produced 'evidence' that Anne had committed adultery on twenty-two occasions, including with her own brother George, Lord Rochford. Most historians agree that all the charges were fabricated.

Anne's execution at 8 am on 19 May 1536 was the first public execution of an English queen.

A series of executions

On 2 May Anne was arrested and transported to the Tower of London to await trial. Over the next few days, five of her co-accused, including her brother, were also arrested and incarcerated. All, including Anne, were found guilty and condemned to death. On 17 May the men were executed, even as Cranmer annulled Henry's marriage to Anne and declared their daughter Elizabeth a bastard. Anne was executed two days later, not by the usual rusty axe, but by an expert French swordsman whom Henry, in a gesture of 'compassion', had retained for a fee of £24. On the scaffold she made a speech in praise of Henry, probably in an attempt to protect Elizabeth. She was buried in the Tower's chapel of St Peter. The next day, 20 May 1536, Henry and Jane Seymour were formally betrothed. Jane gave birth to a son, Edward, on 12 October 1537, and died twelve days later from an infected placenta.

Aftermath

Henry went on to plunder many of England's churches, and confiscate their assets and land. The reformation of the church under Thomas Cromwell continued as Henry gradually attained more power than any other English monarch before or since. But by the time of his death on 28 January 1547, Henry had become paranoid, obese and generally unsightly—the result of a life of dissipation, over-indulgence and debauchery. The many portraits of him over the years attest to this gradual deterioration.

His reputation also suffered because of the many people he had put to death—it is estimated that he had executed more than 70,000 people, including two of his wives—and the fact that he had virtually bankrupted the country by waging continual wars. He is the perfect embodiment of nineteenth-century English historian Lord Acton's dictum: 'Power tends to corrupt; absolute power corrupts absolutely.'

1572

RIVERS OF BLOOD FLOW ACROSS FRANCE

On Sunday 24 August 1572, tensions between French Catholics and the Huguenots erupted when the court assassinations of Admiral Gaspard de Coligny and other Protestant leaders, led to the Parisian mob taking to the streets and continuing the frenzied slaughter, targeting Protestants across the city. The unbridled massacre that spread across the land become known as one of the most violent and savage episodes of French history, as rivers from the Seine to the Rhone flowed with the spilled blood of murdered Protestants.

THE ST BARTHOLOMEW'S DAY MASSACRE

Saint Bartholomew was not a day, but a season.

JULES MICHELET, HISTORIAN

The French Wars of Religion were an ongoing conflict between French Catholics and the Huguenots that erupted in 1562 with a massacre of Huguenots by French troops in the town of Vassy outside Paris. The Huguenots (the origins of the name remain uncertain) were French Calvinist Protestants. Their beliefs were based on the notion that salvation could be achieved through individual faith alone, without a Church hierarchy as intermediary. The religious conflict would continue, albeit with numerous periods of ebb and flow, until 1598. Catholic France was first confronted with Protestant ideology in the 1520s, but Protestantism had failed to attract the level of support in France that it had in England and throughout Scandinavia. Furthermore, it was strenuously opposed by the French monarchy and much of the country's Catholic nobility.

There were seventeen million Roman Catholics in France in the 1560s and just over a million Huguenots; yet, despite this seeming disparity, life in sixteenth-century France was being increasingly characterised by rising Catholic–Protestant tensions. In 1561, the sermon of a Protestant minister preaching in the city's 5th arrondissement was interrupted when a group of Catholics rang the bells of a nearby church to drown him out. In the melee that followed, more than a hundred people, mostly Huguenots, were killed. The following year a force of sixteen thousand men, led by Catholic nobleman Anne de Montmorency, defeated an eighteen-thousand-strong Huguenot army at the Battle of Dreux. Tensions subsided however with the signing of the Edict of Saint-Germaine in 1570, engineered by Catherine de Medici to promote tolerance between the country's Protestant and Catholic factions.

A royal marriage brings rising tensions

Although it was a walled city, religiously conservative, and an intellectual and religious bulwark against Huguenot encroachment, Paris was not immune to Protestant influences. In August of 1572 hundreds of Huguenots had flooded into the city to celebrate the marriage of Marguerite of Valois, the Catholic sister of the King of France, Charles IX, to the Huguenot Henry III of Navarre, which was to take place with the usual pomp and ceremony on 18 August. In sixteenth-century Europe marriage was often seen as a means to overcoming religious differences and to create convenient alliances, but this was not destined to be one such occasion. The proposed marriage of Marguerite and Henry brought consternation to the city's Catholics. Henry, though baptised a Roman Catholic, had been raised a Protestant by his mother Queen Jeanne III, the inspiration of the French Huguenot movement. Jeanne III had declared Calvinism (a form of Protestantism inspired by religious reformer John Calvin) to be the official religion of Navarre, a small kingdom on the Atlantic coast straddling the Pyrenees between France and Spain. Henry had only recently ascended to the throne upon his mother's death in June, and French Catholics were nothing short of horrified at the prospect of Henry, through marriage, placing himself in line to become a future king of France.

Catherine de Medici, the mother of King Charles IX, had pushed hard for the marriage between her daughter and Henry. Never claiming to understand Huguenot theology or motivations, she appeared to be driven only by a desperate desire to further the interests of her own line, the House of Valois, with little regard to the wider consequences of the marriage. Though she failed to gain papal approval for the union, Catherine nevertheless convinced Cardinal de Bourbon to marry the couple, and the day of the wedding came and went without incident—even though the ceremony at Notre-Dame cathedral was boycotted by the Paris *Parlement*. Three days later, on 21 August, long-simmering hatreds were brought to the boil with a failed assassination attempt on the Huguenot leader Admiral Gaspard de Coligny, political head of the Calvinist Party. Coligny had remained in the French capital to discuss Huguenot grievances over the Edict of Saint-Germaine and was returning to his rooms at the Hôtel de Béthisy when he was shot in the arm by an unknown assailant.

The admiral was carried to his lodgings, where a bullet was taken from his elbow and a pair of scissors was crudely used to amputate an injured finger. Coligny, who was among the most respected of the Huguenot leaders and enjoyed a close relationship with King Charles, was visited by the king who gave the admiral his word—very likely born out of fear of imminent, city-wide Huguenot reprisals—that whoever was responsible for the shooting would be quickly and unsympathetically brought to justice. The king and Coligny were undoubtedly close friends. But there were some in the French government, and in particular the aristocracy, who thought them too close, and they worried about the implications for Catholic France should Coligny convince Charles to convert to Protestantism. The capital had long been rife with rumours that the Prince of Condé, Louis de Bourbon of the Protestant House of Bourbon, planned to kidnap Charles and convert the impressionable, twenty-two-year old king to Protestantism once away from the influence of his advisors. With so many Huguenots still in Paris in the wake of the royal wedding, circumstances had delivered those in the government of Charles IX an unprecedented opportunity to eliminate the entire Huguenot leadership with one swift, decisive blow.

Huguenot leadership is eliminated

On the morning of Sunday 24 August, St Bartholomew's Day, Coligny and dozens of others in the Huguenot hierarchy were murdered in a series of coordinated assassinations that could only have been organised at the very highest levels of the French government, although whether or not Charles himself had personal knowledge of the plot remains open to question. The signal to commence the killings came with the ringing of the church bell at Saint

RIGHT: The rampage began with Huguenot leaders hunted down and murdered, even in their own homes.

Germaine l'Auxerrois not far from the Louvre. Coligny ordered his valet to assemble the guards the king had made available for his protection, but was horrified to learn it was these very guards who now were intent upon ending his life. When confronted by his assassin, the fifty-six-year-old Coligny is said to have pleaded, 'Young man, reverence my grey hairs', but to no avail. He was stabbed in the chest with a dagger, his body thrown from an upper storey window. Moments after his lifeless corpse struck the pavement below, his head and hands were severed from his body and the head taken to Catherine de Medici. Hours later, the decapitated torso of Gaspard de Coligny was seen on the end of a rope being dragged by groups of ragged-looking children around the streets of Paris. It was finally brought to the gallows at Montfaucon and strung up ingloriously by the heels. Catherine later had his head embalmed and sent to Pope Gregory XIII, though there is no historical document that suggests he ever took receipt of it. Nevertheless, Gregory was so delighted by the news of Coligny's demise that he ordered hymns of praise to be sung throughout Rome.

Meanwhile Coligny's fellow Huguenots were being killed wherever they were found. François III de La Rochefoucauld, a confidant of Coligny and member of a famous French noble family that could trace its aristocratic roots back to 1019, had dined with King Charles himself just the previous evening—and yet he was stabbed in the heart after six masked men burst into his room. Charles de Teligny, a member of the staunchly Huguenot Rouerque family and son-in-law of Admiral de Coligny, was killed by a musket shot in the corridors of the Louvre after he refused to recant his Huguenot beliefs. The Marquis de Renel was chased to the bank of the River Seine before being shot by his own cousin, Louis de Bussy d'Amboise, as he attempted to cast off in a boat. His body was then thrown into the river.

Slaughter of the Huguenots

Contemporary and historical accounts are in agreement that these targeted slayings were a premeditated act calculated merely to eliminate the Huguenot leadership; they were never meant to escalate into a citywide conflict. Catholics and Huguenots had already fought three civil wars, and nobody wanted a fourth. What was to follow, however, no one was able to foresee. Historians suggest that when the head of Coligny was put on a spike and shown to the Paris mob, it released a rage that had been simmering for decades. In the mistaken belief they were acting on behalf of their king, the mob took over from the royal troops and began seeking out and killing the city's Huguenots. What followed was unbridled slaughter.

Peter Ramus, the French humanist and reformer who had converted to Protestantism in 1561, spent the first two days of the massacre hiding at the back of a bookshop on the Rue St Jacques before making his way under cover of darkness to his home, where he was found and stabbed to death on 26 August. The wife of King Charles' very own *plumassier*, who was in charge of the king's ornamental plumage and feathers, was taken from her home on the Notre Dame bridge, a well-known Protestant enclave, stabbed, and thrown still alive into the river. Paris had become a city in which reputations and innocence counted for nothing. The young and the old, women and children, were dragged from their homes and killed in the streets. Horse-drawn carts soon filled with the bodies of the slain and were hauled to the River Seine, into which they were thrown without ceremony. One particularly gruesome story tells of a little girl whose parents were both killed before her. She was then dipped in their blood and cautioned that the fate that befell her parents would also be hers if she ever dared to become a Huguenot. Paris had gone mad.

Such vast numbers of bodies were thrown into the river and left there for so long that the city's residents refused to eat fish taken from the river for months to come. The injured, bound hand and foot, were thrown still breathing from the city's bridges. Doors were battered down and citizens were dragged into the streets regardless of what their religious convictions might be. Huguenot houses were burned to the ground, reflecting the Catholic belief that fire purifies heresy. Even the entrances to the king's palace became smeared with blood. Huguenots fled their homes in the thousands and were even chased from the gates of the city into the surrounding countryside.

Estimates of the total number of deaths varied widely. Official records of the numbers killed were never kept, and there was the problem of the many wild and exaggerated claims of slaughter, each one more gruesome than the last. A local butcher near the Pont Neuf boasted to the king that he had gloriously dispatched one hundred and fifty Huguenots in a single evening. One man, a gold and silver artisan called Crozier, boasted that he'd killed four thousand Huguenots by dressing himself as a hermit and luring them into his hermit's enclave where he then proceeded to murder them one by one. What is not in dispute is that city officials offered its gravediggers a premium to bury the growing piles of corpses that littered the city's streets.

Violence spreads to towns and villages

In the wake of the massacre King Charles wrote to the governors of France's provinces and regional cities stressing that what occurred was not the result of religious intolerance but a response to a direct and personal threat posed by Admiral de Coligny and his followers upon the royal family. He directed that any armed retaliation by Huguenots in the provinces should be handled with care and diligence and not be used as a further pretext for murder. Over the course of the following six weeks, however, the exact opposite was to happen. The violence in Paris was repeated throughout the towns and villages of France. In Rouen in Normandy, those Huguenots able to escape the killing fled the city, taking its Protestant population from more than sixteen thousand to just over three thousand. Similar accounts were received from Tours, Angiers, Toulouse, and all the way to Lyon in the south. In Lyon almost the entire Huguenot population of five thousand were killed, maimed, or forced to flee for their lives. Among the dead was the French composer Claude Goudimel. The River Rhône flowing south from Lyons, like the Seine, was so polluted by corpses that downstream in the Mediterranean city of Arles the people refused to drink its water.

There were massacres in Orleans, Bordeaux, Angers, and also in Nîmes. At Nîmes, five years earlier, Huguenots had proved they were capable of those same murderous excesses when they massacred one hundred Catholics in 1567. In the town of Meaux, northeast of Paris, about two hundred Huguenots were herded into the town's prison, then brought out one by one into its central courtyard where they were either stabbed or beaten to death. The Duke of Anjou (one of a group of powerful nobles opposing the Huguenots) wrote a letter to Count de Montsoreau, the governor of Saumur in the Loire Valley, which said, in part: 'You must go at once to Saumur with all your supporters and kill any Huguenots you find there'. Across

France anywhere between five thousand and fifty thousand people were murdered, depending upon whether one chooses to believe the accounts of Roman Catholic apologists or Huguenot survivors. The general consensus of modern scholars puts the figure at around twenty thousand.

The atrocities of the Saint Bartholomew's Day massacre, however, do not tell the whole story. Amidst the bloodshed there were also many isolated acts of defiance, heroism and tolerance. The governor of Auvergne, for instance, thought a letter given to him, supposedly signed by the king, ordering him to kill the Huguenot

In one of the most horrifying holocausts in history, as many as fifty thousand Protestants were killed in the massacre.

population there, to be a forgery and refused to hand them over. The governor of Bayonne, Viscount Orte, responded to an order to round up the Huguenots there by writing a letter to King Charles claiming not to be able to find a single executioner among Bayonne's citizenry willing to carry out the deed.

Aftermath of the massacre

The consequences of the Saint Bartholomew's Day massacre were far reaching. Huguenots, who had always believed in the good faith of the monarchy, did so no longer. Their trust had been irrevocably betrayed and their leaders began referring to Catherine de Medici as 'that Jezebel'. They abandoned their founder John Calvin's injunction to remain loyal subjects to their king and took up the revolutionary's mantra of justifiable rebellion should a king or queen sufficiently disregard what is in the best interests of their subjects. Huguenot leaders who previously enjoyed little or no influence in decision-making because of their radical, militant positions were once again being listened to. The massacre may have brought joy to the papacy in Rome, but the general response amongst France's Protestant allies and Catholics abroad was that of horror and disgust.

Throughout September 1572, with their leadership now decimated and their way of life in disarray, Huguenots withdrew to their provincial fortress towns such as Nîmes and La Rochelle, accompanied by thousands of moderate Catholics. In the country's southwest hundreds of sympathetic Catholics were seen alongside Huguenots fleeing Toulouse for the nearby Protestant stronghold of Montauban, and before the end of the year the Catholics and Huguenots of France would be embroiled in yet another bloody civil war, ignited when the nominal capital of the Huguenots, La Rochelle, denied the king their taxes as a protest against the massacre.

War was declared on the port city in November 1572 and it was laid siege to in February 1573. By May, however, with the city continually being resupplied from the sea and after heavy losses on both sides, the siege was abandoned. Over the next seven years there would be three more bloody conflicts—the Fifth War (1576), the Sixth War (1577), and finally the Seventh War (1580), culminating in the ascent to the throne of the Protestant king, Henri de Navarre.

1614–15

SHOGUN ANNIHILATES OPPOSITION

Tokugawa Ieyasu was the founder of the Tokugawa shogunate of Japan, which ruled from 1600 until 1868. Tokugawa seized power in 1600, received his appointment as shogun in 1603, and ruled Japan until his death in 1616. In 1615, although he was the supreme Samurai of Japan, Tokugawa could not rest knowing that some of his enemies from earlier days still lived, and determined to stamp out any chance of future conflict. Thus began the Siege of Osaka, a series of battles undertaken by Tokugawa against his old rivals, the Toyotomi clan, which ended the last major armed opposition to the shogunate's establishment.

TOKUGAWA AND THE SIEGE OF OSAKA CASTLE

Look upon the wrath of the enemy. If thou knowest only what it is to conquer, and knowest not what it is like to be defeated, woe unto thee; it will fare ill with thee.

TOKUGAWA IEYASU

In Japan, the period from the mid fifteenth century through to the beginning of the seventeenth century is known as the Age of Warring States. It was an era of sporadic civil wars fought between feudal lords called *daimyo* that ended with the siege of Osaka Castle in 1615. The daimyo fought one another in open defiance of the nominal rule of the emperor and the country's shoguns or military dictators, whose influence had been in decline for more than a century.

Born in 1536, Toyotomi Hideyoshi joined the Oda clan as a servant and sandal bearer, and rose to become a trusted general to Oda Nobunaga, one of the country's pre-eminent warlords. In a country long beset by feudalism Nobunaga was slowly establishing himself as one of Japan's most influential leaders, aided by Hideyoshi, who proved himself an adept negotiator and military strategist, convincing many samurai ('those who serve') to defect to Nobunaga and thus avoiding many a bloody conflict. Hideyoshi also presided over many pivotal battles and conquered the western Chugoku region for Nobunaga in 1576. By the time of Nobunaga's death in 1582 he had conquered more than a third of the country. Hideyoshi then became

Nobunaga's successor, though because of his peasant origins could never hope to become a shogun. Nevertheless he did achieve the title of retired regent, or *taiko*, and in 1583 he began the construction of a castle at Osaka.

Construction of the castle begins

The Osaka castle would be based on the design of Nobunaga's great castle at Azuchi. It would mimic its extensive use of granite blocks in its 6-metre (20-foot) defensive walls and would have a massive central tower to afford its cannons maximum range; a series of irregularly shaped battlements would provide its defenders with a multitude of retaliatory options when under siege. There would, however, be one significant difference. Osaka castle would be on a far grander scale than Azuchi, and would be the most impressive castle ever constructed in Japan.

The castle, when completed, must have seemed impregnable. A complex arrangement of wet and dry moats surrounded inner walls that rose behind each other in tiers topping out at a staggering height of 120 metres (393 feet). Its central tower (*tenshu*) rose up five storeys and was part of an integrated series of multi-layered defences that included towers and ramparts, all set within an outer perimeter wall with a circumference of almost 14 kilometres (9 miles). Immediately to its west was the Sea of Japan; to its north, the convergence of the Yamato, Temma and Yoda rivers created a muddy expanse of rice paddies and shoals that made any approach all but impossible. To the east, the Huano River provided a further natural barrier.

The growing power of Ieyasu Tokugawa

When Hideyoshi died in 1598 he left behind his only son, the five-year-old Hideyori. Hideyoshi had established a Council of Five Elders to rule in his son's place until he came of age, and of those five one was Tokugawa Ieyasu. Tokugawa, born in 1543, was an old ally of Nobunaga. He emerged as the dominant member of the council and cleared his way to become Japan's undisputed shogun after the Battle of Sekigahara in October 1600, which led to him consolidating his power throughout western and central Honshu. In 1603 Tokugawa revived the title of shogun and established the Tokugawa shogunate. He also arranged for his daughter to marry Hideyoshi's heir Hideyori, then just ten years old, in the hope of averting an eventual conflict. However, a confrontation between the ageing Tokugawa and the young Hideyori, whom Tokugawa had allowed to remain in his father's castle in Osaka, became increasingly likely. In 1611, after a meeting in Kyoto in which Tokugawa could see for himself the threat posed by his young rival (and the Toyotomi clan that he headed), he began to devise a plan that would remove Hideyori from his castle stronghold.

By mid 1614 it was clear to everyone that war was inevitable—with the exception of the somewhat naïve Hideyori, who even refused a delivery of English gunpowder because he couldn't foresee a use for it. When Tokugawa heard that Hideyori had turned the carts of gunpowder away from the gates of Osaka Castle he astutely purchased the gunpowder himself, as well as five British guns, which included four 1800-kilogram (4000-pound) giants that could shoot 8 kilograms (18 pounds) of shot and were considered superior in range and firepower to their smaller Asian alternatives. By July Hideyori had learned that Tokugawa was planning an assault on the castle and sent out a call for *ronin*, wandering samurai and swordsmen not aligned to any master or feudal lords, to join him in the defence of the Toyotomi clan. In no time at all the young Hideyori had almost ninety thousand men at his disposal, veteran fighters mostly, who had previously refused to align themselves with anyone but who now had thrown their lot in with the House of Toyotomi. Some of Hideyori's new recruits were Christian samurai who had suffered sporadic periods of persecution under Tokugawa's rule and considered him to be a 'devil of war'. There were also thousands of men who had been ruthlessly displaced by Togukawa's men after the Battle of Sekigahara fourteen years earlier. This decisive battle had been vast in its scale, and there were many who were eager for an opportunity to exact some revenge.

All that Hideyori was lacking was a commander able to lead his men in battle. Although he had been trained in many of the disciplines of the samurai, the one thing he lacked was experience on the battlefield. Though unable to find anyone with the sort of battlefield experience he was looking for, Hideyori was fortunate in acquiring Sanada Yukimura, a defensive specialist who helped turn the already heavily defended castle into an impenetrable edifice. One of Yukimura's first ingenious acts was to trade thousands of

Portrait of Shogun Tokugawa Ieyasu in court dress.

his men's samurai swords for spades—and to put the samurai to work beyond the castle walls digging a ditch linking the Nekoma Stream with the Ikutama Canal just beyond its western wall. This created a moat more than 72 metres (236 feet) wide and 11 metres (37 feet) in depth. He also built an outer wall or barbican. Despite Yukimura's emphasis on defence, however, he also had something of a reputation as an audacious offensive tactician; he tried in vain to persuade Hideyori to launch a raid on Kyoto and to convince the emperor to declare Tokugawa a traitor. But Hideyori rejected the plan, preferring instead to ensconce himself behind the walls of his castle and wait for Tokugawa to come to him.

The Winter Siege

In November, with almost one hundred and ninety-five thousand troops at his disposal, Tokugawa began what was to become known as the Winter Siege, focusing on eliminating a number of outposts east of Osaka Castle that guarded the castle's approaches and looked over its various supply routes. The first to fall, on 19 November, was Kizu Fort, a small cluster of fortifications at the mouth of the Kizu River garrisoned by eight hundred men; six days later the village of Imafuku with its six hundred defenders was taken. Tokugawa's forces were well armed and many carried arquebuses, low-velocity Portuguese-designed muzzle-loading muskets that fired shot that could pierce armour if fired at very close range. More of Hideyori's outposts succumbed to Tokugawa's samurai, and by the beginning of December the armies of the Tokugawa shogunate had marched within sight of Osaka Castle.

Despite repeated shows of strength and a string of small victories, Tokugawa decided he would attempt to infiltrate into Osaka Castle

and take it by stealth rather than rush headlong into an armed conflict. He had successfully managed to bribe a low-ranking commander, Nanjo Tadashige, who promised he would open the castle gates and permit the shogun's troops entry. The bribe, by all accounts a moderate sum at best, came close to paying off, but Tadashige's treasonous act was uncovered at the eleventh hour and he was executed.

On 20 December Tokugawa, still keen to avoid a long siege and costly battle, initiated a series of overtures to Hideyori by dispatching a merchant from Kyoto to the castle gates with the offer of a negotiated settlement. No reply was received. More offers were sent, but each one was met with silence.

Tokugawa advances on the castle

Now impatient to test the defensive capabilities of the castle, Tokugawa decided he would make an attack on its southern flank, which just happened to be the one commanded by Yukimura, who was defending the southern perimeter with more than seven thousand men. Tokugawa launched the assault in two waves, the first with twelve thousand troops under the command of Maeda Toshitsune, an able but unremarkable general, and the second consisting of ten thousand Red Devils from the Ii clan, commanded by Ii Naotaka and Tokugawa's grandson, Matsudaira Tadanao.

On 3 January Toshitsune's samurai began to advance. The red flags attached to the tops of poles fastened to their backs waved in the breeze as a single, undulating river of red. They approached the walls of the castle in tight formation but were driven back under a withering onslaught of arrows and musket fire as they were scaling the castle walls. Naotaka's Red Devils, with their trademark red breastplates, fared a little better, managing to penetrate the castle's Hachomeguchi gate and the outer defences constructed by Yukimura known as Sanada's Barbican, further along the southern flank. Their progress, however, was halted by more than eight thousand heavily armed Toyotomi troops under the command of Kimura Shigenari who fell upon the Red Devils' tightly packed formations. Hundreds were felled by Shigenari's muskets, and lead shot from the defenders of the pierced barbican wall, and the Red Devils were forced into a headlong retreat that turned into a rout. The attack had been a disaster, but Tokugawa was not easily dissuaded. On the following day, another attack was mounted, this time on the Tanimachiguchi gate, by a four thousand strong force led by Todo Takatora, a loyal and fearless samurai whose family had been in allegiance with the Tokugawa clan since the mid 1590s. Takatora's troops managed to briefly gain a foothold on the castle ramparts, before they too were driven back in yet another fierce counterattack. Tokugawa was now convinced that the castle would not fall to assaults by ground troops.

At the same time as the failed attacks were taking place, Tokugawa had ordered the construction of a network of ramparts and battlements that had all but encircled the castle, into which he now began to place his three hundred cannon. The time had come to demonstrate the massive superiority he enjoyed in artillery over his besieged opponent. The majority of his cannon were of English and Dutch origin and included 3½-inch sakers and 5½-inch culverins (around 9 centimetres and 14 centimetres respectively). These cannon were both capable of long-range bombardment and far superior to Hideyori's smaller, breech-loading swivel guns, which were barely able to fire beyond their own outer defensive walls.

On 8 January the bombardment began, but it soon became apparent that even Tokugawa's culverins were no match for the thick walls of Osaka Castle. Although the bombardment was unsuccessful, it did have the effect of significantly unnerving Hideyori's mother, who now urged her son to seek a diplomatic end to the siege.

Diplomacy was also on the mind of Tokugawa. Although he had his enemy surrounded and his own troops dug in, he was looking forward to a long and tedious and morale-sapping siege in what had so far been a bitterly cold winter. Tokugawa offered Hideyori any fiefdom in Japan as well as a guaranteed revenue should he voluntarily leave Osaka Castle. He also insisted that Hideyori allow him to fill in the castle's moat and demolish the barbican. Finally, on 22 January, Tokugawa received a letter signed by Hideyori saying he was prepared to put aside any thoughts of rebellion against the Tokugawa shogunate, and Tokugawa agreed to withdraw his troops. The Winter Siege, or *Fuyu no Jin*, had come to an end.

The stage is set for the Summer Siege

Hideyori, however, had been emboldened by his successful resistance and chose to remain defiant. In Tokugawa's absence Hideyori made repeated attempts to interfere with the filling in of the castle moat, and spent the spring of 1615 gathering even more troops to his side. By the end of April he began striking out again at Tokugawa's outposts, setting the stage for the *Natsu no Jin*, the Summer Siege, which would prove to be the final act in the siege of Osaka Castle and bring about the end of Hideyori's stubborn defiance.

The Summer Siege began as a series of running battles as Hideyori went on the offensive—but things did not go well for him. On 24 May, on the approaches to the Tokugawa stronghold of Wakayama Castle, a force of five thousand men loyal to Tokugawa defeated Hideyori's three thousand men. On 2 June, not far from the imperial tombs at Domyo-ji, a further force of three thousand—this time commanded by Sanada Yukimura—confronted the ten-thousand-strong army of one of Tokugawa's most accomplished strategists, Date Masamune, and suffered heavy casualties. Yukimura retreated hastily to the supposed

During the siege of Osaka, Tokugawa wiped out the Toyotomi family, effectively eliminating any rivals to his reign.

safety of Osaka Castle, but when he arrived was confronted with the sobering sight of 150,000 Tokugawan samurai in the fields to the south of the castle preparing for one mighty, final assault on Hideyori's stronghold. The coming battle, the Battle of Tennoji, would be the last large-scale samurai confrontation in Japanese history.

Yukimura steeled the remnants of his army for one last fight but was himself suffering from exhaustion and unable to go on. When confronted by a Tokugawa samurai, Yukimura admitted who he was and slowly removed his helmet. Moments later, in full view of his troops, he was beheaded.

A brutal conclusion

Tokugawa then ordered the commander of the Red Devils, Ii Naotaka, to fire on the castle's wooden keep with his artillery. Soon flames were engulfing the castle's inner courtyards. Hideyori, in one last desperate attempt at freedom, rode out to confront the enemy but was literally chased back into the castle, allowing the enemy at his heels to enter the grounds. The following day the once impregnable Osaka Castle was in flames. Almost all of its defenders were slaughtered, including Hideyori's mother, his young son (who was, ironically, Tokugawa's grandson), and Hideyoshi's wife, Yodogimi. Hideyori committed *seppuku*, a traditional samurai suicide involving disembowelment.

With the final destruction of the powerful Toyotomi line, the Tokugawa clan was able to establish an uninterrupted line of shogunate rule, ushering in a period of relative peace and prosperity in Japan that would last for more than two and a half centuries. Tokugawa Ieyasu proved to be a master politician as well as a fine military strategist who won far more battles than he lost and possessed a sweeping vision for a unified Japan. Not long after the siege of Osaka Castle, Tokugawa retired to Sunpu Castle, where he died on 1 June 1616. In 1617 his remains were taken to Nikko Tosho-gu shrine in Tochigi Prefecture, where they remain to this day.

1692

SALEM WITCHES TO HANG

The Salem witch trials were a series of hearings and trials to prosecute people accused of witchcraft in colonial Massachusetts, held between February 1692 and May 1693. With fear and paranoia sweeping the young colony, over 150 people were arrested and imprisoned, with even more accused but not arrested. The court convicted twenty-nine people of the capital felony of witchcraft. Nineteen of the convicted, fourteen women and five men, were hanged.

THE SALEM WITCH TRIALS

If it was the last moment I was to live,
God knows I am innocent of any thing of this nature.

ELIZABETH HOWE, EXECUTED 19 JULY 1692

The Salem witch trials hold great historical significance for America. They mark a defining moment in the shift from Puritanism, with its values of kinship, minimalism and devoutness, to the new, evolving world of individualism, sophistication, competition and freedom of personal belief. They also clearly illustrate the methods by which human groups initiate, rationalise and escalate persecution. Because so few people were involved, the trials illustrate with particular clarity the processes that humans have always tended to use against those they wish to marginalise, demonise or annihilate.

Witch hunts were the result of superstition and a general climate of persecution. In seventeenth-century Salem, as elsewhere, fear of the devil—and of divine punishment for heresy—led to an environment where many feared the influence of witches on god-fearing members of Christian society. Witches were believed to reject Jesus Christ, worship Satan and make contracts with him in return for riches or supernatural powers. They were also believed to fly at night to secret trysts, or 'sabbats', where they indulged in orgies, defiled crucifixes and used demons to help them undertake various evil acts. They supposedly changed form into other humans or into animals, and abducted children in order to eat them. No doubt some people did worship the devil or try to use witchcraft to cause harm, but despite the lack of any empirical evidence, sorcery and other specifically defined 'supernatural acts' were forbidden under law in Europe and America.

Early signs of discord among the faithful

Many of Salem's citizens were descended from the Pilgrim Fathers, plain-living English Puritans who had sailed to nearby New Plymouth in the *Mayflower* in 1620 to escape persecution at the hands of the recently formed Church of England. By 1690 a commercial elite was developing as debate raged over how independent the small Salem Village (now Danvers) community should be from New Plymouth. Two of Salem Village's most prominent families, the Porters and the Putnams, were involved in a power struggle over control of the village and its church.

Harvard University dropout and failed businessman Samuel Parris, following the invitation of Putnam clan leader Thomas to take up the position of minister at the Salem Village church, arrived in Salem with his family in 1689. He accepted the position, but only after negotiating an unprecedentedly generous contract which, among other things, required the parishioners to supply him with free firewood. Putnam also agreed that Parris could own the pastor's house, which traditionally remained the property of the town. The appointment outraged the Porters and many other community members.

The first 'symptoms' of witchcraft are manifest

In January 1692 Parris' daughter Betty and niece Abigail started having strange seizures— throwing things about, gibbering incoherently, contorting their bodies and crawling under furniture. The following month Parris' Caribbean slaves, John Indian and his wife Tituba, used their knowledge of voodoo to bake a 'witch-cake' with the girls' urine, which they fed to the family dog. This was designed to break whatever spell was affecting the girls, as dogs were commonly believed to be 'familiars' (servants) of Satan. Soon other children, including Mary Lewis, Ann Putnam and Elizabeth Hubbard, began to exhibit similar symptoms of madness. When pressed, they accused Tituba and two others, Sarah Osborne (who had married her black slave and rarely attended church) and Sarah Good (who was poor and often begged food from her neighbours), of bewitching them. The three women (all fitting the stereotype of a witch) were charged with witchcraft, interrogated for several days by magistrates, then jailed on 5 March.

The two girls then accused a respectable churchgoer, Martha Carey, of bewitching them. On 21 March she was examined and imprisoned. On the same day Ann Putnam's mother, also named Ann, began having similar seizures, and blamed seventy-one-year-old Rebecca Nurse. Three days later Rebecca was imprisoned, along with Sarah Good's four-year-old daughter Dorcas. By the end of April, as the accusations, examinations and imprisonments continued apace, twenty-three more alleged witches had been imprisoned. They included John Proctor and his wife Elizabeth, Bridget Bishop, Mary and Phillip English, and Giles Corey. Several of them had been accused by Thomas Putnam. On 4 May, George Burroughs, who had served as Salem Village preacher between 1680 and 1683, was arrested in nearby Maine following allegations of witchcraft, and imprisoned in Salem.

The accused are tried

On 14 May Sir William Phipps arrived from England to take up his appointment as governor of Massachusetts, accompanied by Increase Mather, who became a minister in Boston. By the end of May about forty more people had been imprisoned in Salem. On 2 June Governor Phipps appointed a court, led by Deputy Governor William Stoughton, to try the alleged witches. If found guilty, the only way an accused could avoid the death penalty was if they were pregnant, or had pleaded guilty in the first place. Bridget Bishop was found guilty of witchcraft and, on 10 June, became the first fatality when she was hanged on Salem's Gallows Hill. Nathaniel Saltonstall, a member of the judges' panel, resigned the same day. Increase Mather and his son Cotton produced a report titled *Return of the Ministers Consulted*, which advocated both 'caution' and 'speed and vigour' in the witchcraft trials. On 29 June Sarah Good, Rebecca Nurse, Sarah Wildes, Susannah Martin and Elizabeth Howe were tried and found guilty; they were hanged on 19 July.

John Proctor, a farmer who had been outspoken against the witchcraft proceedings from the outset, was also the first male accused of witchcraft. On 5 August, he and his wife Elizabeth, along with George Burroughs, John Willard, George Jacobs and Martha Carrier, were brought to trial and found guilty. All but Elizabeth (spared because she was pregnant) were hanged on 19 August.

Between 9 and 17 September, fifteen more Salem residents were tried and condemned to death. Five were spared, either because they confessed or were pregnant, but on 22 September Martha Corey, Mary Easty, Margaret Scott, Alice and Mary Parker, Ann Pudeator, Samuel Wardwell and Wilmott Reid were hanged. These would be the last hangings. On 19 September Giles Corey, who had refused to enter a plea or attend the court, was pressed to death—the statutory penalty for refusing to stand trial, which until then had never been used in Massachusetts. Corey, a supporter of the Porter faction and critic of the entire proceedings, had been accused by Ann Putnam and imprisoned in April. He was stripped naked and a board was placed upon his chest. As more and more boulders were added to the board in an attempt to elicit a confession, he asked only that more weight be added in order to hasten his death.

Hysteria spreads throughout Massachusetts

By now members of nearby communities in Andover, Ipswich and other rural areas of Massachusetts were being accused, arrested and examined as the witchcraft hysteria spread. In October the afflicted girls were summoned to Andover, then Gloucester, where they made more than fifty accusations. But they went too far,

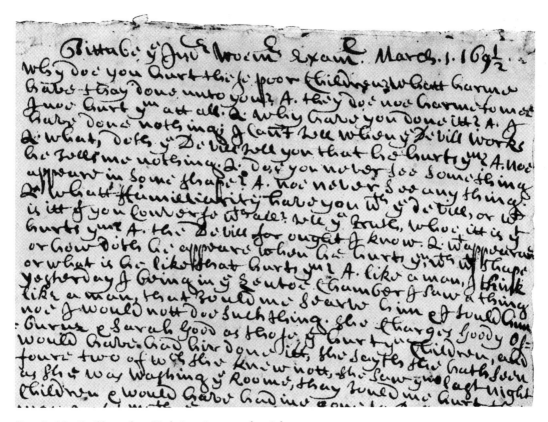

Record of the Caribbean slave Tituba's testimony at the trials.

stimulating a backlash when they named several highly respectable and prominent churchgoers (as many of the Salem accused had indeed been), including Lady Phipps, the governor's wife. Many of those who disagreed with the whole proceedings had remained silent, noting the deadly fate of John Proctor and others who had spoken out. The young accusers had been particularly harsh in their accusations against anyone who cast aspersions on their allegations.

On 2 October Increase Mather preached a sermon called 'Cases of Conscience Concerning Evil Spirits Personating Men', which shed grave doubt on the accuracy of 'spectral visions' such as were claimed by the Salem girls. He said: 'It were better that ten suspected witches should

George Jacobs pleads for mercy after he is accused by his grand-daughter Margaret (centre), acting to save her own life.

escape, than one innocent person should be condemned.' Five days later, merchant and astronomer Thomas Brattle wrote a long letter to an unknown recipient, which argued fervently against the trials and convictions. We may assume that he intended it to be circulated in the hope of influencing Governor Phipps over the future of the trials. He wrote 'I cannot but condemn this method of the justices, of making this touch of the hand a rule to discover witchcraft; because I am fully persuaded that it is sorcery, and a superstitious method, and that which we have no rule for, either from reason or religion.'

Voices of reason

At last voices of reason were starting to be heard above the hysterical tumult. Finally, on 12 October Governor Phipps forbade any further imprisonments at Salem, and on 29 October officially dissolved the court. In November the afflicted girls were again summoned to Gloucester, but this time their fits and accusations were ignored. After this they did not make, nor were asked for, another accusation. In May 1693 Phipps ordered the release of all the convicted witches remaining in jail, thus ending the entire sordid episode. Nineteen people had been hanged and one pressed to death, while five had died in jail.

Aftermath

Though the trials and their attendant horrors had come to an end, the repercussions were felt for years to come. The burden on the accused and their families was severe. In addition to the great emotional distress they had suffered, there were economic consequences. Those who remained in jail were obliged by law to pay for their food and 'lodging'. Until these debts were discharged, they could not secure their release. Also, many had their properties confiscated by the authorities. Fields and their crops were left untended or laid to waste while buildings fell into disrepair.

In the years that immediately followed, Salem failed to prosper, and many saw this as punishment for the great wrongdoing perpetrated by the accusers. Relationships between the Reverend Samuel Parris and his community had been irrevocably undermined, and three years after the trials ended the disgraced minister agreed to remove himself from his post.

On 25 August 1706 Ann Putnam recanted her accusations, in the form of a confession read out to the Salem congregation by the Reverend Thomas Green, who had replaced Parrish. She did not take responsibility for her actions, but at least blamed her delusions on Satan, rather than on humans. Her confession said, in part:

I desire to be humbled before God for that sad and humbling providence that befell my father's family in the year about '92 ... it was a great delusion of Satan that deceived me in that sad time, whereby I justly fear that I have been instrumental, with others, though ignorantly and unwittingly, to bring upon myself and thus land the guilt of innocent blood ...

1788

CONVICT COLONISERS LAND IN BOTANY BAY

On 26 January 1788, the First Fleet of transported convicts arrived in Australia after an eight-month journey from England. Approximately 600 officials, soldiers and crew, and nearly 800 convicts, found themselves in a land largely uncharted. Twenty-eight years earlier Captain Cook had sailed to Australia and mapped some of its eastern coastline—it was on his reports that England formed the idea of transportation to Australia. Instead of the lush pastures described by Cook, however, the First Fleeters found a hot, dry, infertile country unsuitable for small farming—putting the future of the colony in jeopardy before they had even settled in.

THE FIRST FLEET

The clearing the ground will be a Work of time & it will be four Years at least, before this Colony will be able to support itself, & perhaps no Country in the World affords less assistance to first Settlers. still, My Lord, I think that perseverance will answer evry purpose proposed by Government, & that this Country will hereafter be a most Valuable acquisition to Great Brittain from its situation.

CAPTAIN ARTHUR PHILLIP, LETTER TO THE MARQUIS OF LANSDOWNE, 3 JULY 1788

On 18 August 1786 English home secretary Thomas, Lord Sydney of Whitehall, wrote to the Lords Commissioners of the Treasury outlining his plan to overcome the growing problem of chronic overcrowding in English gaols. Felons had previously been sent to North America, but that option had been closed after the American victory over the British in the War of Independence in 1776. The gaols were full to overflowing, as were the numerous rotting prison hulks moored in various harbours and rivers. England was undergoing an industrial revolution which saw a transition from an agrarian-based economy to an industry-based one centred in cities, towns, factories and workshops. By the late eighteenth century this revolution was well under way, with the result that millions of workers had lost their jobs, to be replaced by machines. While the rich were getting richer, the unemployed working class was growing in leaps and bounds.

England's jails overflow

London's population had doubled between 1750 and 1770 as people flocked from the countryside to seek non-existent work. Many resorted to what we would call petty crime, most often theft of food and other essentials. The government's response was to introduce the death penalty for numerous crimes, including smuggling, forgery, burglary, larceny by servants, petty theft and horse-stealing. But judges were reluctant to send offenders to the gallows, and they commuted many sentences to transportation to America, even after that was no longer possible.

In 1770, acclaimed English explorer Captain James Cook led an expedition to the South Seas during which he discovered new lands and claimed territories for Britain. He had made landfall at Botany Bay, on the east coast of the continent that would be named Australia. His official botanist, Joseph Banks, had returned with hundreds of new plant species. As the government considered its options for transportation, the *Journal of the House of Commons* recorded Banks' opinion:

… the place …, best adapted for such a purpose, was Botany Bay, on the coast of New Holland, in the Indian Ocean, which was about seven months voyage from England, that he apprehended there would be little possibility of opposition from the natives, as during his stay there in the year 1770, he saw very few and did not think there were above fifty in the neighbourhood, and had reason to believe the country was very thinly populated,

*those he saw were naked, treacherous, and armed
with lances, but extremely cowardly...*

The transportation solution

Lord Sydney was secretary of state for the Home
Office in the government of William Pitt the
Younger and was responsible for solving the
convict problem. He became an advocate for
transportation to Botany Bay, and Parliament
adopted his recommendations, less than a year
before the departure of the largest migration
fleet in history.

The great southern land was already
well known in Europe before Captain Cook's
exploration—more than fifty Dutch, Portuguese
and Spanish ships had landed on various parts
of the continent over the previous three hundred
or so years, but none had set up colonies. Britain
hoped by settling the land to solve their convict
problem and claim the land outright.

The fleet comprised the naval escorts HMS
Sirius and HMS *Supply*, the convict transports
Alexander, *Charlotte*, *Lady Penrhyn*, *Friendship*,
Scarborough and *Prince of Wales*, and the
food transports *Golden Grove*, *Borrowdale*
and *Fishburn*. The largest, the *Alexander*, was
just 35 metres (115 feet) long and less than
10 metres (33 feet) wide. The fleet was placed
under the command of Captain Arthur Phillip,
a relatively undistinguished naval officer who
nonetheless turned out to be a good choice;
he would also become the first governor of the
colony of New South Wales. On board were more
than 1400 passengers, including nearly 800
convicts, several hundred soldiers, marines and
officers, some family members and the ships'
crews. Of the convict contingent, nearly 200
were women, important to the colony according
to Lord Sydney because 'without a sufficient
proportion of that sex it is well known that it
would be impossible to preserve the settlement

from gross irregularities and disorders'. The fleet
also took tools that would be needed to create
the new settlement, including 300 chisels, 175
saws and hammers, 140 knives and drills, and
an assortment of wheelbarrows, grindstones,
fish hooks and ploughshares.

Almost 60 per cent of the convicts had
been sentenced for stealing food or other goods
of relatively minor value. Thirteen per cent
had been convicted of breaking and entering
or burglary, and 15 per cent were guilty of
highway robbery, robbery with violence or grand
larceny. The remainder had been sentenced
for swindling, receiving stolen goods, forgery
or some other crime. A West Indian, Thomas
Chaddick, was sentenced to seven years'
transportation for stealing twelve cucumber
plants. Thirteen-year-old Elizabeth Hayward
was transported for stealing a silk bonnet and a
linen gown worth seven shillings.

The First Fleet sets sail

In late 1786 the convicts began to be loaded
onto the ships. They were shackled below
decks, and many died of disease or malnutrition
even before the fleet departed. Finally, on the
morning of 13 May 1787, the First Fleet left
Portsmouth Harbour, bound for New Holland.
Less than a week into the voyage, the crew of
the *Friendship* went on strike, demanding an
increase in daily meat rations from one and
a half to two pounds. But it was not physical
hunger that the sailors wanted to satisfy—
even though a wall had been built to separate
the crew and convicts, the sailors had already
knocked a hole in it; their intention was to use
the meat as a bribe for sexual favours from the
female prisoners. Phillip refused to increase the
rations, but promised a pay rise.

By the time the fleet reached Tenerife in the
Canary Islands to re-stock with fresh food and

water, eight convicts had died of pneumonia and dysentery, but thereafter the general health of the prisoners improved. From Tenerife the fleet sailed to the Cape Verde Islands off the west coast of Africa, where they planned to replenish their supplies, but Phillip decided against landing due to light winds and strong currents. They headed across the Atlantic to Rio de Janeiro, enduring plagues of rats and insects in the stifling tropical conditions. Phillip compassionately ordered the opening of the hatches above the convict quarters after many of the prisoners began suffering from dehydration, fainting fits and convulsions.

The conditions below decks were generally atrocious. Most of the time the prisoners were locked up in total darkness as the risk of fire prevented the use of candles or torches. Lice, fleas, cockroaches and other vermin flourished on all the ships, and the rotten water in the bilges filled the airless quarters with an overpowering stench. The open-air exercise areas were only a few metres long because convicts were prevented from reaching the quarterdeck by a high wooden wall topped with metal spikes. John White, chief surgeon of the First Fleet, reported that 'when the hatches were taken off the stench was so powerful that it was scarcely possible to stand over them'.

The fleet reached the Portuguese-run port of Rio de Janeiro on the east coast of South America on 6 August. Phillip was very well received, having previously served in the Portuguese navy in its war with the Spanish. The ships were repaired, particularly the flagship *Sirius*, which was leaking badly. The convicts were held below deck, but the crews enjoyed shore leave during the month-long stay. They stocked up on rice, coffee, cocoa, fresh meat, various fruits and vegetables and 65,000 litres (over 14,000 gallons) of rum.

On 4 September the ships set sail on the prevailing westerly breeze for the Cape of Good Hope at the southern tip of Africa. The weather mercifully cooled, but at times the seas were so rough that Lieutenant Ralph Clark wrote that 'those marines sleeping with the convict women were washed out of their beds'. They arrived at the Cape on 13 October, staying for four weeks and stocking up with provisions that included over five hundred animals—cattle, pigs, horses, poultry, goats and sheep—for use not only as food on the voyage, but also to stock farms at the new colony.

On 13 November, aided by brisk westerlies, they set off across the Indian Ocean on the final, longest leg of the voyage. There was a general outbreak of dysentery, which caused the death of a marine private named Daniel Creswell. At the end of November, Phillip split the fleet into two, the fastest ships going ahead to scout for suitable locations for the new settlement. The *Supply*, along with the three fastest transport ships, set off with some convicts who had carpentry or gardening skills to help prepare for the arrival of the others. On 3 January 1788 the leading group saw land which they knew to be Van Diemen's Land (now Tasmania), discovered and mapped by Dutch explorer Abel Tasman in 1642. It took them another two weeks, struggling against northerly winds, to sail the thousand kilometres (620 miles) to Botany Bay, where their gruelling voyage finally ended on 18 January.

Landfall at Botany Bay

The new arrivals' first encounter with the natives was friendly. They were naked and armed with spears, but pointed the unarmed newcomers to a freshwater stream. These good relations would not last for long. The second division arrived just the next day, having encountered much more favourable conditions en route. The voyage had actually been very successful—no ships were lost, and fewer passengers died than on most of the fleets that would bring about 160,000 more prisoners to Australia over the next fifty years (the exact number is unknown, due to lack of accurate records). Just sixty-nine people had died—many before the fleet had left Portsmouth—of the more than fourteen hundred who had set out. They included forty convicts, five children of convicts, one marine, a marine's wife and a marine's child.

When the Aboriginal people saw the extra ships arriving in Botany Bay, they gathered in larger numbers around the shore, brandishing spears and shouting *'Warra, warra'* ('Go away'). These are the first recorded words spoken by black to white in Australia. Several spears were thrown; one of the marines answered with a blank pistol shot. But soon peace was made, as the Aborigines admonished the spear-throwers and accepted conciliatory gifts of beads from Phillip.

Phillip quickly decided that Botany Bay, with its poor shelter and sandy, barren soil, was unsuitable for settlement. On 21 January he and a group of his men sailed north and entered Port Jackson, which Cook had mentioned in passing, but did not enter. Phillip called it 'the finest harbour in the world'; Chief Surgeon White was even more enthusiastic, dubbing it the finest 'in the universe'.

They explored several coves, eventually finding a hospitable location with deep water close to the shore, and fed by a small river. Phillip named it Sydney Cove. Arthur Bowes Smith, captain of the *Lady Penrhyn*, wrote:

The finest terra's, lawns and grottos, with distinct plantations of the tallest and most stately trees I ever saw in any nobleman's ground in England,

cannot excel in beauty those which I saw. Nature now presented to our view ... the stupendous rocks from the summit of the hills and down to the very water's edge hang'g over in a most awful way from above, and form'g the most commodious quays by the water, beggard all description.

Early hardships

They returned to Botany Bay and, on 25 January, after being delayed for several days by a fierce storm, the fleet set sail for Port Jackson and began to set up the new outpost—the most distant colony ever established by a founding state. The next day Phillip raised the British flag and the new settlers began unloading the ships, starting with the livestock that had not starved or been eaten on the way. The female convicts were left on board as land was cleared and a tent town erected. On Sunday 3 February the chaplain, Reverend Richard Johnson, conducted the first church service under a large tree overlooking the bay. Ten days later the female convicts were brought ashore during a wild storm, giving rise to scenes of unrestrained licentiousness as the seamen shared their grog rations. The officers were powerless to keep apart the men and women; as Surgeon John Smith wrote: 'it is beyond my abilities to give a just description of the scene of debauchery and riot that ensued during the night' and Captain Watkin Tench recorded: 'when landed their separation became impracticable, and would have been, perhaps, wrong ... What was to be attempted? To prevent their intercourse was impossible'.

The first few weeks were marked by numerous summer storms. On 1 February, marine Ralph Clark wrote: 'I never slept worse my dear wife than I did last night—what with the hard ground, spiders, ants and every vermin you can think of was crawling over me'. The fierce summer winds killed many of the newly planted crops as the temperature reached 109°F (43°C). The local gum trees turned out to be difficult to use for building, their timber so hard that English tools were barely strong enough to make an impression.

The newcomers could have gleaned much useful survival information from the Aborigines, but their attitude of racial superiority prevented them from seeking advice, even though the British government had sought good relations with the locals: 'to conciliate their affections, enjoining all our subjects to live in amity and kindness with them'. By and large the two groups kept out of each other's way at first, although later in the year there were several incidents where Aborigines or settlers died, usually following theft of each other's property. Hostilities gradually increased, leading to the uneasy relationships that would endure for the next two centuries. Imported cholera and influenza, previously unknown, also took a terrible toll

The First Fleet explored coastal inlets in Sydney Harbour before settling in Camp Cove.

on the locals, who had no resistance to these diseases. Although this was accidental, and the settlers had no wish to add tribal warfare to the colony's numerous problems, within a year the surrounds of Sydney cove were littered with decomposing native corpses.

Morale in the fledgling settlement was appalling, fuelled by hunger, malnutrition, disease, and by cruelty inflicted by officers on marines, and marines on convicts. Realising that the colony faced starvation unless more stores arrived soon from England, Phillip allocated the same rations to convicts and employees alike, regardless of status—this caused further resentment. Things would not start to improve until the arrival of the Second Fleet in June 1790.

Yet despite these brutal and unpromising beginnings, the colony very slowly began to prosper. Army officers were given land, many

LEFT: Of the 1400 or so who landed, nearly 800 were convicts, the remainder marines and officials.

assisted by convicts who, on emancipation, acquired their own smallholdings. The young country attracted new settlers wishing to take advantage of the opportunities offered by cheap land and labour, and a range of other commercial enterprises.

Convicts continued to be transported to Australia but, by the mid nineteenth century, attitudes towards transportation had begun to change. There were many more free immigrants living in Australia, along with a number of former convicts, and they were concerned about the negative influence of a large criminal population in the increasingly prosperous colony. In Britain, social reformers voiced their concern at arbitrary and inconsistent sentencing and the inhumane treatment of prisoners aboard the convict ships. The number of transportation ships dwindled until, in 1868, eighty years after the arrival of the First Fleet in Botany Bay, the last convict ship left Britain for Australia.

1836

BRAVE TEXAN REBELS DEFEND TO THE DEATH

The Battle of the Alamo was a pivotal moment in the war of independence between Texas and Mexico. The Mexican forces descended on San Antonio on 23 February 1836 and the Texans retreated into the old missionary complex, the Alamo. Over the next twelve days, Mexican troops continued to muster and reached numbers up to 2000 while over 180 defenders holed up inside the fortress walls under the joint command of William B. Travis and James Bowie. On the thirteenth day the Mexicans stormed the Alamo and all the defenders were killed.

THE BATTLE OF THE ALAMO

When gallant Colonel Travis, Drew a line down in the sand,
Everyone stepped over, But one solitary man.
They called him Rose the Coward, And they called him Yellow Rose,
But it takes bravery to stand alone, As God Almighty knows.

FROM THE TRADITIONAL SONG 'MOSES ROSE OF TEXAS',
AUTHOR AND DATE UNKNOWN

Late in the evening of 5 March 1836, so the story goes, Lieutenant-Colonel William B. Travis, the commander of a small garrison of over one hundred and eighty volunteers manning the Alamo mission in Texas, called them together, took out his sword, and drew a line in the sand. He then asked anyone who wished to stay and face the army of the Mexican General Antonio López de Santa Anna—which by then had all but surrounded their isolated outpost—to cross the line and stand with him. But he warned that whoever did so faced the likelihood of being killed or captured. All but one, a former lieutenant in Napoleon's Grande Armée named Moses Rose, stepped over the line and into history. Later that same evening Rose made his own way into history, crossing silently through the Mexican lines to freedom and everlasting notoriety as the so-called Coward of the Alamo.

No documentary evidence survives to support the 'line in the sand' story. It may well be apocryphal. Rose, who settled in Louisiana and eventually faded from history, later swore that Travis did indeed draw the line, and Susannah Dickinson, the wife of the Alamo's artillery officer Almaron Dickinson and one of twenty women and children to survive the battle, also claimed to have seen Travis draw his sword and use it to make a sweeping gesture in the sand. That such an incidental moment should achieve the mythic proportions it has in the history of America—and of Texas in particular—might at first glance seem surprising, but nothing about the Alamo story is inconsequential. In the reverential retelling of the events leading up to 6 March 1836, every decision, every command, every gesture and every shot is an intrinsic piece of the legend and a treasured reminder of what it means to live free.

The Alamo's Spanish origins

In the early 1700s the Spanish government controlled a large area that swept north from Mexico and included present-day Texas. It began to establish a series of Catholic missions across eastern Texas that were intended to serve as a buffer against the growing French settlements in Louisiana. The isolation of the missions, however, required the establishment of a way station to assist in the adequate provisioning of these new outposts, and in 1718 an expedition led by Martin de Alarcon, the governor of Spanish Texas, arrived at the banks of the San Antonio River. Construction soon began on a new mission, San Antonio de Valero. When floods from a gulf hurricane demolished the mud and straw structure in 1724, it was relocated to the other side of the river, which was less prone to flooding. Over the following decades this building grew into a collection of more than thirty adobe structures that included storerooms, homes for its missionaries and its growing population of Indian converts, and a chapel.

The mission complex was continually being reinforced and strengthened to withstand raids by the local Apache and Comanche Indians, but, with the population overwhelmingly converted to Roman Catholicism, the mission, which had been secularised in 1793, was abandoned.

Early in the new century the old mission was given a new name, the Alamo, most likely after a nearby grove of cottonwood trees known as *alamo* in Spanish. Responsibility for the mission was transferred from Spain to Mexico after the Mexican Revolution in 1821.

Texas colonists take over the Alamo outpost

In a series of battles and sieges during 1835, Texan revolutionaries inflicted a series of defeats upon the Mexican military culminating in the Siege of Bexár, staged in San Antonio de Bexár (present-day San Antonio), Texas. The Mexican forces, under General Martín Perfecto de Cos, brother-in-law of Santa Anna, surrendered on 10 December and, four days later, Cos marched his remaining eight hundred troops from San Antonio back to Mexico. This defeat represented the end of any Mexican armed presence in Texas and led many Texans to believe that the days of armed conflict with Mexico were over.

James Clinton Neill, a Texas revolutionary and politician, took command of the old mission on 21 December 1835. He was appalled at what he found and immediately set about strengthening its defences. Neill had inherited a strategic outpost that was woefully undermanned and lacking in even the most basic of supplies. He wrote to Sam Houston, then a major general in the Texas army and soon to be the first president of the Republic of Texas, pleading for extra provisions as well as an increase in the numbers garrisoning the outpost, which he claimed wouldn't last four days if placed under siege. 'Unless we are reinforced and victualled,' he wrote, 'we must become an easy prey to the enemy, in case of an attack'.

But no help was forthcoming. Instead, on 19 January, Jim Bowie, the legendary Texan pioneer and soldier, arrived with fifty men and a note from Houston to salvage the mission's artillery and blow the Alamo to pieces—a difficult order to obey when a shortage of horses meant hauling artillery away on gun carriages was next to impossible. Both Bowie and Neill, convinced of the mission's strategic importance, thought the order ridiculous and replied they would rather perish defending it than surrender it to the enemy. On 26 January, the mission's garrison passed a resolution in which they vowed to defend rather than destroy the mission.

Tennessee's Davy Crockett rides into town

In early January Davy Crockett had arrived in Texas from his home in Tennessee and signed an oath to defend the Provisional Government of Texas (declared in November the previous year) for a period of six months. He and a small group of Tennesseans rode into the town of San Antonio on 6 February and were met there by Jim Bowie. Bowie convinced them to ride with him to the Alamo as volunteers. On

Davy Crockett, folk hero, frontiersman and defender of the Alamo, shown in heroic pose.

14 February James Neill went on furlough to visit his sick family in Bastrop and to seek out supplies and reinforcements. He left the Alamo under the command of the garrison's highest ranking officer, William B. Travis, a cavalryman who had arrived at the mission the previous week with thirty volunteers. Twelve days later fourteen hundred troops under the command of the self-styled 'Napoleon of the West', General Antonio López de Santa Anna, arrived to reassert Mexican control over its rebellious northern state.

Santa Anna was one of the great and enduring figures in Mexican history. Born in Vera Cruz on 21 February 1794, he joined the colonial Spanish Army in 1810 and rose to the rank of captain. In 1822, together with Guadalupe Victoria, he signed the Plan de Casa Mata, which led to the abolition of the monarchy and the establishment of the Republic of Mexico. In 1828 he took part in the coup that overthrew the government of President Manuel Gómez Pedraza and in 1833 was elected president of Mexico. Far more than just another general, Antonio López de Santa Anna was the embodiment of the Mexican nation.

Extending over a hectare (3 acres), the collection of buildings that constituted the mission complex (it included palisades, barracks and a chapel) had been fortified over the years to withstand attacks by Indian raiders—but its walls and defences were ill-equipped for the artillery that Santa Anna was bringing. Its perimeter of over 400 metres (almost 1300 feet) would also be impossible to adequately defend with the number of men at Travis' disposal. Furthermore, there were no firing ports (or openings) built into its walls through which a rifleman could project the barrel of his gun and shoot while still being protected. This meant a walkway had to be constructed that allowed its defenders to shoot over the walls; however, this left their upper bodies horribly exposed to enemy fire.

Santa Anna's unexpected advance

Santa Anna, however, was so enraged by what he saw as nothing more than armed acts of rebellion against the Mexican government that he wrote a tersely worded letter to the US president, Andrew Jackson, stating that he regarded any 'foreigners' who might be captured in future battle to be 'pirates' and they would be treated accordingly. He would be taking no prisoners. The letter reached Washington in January but seems not to have been widely circulated. It is all but certain that the volunteers within the walls of the Alamo had little idea that, once they stepped over Travis' line in the sand, their chances of survival were nil. By mid-February Travis had heard talk that Santa Anna was marching in the direction of San Antonio but wasn't expecting him to advance north until early spring and discounted rumours of his approach as unfounded. It proved to be a grave miscalculation. On 16 February Santa Anna crossed the Rio Grande and, on the evening of 21 February, with his troops camped along the banks of the Medina River just 40 kilometres (25 miles) away, all but ten of the Alamo's garrison were enjoying a raucous night with the residents of San Antonio celebrating the birthday of George Washington.

On the evening of 22 February Santa Anna arrived at Leon Creek, a mere 13 kilometres (8 miles) from the Alamo and word of his advance spread to the residents of San Antonio. When scouts sent out by Travis returned claiming to have seen advance elements of Santa Anna's Delores Cavalry, his volunteers did all they could in what little time they had to fortify their position. Cattle were brought into the compound; food was scrounged from surrounding houses;

and San Antonio's blacksmith shop was raided for anything that might prove valuable in a long siege. Some men, such as Alamaron Dickinson and Jim Bowie, brought family members in to the perceived safety of the mission, and Travis hurriedly dispatched couriers to the garrison at Gonzales 110 kilometres (68 miles) away to plead for reinforcements.

Colonel Fannin's doomed mission

When news of the Alamo's plight reached members of the Provisional Government, recruitment drives were begun and reinforcements assembled, but none would arrive in time to help. Colonel James Fannin Jr left Goliad (to the southeast of San Antonio) on 28 February with more than three hundred men and four cannon, but the rescue attempt would prove a disaster. A shortage of horses meant Fannin was forced to rely on oxen to pull the artillery. Wagons broke down while still within sight of Goliad and the expedition took six hours just to cross the San Antonio River. Oxen wandered off into the night and many of the men under his command had even forgotten to bring any provisions for the journey. Fannin's mission ground to a halt. The defenders of the Alamo were on their own.

The siege began on 24 February. Santa Anna positioned his artillery of 8-, 6- and 4-pound cannon within 300 metres (330 yards) of the Alamo's southern and eastern walls, too far to do any real damage to its defensive walls but intimidating nonetheless. The following day, under cover of artillery shells, Mexican troops moved to within 90 metres (almost 100 yards) of the Alamo's perimeter and took shelter in a series of small mud huts, but were driven out the following morning. On 26 February the Alamo's artillerymen exchanged fire with some Mexican guns until forced to cease firing in order to conserve their low reserves of powder.

The next day, having heard of James Fannin's failed rescue mission, a group of approximately fifty men left Gonzales and reached the Alamo in the early hours of 1 March. Not realising in the darkness that the men were Texans, the Alamo sentries fired at them. One man was wounded, but their pleas quickly convinced those inside that they were Texans, not Mexicans, the gates were opened and the men were allowed in. According to the majority of historical accounts, the Alamo was now garrisoned by over one hundred and eighty men.

Texas declared a republic as troops dig in

In the midst of the siege on 2 March, unbeknown to those inside the Alamo and even to Santa Anna himself, Texas was declared an independent republic by the convention of 1836 delegates meeting at Washington-on-the-Brazos, a small town on the Brazos River in eastern Texas. The men of the Alamo, although they could not have possibly known it, were now fighting not only for their lives, but also for the world's newest nation, the Republic of Texas.

Any hopes those inside the Alamo might have had of holding on until reinforcements could arrive were dashed when, on 3 March, a thousand Mexican troops arrived and paraded through San Antonio's plaza. This brought the total strength of Santa Anna's army to 2400. The Mexicans were in high spirits, celebrating the defeat of a small force of Texans at the Battle of San Patricio, though in truth it was more of a skirmish than a battle, with just twenty Texans killed out of a complement of sixty. Nevertheless, the Mexican marching band played long into the night, and all those inside the Alamo could do was sit and listen.

The final assault

Sporadic artillery bombardments continued throughout 4 March, and on 5 March Santa Anna announced to his staff that the final assault would begin the following day. When his aides asked why he did not prefer to wait until the arrival of his 12-pound cannon he replied: 'What are the lives of soldiers than so many chickens?' So it was, with the mission all but surrounded and with food and water quickly running out, Santa Anna, rather than waiting out the enemy, chose instead to sacrifice his men in a dramatic, bloody and glorious finale.

Defenders of the Alamo are overrun in a withering assault by Santa Anna's troops, leaving only seven Texan survivors.

At 5 am on Sunday 6 March approximately eighteen hundred Mexican troops advanced in formation on the Alamo and were hit with a withering onslaught of cannon and musket fire. Their ranks staggered, but they regrouped and drove relentlessly forward. Travis was among the first to be killed, felled by musket fire while defending the north wall. Abandoning the mission walls the defenders withdrew to the inner courtyard and barracks, but the cause was hopeless. Jim Bowie, bedridden with a mystery illness, was bayoneted to death. The chapel was the last building to fall. Only seven men survived the battle, including by most accounts Davy Crockett, but all seven were subsequently executed on the personal orders of Santa Anna.

The siege of the Alamo had lasted thirteen days and was as much a tragedy as it was a heroic sacrifice. If the Texas Provisional Government hadn't been in such disarray, reinforcements could have been despatched sooner and the slaughter avoided. But it was not in vain. The battle ignited a righteous anger that spread across the fledgling nation, helped inspire a Texan victory at the decisive Battle of San Jacinto (Santa Anna and his troops were thoroughly routed), and etched into American history that famous call to arms: 'Remember the Alamo!'

 # 1879

BRITISH REGIMENTS DEFEAT AFRICAN NATION

The Battle of Ulundi was the final battle in the Zulu Wars, ending two years of bloodshed initiated by the British to remove the last challenge to their imperial power in southern Africa. Zululand had become a powerful kingdom under the rule of the warlord King Shaka in the early nineteenth century, but by the 1870s European colonial expansion was starting to hem it in. Ulundi was the decisive battle that finally broke the military power of the Zulus. Facing the estimated 20,000 Zulus were 4000 British troops and two Gatling machine-guns. Within half an hour the last stand of the Zulus had come to an end and the Zulu nation was defeated.

THE ZULU WARS

An assegai [spear] has been thrust into the belly of the nation, there are not enough tears to mourn for the dead.

CETSHWAYO KAMPANDE, AFTER HIS VICTORY AT THE BATTLE OF ISANDLWANA

When the great Zulu ruler King Shaka kaSenzangakhona was assassinated by members of his own family in a coup in 1828 he is said to have used his dying breaths to warn them that they would never rule the land as he had done. White men, he said prophetically, would one day come 'like locusts' and devour the kingdom that he had created.

Although the Dutch had settled the southern regions of the African continent as early as 1652 and the British gained their foothold around Cape Town in 1806, the landlocked kingdom of the Zulu had remained unaffected by European colonialism. A former Royal Navy lieutenant, Francis Farewell, established the first commercial ties with King Shaka in 1824. Natal was annexed to the Crown in 1843 and for the next thirty years the relationship between the colonial British and the kingdom of Shaka kaSenzangakhona was amiable and profitable.

When diamonds were discovered in Kimberley in 1868, however, British government strategists began to reassess the traditional view of southern Africa as being little more than a colonial backwater and began to examine ways in which their control of the region could be strengthened.

Britain mounts an offensive

In late 1878 a series of unresolved border disputes between the Zulus and white farmers in the Transvaal provided the British government with the trigger to wipe the Zulu nation from the map of Africa. An ultimatum was handed to Zululand's monarch Cetshwayo kaMpande in December 1878, demanding that the Zulu army and its hierarchy be disbanded, and that certain Zulu warriors responsible for various border incidents involving the apprehension and detention of British citizens be handed over for trial. Cetshwayo did not acknowledge the ultimatum, providing the British with the excuse they were looking for to invade.

On 11 January 1879 the 24th Regiment of Foot under the command of Lieutenant-General Frederick Augustus Thesiger, Second Baron of Chelmsford, invaded Zululand. He divided his force into three columns: the Central Column crossed the Buffalo River at the Rorke's Drift; Northern Column forded the Ncome River 64 kilometres (40 miles) north, and the Coastal Column of 2700 men crossed the Tugela River. The objective of these three columns was the Zulus' royal capital, Ulundi, 60 kilometres (35 miles) to the northeast. Ten days later, on 20 January, after their crossing at Rorke's Drift, the Central Column passed by a hill to the east called Isandlwana, where Chelmsford decided to make temporary camp. Little did he know that the first major battle of the Anglo-Zulu War was just two days away, and that it would end in the worst ever defeat for the British Army in a fight against a technologically inferior enemy.

The Battle of Isandlwana

After ten days of marching, the Central Column had covered just 16 kilometres (10 miles) and made camp beneath the isolated sphinx-shaped hill of Isandlwana, believing that the Zulu army was still days away. Britain, however, was about to be dealt its largest ever military defeat at the hands of a native militia, as twelve thousand Zulu warriors closed in, having covered 80 kilometres (50 miles) in a mere five days, from Ulundi.

On 22 January British scouts discovered twelve thousand Zulus, under the command of Prince Ntshingwayo, one of the most able military strategists in the Zulu kingdom, sitting quietly in a valley adjacent to Chelmsford's troops. The Zulus' original plan was to attack forward elements of Chelmsford's force the following day; now that their position was revealed, Ntshingwayo was forced to issue orders to assume the Zulus' traditional 'buffalo horn' formation. He also chose to bypass Chelmsford's 2500-man strong Central Column, which had marched out at dawn in search of his army, and instead to attack the approximately twelve hundred men left to guard the Isandlwana camp under the command of Colonel Henry Pulleine.

Pulleine was a bureaucrat with little field experience and, instead of organising a defensive perimeter with Isandlwana at their backs, he ordered his troops to assume a standard firing line. It was a decision that would cost his men their lives. The Zulu attack was methodical, swift and brutal and, despite the Zulu 'chest' taking heavy casualties, the 'horns' were able to envelop the British line and break through on both its right and left flanks, at which point the British line collapsed. As discipline broke down small groups of British troops formed into a disparate collection of 'last stands', firing until their ammunition was exhausted and they were simply overwhelmed. Forced back to a tributary of the Tugela River, the last vestiges of Pulleine's battalions were cornered and slaughtered as they tried to make their way across. British losses included 802 non-commissioned officers, 52 officers and 470 native Africans. Only 55 British soldiers managed to escape. Zulu losses were approximately two thousand killed.

As if the losses at Isandlwana were not enough, when Lord Chelmsford's column returned to the encampment they were able to see beyond the Tugela River to where, in the distance, smoke was rising from the old mission station at Rorke's Drift.

Defence at Rorke's Drift

In the afternoon of 22 January, after Pulleine's troops had been encircled at Isandlwana, 4500 Zulus under the command of Cetshwayo kaMpande's younger brother, Prince Dabulamanzi, chose to descend upon the 139 soldiers left to man an old mission station at Rorke's Drift. Commanding officer Lieutenant John Chard of the Royal Engineers had transformed the church into a storeroom and the house of its resident minister, Otto Witt, into a hospital.

In the morning gunshots could be heard coming from the direction of Isandlwana, 21 kilometres (13 miles) away, and the garrison started fortifying the mission by using mealie bags and biscuit boxes to create defensive walls linking the church and the hospital. Five hundred Zulus descended on the mission from the south while the main body attacked the British defences with gunfire from the west and northwest. The hospital became the focus of the battle after Zulu warriors set it alight. The British withdrew from the building, fighting almost hand-to-hand with the advancing warriors as they went. Three patients had to be left behind and were stabbed to death.

Fighting continued until well past midnight, but the Zulus couldn't break the British line despite the British being pushed back into a small fortified area around the old church. Through the night the Zulus would withdraw, engage in a war dance and beat their spears and shields on the ground—and attack again. The following morning, upon seeing the approaching relief column of Lord Chelmsford, Dabulamanzi ordered a withdrawal, and the Zulus turned and left the battle. British casualties were fifteen killed and thirteen wounded, and the battle at Rorke's Drift went into the history books as a classic example of defensive warfare.

Twenty-three Victoria Crosses, the highest military award for bravery in the British Army

British ambassadors return to Lord Chelmsford after meeting with Cetshwayo as the conflict escalates.

(instituted in 1856 by Queen Victoria), were awarded during the Zulu Wars. Of those twenty-three, eleven were awarded at the Battle of Rorke's Drift, the most ever received by a British regiment in a single engagement; another five were awarded to those involved in the defence of the hospital, including Alfred Henry Hook, who was wounded in the scalp by a Zulu spear and retired from the army in June 1880.

Accounts at the time put Zulu losses at 370, but the real figure will never be known. Wounded Zulus were later bayoneted or shot where they lay by the relief force, whose men had witnessed the disembowelment of British troops at Isandlwana. In an interview with the newspaper *Western Mail* in 1914 Samuel Pitts, a private who fought at Rorke's Drift, claimed the actual number of Zulu dead was in the vicinity of 875.

Eshowe, Intombe and Kambula

Also on 22 January, a Zulu force numbering six thousand attempted to block the advance of the Coastal Column, under the command of Colonel Charles Pearson. Pearson was on the way to the KawMondi Mission Station at Eshowe, from where he planned to advance on the capital, Ulundi. Pearson made it into the mission only to be besieged for ten weeks by 12,000 Zulus under the command of Prince Dahilamanzi in what became known as the Seige of Eshowe, until relieved by Lord Chelmsford on 3 April. In that time thirteen hundred Zulus and forty-four British were killed.

To the north of Zululand was a region of disputed territories, with the town of Luneberg at its centre, a white settlement that was under constant threat of a Zulu attack. The decision was made to reinforce the town, and eighteen wagons of supplies and ammunition were despatched, along with the one hundred and six troops of the 80th Regiment under Captain David Moriarty, who would be stationed there until war's end. The wagons, however, began to founder in a series of heavy rainstorms that had swollen the Intombe River and separated the convoy. On 12 March the Zulus ambushed the wagons and killed seventy British troops.

The Battle of Kambula on 29 March is considered the turning point in the conflict, when an attack on the British camp there resulted in the deaths of over a thousand Zulus, with British casualties of thirty-eight killed and forty-three wounded. The Zulus, despite being armed with captured British rifles, were unable to break through the *laager*, a hexagonal-shaped fort of interlocked wagons. The adjacent *kraal* (an Afrikaans word for cattle enclosure) could not, however, keep the Zulus out and was the scene of heavy hand-to-hand fighting before the British troops could withdraw to the relative safety of the *laager*. Despite several Zulu charges on the tightly drawn wagons the British lines held, aided by the canister shells of its artillery projected in a devastating arc that decimated the Zulus' tight formations. When the Zulus were at last forced to retreat they were chased down by cavalry units for more than 12 kilometres (7 miles), constantly being shot at and even speared with their own discarded iron spears.

There were other battles of course, at Hlobane and Gingindlovu, but after Kambula the result was never really in doubt. The Zulus were a motivated, mobile fighting force and their leaders proved themselves adept strategic thinkers, but even the finest strategy is rarely a substitute for superior weaponry. Spears and cowhide shields were no match against Gatling guns, 7-pound (3-kilogram) artillery shells and long-range rifles. But it wouldn't be until the Battle of Ulundi on

4 July that the military power of the Zulus would be smashed once and for all.

British troops approach the Zulu capital

On 4 July 1879 the Frontier Light Horse, a British cavalry regiment consisting of 156 officers and men under the command of Captain Robert Barton of the Coldstream Guards, was steadily advancing across a wide plain toward Zululand's capital of Ulundi. The Frontier Light Horse included forty scouts, seventy Transvaal Rangers, about a hundred Cape Colony volunteers, a contingent of Border Horsemen and more than 250 native troops from the Transvaal. At the same time, 4200 troops under the command of Lord Chelmsford looked on from the surrounding ridges. Chelmsford had been sending out scouts since first light in the hope of locating the army that he knew would be defending the Zulu capital, but by 8 am no sightings of the enemy had been reported. It was now up to the Frontier Light Horse to approach the city and flush the warriors out, and up to Chelmsford to end the six-month-long Zulu Wars.

The Frontier Light Horse crossed the Mbilane stream with nothing, it seemed, between them and the city. But from the surrounding grasslands fifteen thousand troops of the Zulus' inGobamkhosi regiment suddenly arose to the cavalry's north, south and east and began to thump the ground with their feet and shields. If the Zulus had been armed with modern weaponry the Frontier Light Horse would have been slaughtered, but the regiment was able to retreat to the lines of the British infantry before the Zulus could close the noose. As the inGobamkhosi advanced, Chelmsford's infantry formed a defensive square four rows deep, with the first two rows in kneeling positions, supported by rapid-fire Gatling guns and artillery fire directed almost point-blank into the ranks of the advancing Zulus. Discipline saw the British prevail. The sequence of firing—first the front row, then the second, third, fourth, returning to the first again—proved impenetrable, and no Zulu could get closer than 30 metres (33 yards). A reserve of Zulus charged the square's southeast corner but fell to the British 9-pound (4-kilogram) artillery shells and the withering fire from the infantry. It was hardly a fair fight.

When the Zulu ranks finally broke and began to retreat, Chelmsford ordered his cavalry, the 1st King's Dragoon Guards, the veteran 17th Lancers (many of whom had participated in the Charge of the Light Brigade during the Crimean War), the colonial cavalry and a contingent of native cavalry that had been raised in Natal Province, to set off in pursuit. The bloody chase did not end until every Zulu warrior was killed. Not even the wounded were spared the wrath of the British, keen to take their vengeance for the slaughter of their troops at the Battle of Isandlwana. British losses amounted to ten killed and about eighty wounded. Zulu losses were in the thousands. Lord Chelmsford ordered Ulundi to be razed to the ground, and the Zulu capital burned for days. The Anglo-Zulu Wars that began in January of 1879, and lasted for six bloody months, were over.

For the most part the Zulu Wars had been a series of murderous, suicidal charges, with spears and cowhide shields proving no match for rifles and British discipline. In hindsight, of course, had the Zulu leadership been able to depart from their 'buffalo horns' tactics and learn to use the thousands of rifles they

FOLLOWING PAGES: In nearly twelve hours of fighting 120 British troops shot down 500 Zulus at Rorke's Drift.

acquired from their victories on the battlefield, they would certainly have been able to put up more resistance. But to the Zulu a rifle was little more than a kind of super throwing stick, to be fired occasionally but ultimately to be discarded in favour of spears and shields. It was this inability to alter their traditional approach to warfare that helped bring the Anglo-Zulu Wars to a relatively swift conclusion.

Aftermath of the Zulu Wars

In the wake of the Battle of Ulundi the Zulu armies were disbanded and their chiefs submitted *en masse* to British rule. The British withdrew from Zululand shortly after the conclusion of the battle and the once-proud Zulu nation was divided into thirteen separate 'kingdoms' each ruled by pro-British sympathisers. The Zulu king, Cetshwayo, fled but was eventually captured on 8 August and spent the next four years living as an exile on Robben Island. He died in February 1884. On 20 May 1884 the Boers supported the installation of Cetshwayo's son, Dinizulu, as ruler over one of the thirteen kingdoms, but he was never formally recognised by the British.

Tensions between the Boers and the British resulted in the First Anglo-Boer War (1880–81), where the Boer fought to regain the independence in the Transvaal which they'd lost in 1877, and the Second Anglo-Boer War (1899–1902), which saw the Boer republics eventually become British colonies.

1883

KRAKATOA BLOWS ITS TOP

One of the most powerful volcanic explosions in recorded history occurred at Krakatoa in August 1883, when the Indonesian volcanic island erupted with the force of 100 megatons (the Hiroshima bomb was about 20 kilotons). The explosion was heard as far away as the island of Rodrigues of Mauritius, 4800 kilometres (2200 miles) to the west. Tsunamis resulting from the explosion rose to 30 metres (33 yards), and destroyed 300 villages along the coasts of Java and Sumatra and huge waves rippled across the South Pacific. Ash from the explosion rose 80 kilometres (50 miles) into the atmosphere and global weather patterns were affected for a year.

THE ERUPTION OF AN INDONESIAN VOLCANO

Suddenly we saw a gigantic wave of prodigious height advancing toward the seashore with considerable speed ... There, where an instant before had lain the town of Telok Betong, nothing remained but the open sea.

CAPTAIN LINDEMANN ABOARD THE *LOUDON* IN THE SUNDA STRAIT

Beginning in the early morning of 27 August 1883, in Indonesia's Sunda Strait between Sumatra and Java, a series of eruptions, the like of which had never been seen or heard in recorded history, tore through the atmosphere. The explosions of rock and magma that rose from the depths of Krakatoa Island were heard 4800 kilometres (3000 miles) to the west on the Indian Ocean island of Rodrigues and 3500 kilometres (almost 2200 miles) to the south in the Western Australian city of Perth, where citizens mistakenly identified the sound as cannon fire. It was, in effect, a very large cannon. The Krakatoa eruption was the equivalent of 10,000 Hiroshima-style atomic bombs, and the 16 cubic kilometres (3.8 cubic miles) that the island lost that day, quite apart from what collapsed into the caldera, was spread over a staggering 4 million square kilometres.

Unimagined destruction on a vast scale

The cataclysmic events and horrifying statistics that followed the Krakatoa eruption are almost too numerous to name. Estimates of the actual death toll from the explosion and subsequent tsunamis are as high as one hundred and twenty thousand, but it is generally accepted that at least thirty-six thousand people perished in an estimated three hundred villages along the coastlines of the Indonesian islands of Java and Sumatra—in the tsunamis that the eruption generated and the pyroclastic flows that raced across the Sunda Strait and onto the Indonesian coast. Floating pumice in the Sunda Strait was so thick it hampered the progress of ships, and as much as a year later skeletons floating on 'pumice rafts' were being swept ashore on the coastline of East Africa. Twenty-one cubic kilometres (5 cubic miles) of rock and pumice were thrown into the air when two-thirds of Krakatoa disappeared, and the island was reduced in height from 450 metres (1476 feet) above sea level to 250 metres (820 feet) below. Three thousand people, the entire population of the island of Sebesi, Krakatoa's nearest inhabited neighbour 12 kilometres (almost 8 miles) to the north, were killed instantly.

Ash from the eruption fell on the surrounding islands and killed every living thing, every blade of grass and every insect. The ash cloud rose to a height of 80 kilometres (50 miles) and then began to spread around the globe, darkening the skies and resulting in spectacular red sunsets that prompted the great English poet of the Victorian era, Alfred, Lord Tennyson, to compose the poem 'St Telemachus', which read in part:

Had the fierce ashes of some fiery peak
Been hurled so high they ranged about the globe?
For day by day, thro' many a blood-red eve,
The wrathful sunset glared.

Tidal surges, possibly caused by the shockwaves that travelled seven times around the earth, were recorded in Alaska and the english Channel, and ships anchored in the coastal waters off South Africa swayed at their moorings. Krakatoa was a global event such as the modern world had never seen, and its effects on climate and vegetation would last for years.

Anatomy of a cataclysm

The eruption of Krakatoa was thousands of years in the making. Krakatoa Island, Verlaten Island, Lang Island and a small volcanic outcrop called Polish Hat were all that remained after the eruption of Ancient Krakatoa approximately 60,000 years ago. In 1883 Krakatoa Island was home to three volcanoes: Danan, Rakata and the most active, Perboewetan. Since the collapse of Ancient Krakatoa, the chambers beneath these three volcanoes had slowly been filling and heating up, resulting in the build-up of enormous amounts of pressure. Three months before the eruption smoke began rising from Perboewetan for the first time in more than two hundred years, reaching a height of over 10 kilometres (6 miles). Steam began venting from the volcano's slopes and shockwaves from the explosions rattled windows in the capital of Batavia. Towards the end of May all measurable volcanic activity had subsided. On 27 May, eighty-six volcano watchers arrived at

Krakatoa Island on the *Loudon,* climbed to the eastern rim of Perboewetan's crater and peered into its black heart—a remarkably foolish act by any standard. On 16 June a series of small eruptions began anew. More steam vents had formed between Perboewetan and Danan to the south, and the eruptions became so intense that high tides were reported in several Javanese and Sumatran ports. By 19 June much of Perboewetan's upper cone had been blasted away.

In early August a Dutch engineer, Captain H. Ferzenaar, visited Krakatoa and noted that two new steam vents had opened up on the north face of Danan and that part of its crater had collapsed. He also recorded that an additional vent had opened on Perboewetan and went on to write in his diary that, in his opinion, it was now too dangerous to send anyone onto the island; and, indeed, Ferzenaar was the last human being to leave a footprint on Krakatoa. The Sunda Strait had busy shipping lanes, which ensured that Captain Ferzenaar's sighting would not be the last. On 12 August a Dutch ship, the *Prins Hendrik,* reported columns of steam and ash rising 3500 metres (2 miles) into the atmosphere.

Karakatoa's explosions shake the world

By 26 August the eruptions were virtually continuous. Ships within a 20-kilometre (12-mile) radius of the island began to report heavy falls of volcanic ash as well as large pieces of solidified volcanic rock crashing onto their decks. The volcanic rock, or pumice, was the result of rapid cooling and depressurisation. In Batavia that afternoon, ash was reportedly falling in the streets, while pressure gauges in the city recorded increasingly violent explosions throughout the day and into the evening. The explosions were so loud they woke people from their sleep in Australia's Northern Territory. During this first phase of the eruption, which lasted until the early hours of 27 August, it is estimated that between 8.5 and 12.5 cubic kilometres (2–3 cubic miles) of pumice, rock and magma were ejected into the atmosphere. As spectacular as this undoubtedly was, it was nothing in comparison to what was soon to come.

At 5.30 am on 27 August the first of a series of four massive explosions began to tear Krakatoa Island apart. The explosions were of such intensity that they shattered the eardrums of sailors on ships in the Sunda Strait. Then, at 10.02 am, Perboewetan and Danan collapsed and the island began to disintegrate. Rock fragments (tephra) mixed with superheated ash raced down the flanks of the volcanoes towards the sea and were propelled as far as 40 kilometres (25 miles) across the Sunda Strait—with such ferocity that they did not stop until they hit the Indonesian coast. This pyroclastic flow reached temperatures in excess of 700°C (1300°F)—temperatures so extreme that it boiled the seawater over which it was moving, allowing the gases to ride a self-made cushion of air that increased the speed and the distance it was able to travel. The pyroclastic flow didn't stop until, like the tsunamis, it hit the coastline which was only 40–50 kilometres (25–30 miles) away. It is estimated that around 4500 people who were fortunate enough to survive Krakatoa's tsunamis were soon afterward burned alive by its gases.

The force of the pyroclastic flow's impact becomes obvious when one reads the testimony of the Beyerinck family. Willem and Johanna Beyerinck and their three children lived in the Sumatran coastal town of Ketimbang but also had a small hut on the slopes of Radja Bassa 400 metres (1312 feet) above the village.

Willem was the area's comptroller, a civil servant responsible for the dispensing of law and order, and tax collection on behalf of the Dutch colonial government.

One family's story of loss and survival

A detailed diary kept by Johanna Beyerinck provides a valuable insight into the events of 26 and 27 August 1883 and the ordeals she suffered in the week that followed until her family's rescue on 1 September.

By 26 August the rumblings of Krakatoa had filled Johanna with a sense of dread. Unable to ignore her feelings, she convinced her husband Willem to make his apologies at the opening of a small market in the nearby village of Tjanti, and they returned home to their government house in Ketimbang. That afternoon, with Krakatoa obscured by thick black smoke that was hiding an ominous, blood-red sun, Johanna again pleaded with Willem, this time to make for a small hut the family had above the town outside the small village of Amboel Balik. Though initially concerned at creating a panic should the populace see him fleeing into the hills, increasingly erratic wave surges convinced Willem to head for higher ground.

That evening at 8 pm, as the family were busily packing their suitcases, a small tsunami struck their house, demolishing the staircase and hastening their departure. Three thousand villagers joined them. It took three and a half hours to reach the hut, trudging through ankle-deep mud, and when they got there Johanna put her exhausted children to bed as the terrified villagers huddled outside. By this time the roof

RIGHT: A view of Krakatoa during the 1883 eruption—one of the most catastrophic explosions in recorded history.

was covered in a thick layer of ash and pumice, which continued to fall throughout the night and, unbeknown to those inside, began to kill those outside the hut in their hundreds.

During the night, a thousand people perished in the ash and pumice that fell on and around the Beyerincks' hut, preserving the victims just as they had been when they drew their last breaths. Bodies, Pompeii-like in their last desperate, grotesque and pathetic poses, were everywhere. A week after the skies cleared, the body of a man was found, his arms stretched out in front of him as he tried in vain to crawl through the choking fumes that took his life. The deaths of the Ketimbang villagers on Radja Bassa were the only recorded deaths attributable to the eruption itself, not to its many after-effects.

The next morning, 27 August, the day of the final eruption, Johanna Beyerinck emerged from her hut to see fire raining down from the sky. Some of the surviving villagers raced to Ketimbang, only to return a few hours later with the news that the entire village had been washed away. Then, at precisely 10.02 am, the eruption and the shockwave that travelled around the world launched a pyroclastic flow that surged towards the Sumatran coast. Miraculously, it had drained itself of its deadly intensity just as it reached the front door of the Beyerincks' hut.

Johanna, protected by the walls of the hut, described how her sarong was almost burned from her body, and how the hot ash was so thick she could barely see her hand in front of her face. Willem closed the door to the hut and plunged the family into darkness. The ash took its toll on the couple's three-and-a-half-year-old son who died the next day. Overcome with grief and unable to stand the confines of the increasingly suffocating room any longer, Johanna stumbled out into what was once a green, verdant forest and was now a grey, still world devoid of life. It was only then that she noticed large swathes of skin hanging from her body.

Reports of the eruption swept the world. This is the front page of the Illustrated London News *from 8 September.*

I noticed for the first time that my skin was hanging off everywhere, thick and moist from the ash stuck to it. Thinking it must be dirty, I wanted to pull bits of skin off, but that was still more painful. My tired brain could not make out what it was. I did not know I had been burned. Worn out, I leaned against a tree.

FROM THE DIARY OF JOHANNA BEYERINCK, 1883

Tsunamis of rock and molten ash

The four explosions on 27 August that ripped Krakatoa Island apart each created its own tsunami, generated by several cubic kilometres of rock and magma entering the ocean and displacing equal volumes of water that then raced towards the low-lying villages of Java and Sumatra with devastating speed. They were reportedly over 30 metres (100 feet) high. Nine out of every ten people killed that day lost their lives to the monstrous tsunamis, which were of such ferocity that the steamship *Berouw* was picked up and deposited more than one and a half kilometres (almost a mile) inland, with its entire crew of 28 subsequently lost.

Blankets of pumice choked the waterways of the Sunda Strait for weeks afterwards. Hundreds of bodies were washed up on Javanese and Sumatran beaches and thousands of head of cattle were swept into the sea. Sailors described how buckets lowered over the sides of their ships would come back up laden not with water but with a thick sludge of pumice and ash; they told of floating pumice, thick enough to carry tree trunks, that was still being found on the world's oceans more than two years after the eruption. The sulphur dioxide propelled into the atmosphere mixed with water vapour to produce vast amounts of sulfuric acid—on such a scale that for the twelve months after the eruption it is estimated the amount of sunlight reaching the earth was reduced by as much as 13 per cent, and the earth's temperature dropped by almost half a degree Celsius.

Willem and Johanna Beyerinck, their two remaining children and some two thousand native Indonesians stayed for three nights on Radja Bassa before deciding to make their way down from their mountain sanctuary and back towards the coast. They passed paddy fields and collapsed villages and along the way met a group of survivors who had taken refuge in a nearby river.

Progress down the mountain was slow but, on 30 August, the Sunda Strait came into view and the sun was at last visible through the clouds of ash. Johanna stood and faced the sun, and gave thanks to God for delivering her family. On 1 September the ship *Kederie*, which had been trying for days to find a path through the choking sludge of volcanic pumice to the coast, finally managed to get a boat to shore where the village of Kali Antoe used to be and where the Beyerinck family and the survivors of Ketimbang had emerged, blistered and bloodied, from the jungle.

Why Krakatoa?

The islands of the Sunda Strait and the islands of Java and Sumatra sit over two convergent tectonic plates, the Indo-Australian Plate and the Asian Plate, with the crust of the Indo-Australian Plate pushing beneath the Asian Plate to its north along the Sumatra–Java trench. As the rocks of the uplifted Asian Plate slip across the Indo-Australian Plate, its rocks are heated by friction and begin to melt, occasionally rising to the surface in the form of molten magma and ending their journey in the form of a volcanic eruption. Volcanoes of this type often occur along oceanic trenches and are known as 'andesites', after the volcanic Andes Mountains in South America which were formed in the same manner.

Along the line of the Sumatra–Java trench a string of islands has been born, including Krakatoa and Anak Krakatoa, the 'child of Krakatoa', which first broke the surface in 1927 and is today in an almost constant state of eruption and growing at the rate of 6.8 metres (22 feet) a year.

THE NATIONAL BULLETIN

LEFT: Soldiers walk through the Belgian town of Ypres, reduced to rubble, during World War I.

1912

THE *TITANIC* GOES DOWN

On 10 April 1912, the *Titanic*, largest ship afloat, left Southampton in England on her maiden voyage to New York City. She was touted as the safest ship ever built—so safe that she carried only 20 lifeboats, enough to provide accommodation for only half her 2200 passengers and crew. Four days into her journey, at 11.40 pm on the night of 14 April, she struck an iceberg and slowly began to go down. The next morning, the liner *Carpathia* rescued 705 survivors: 1522 passengers and crew were lost. The sinking of the *Titanic* ranks as one of the worst peacetime maritime disasters in history and the story made headlines around the world.

THE SINKING OF THE UNSINKABLE SHIP

I cannot imagine any condition which would cause a ship to founder. I cannot conceive of any vital disaster happening to this vessel. Modern ship building has gone beyond that.

CAPTAIN SMITH, COMMANDER OF *TITANIC*

On 31 May 1911, the hull of the world's largest luxury liner, the *Titanic*, was launched in the River Lagan in Belfast, Ireland. Her manufacturers, Harland & Wolff, boasted that she was 'virtually unsinkable'. It was not their custom to have ship-naming ceremonies, so rather than the traditional smashing of a bottle of champagne across the bow of the ship, three rockets were fired into the sky. The large crowds along the river bank cheered as the ship's 26,000-tonne hull began to slide down its greased slipway into Belfast Harbour.

The next day the *Belfast Morning News* published the following editorial comment:

… It is difficult to understand why the owners and builders named the ship Titanic. *The Titans were a mythological race who came to believe they'd conquered nature, who thought they'd achieved power and learning greater than Zeus himself, to their ultimate ruin. He [Zeus] smote the strong and daring Titans with thunderbolts; and their final abiding place was in some limbo beneath the lowest depths of the Tartarus, a sunless abyss below Hades.*

Statistics of titanic proportions

The gigantic ship had become the talk of the town as her 269-metre (882-foot) long hull took shape on the river bank, held together by more than three million steel rivets. Over the ensuing months the empty hull was transformed into an ornate floating palace. Twenty-nine boilers and one hundred and fifty-nine furnaces were installed to provide the steam power for the ship's engines. Carpenters, metalworkers, engineers and decorators spared no expense as they installed first-, second- and third-class cabins, restaurants and ballrooms, a gymnasium, library, hospital and the world's first on-board swimming pool. State-of-the-art electronic navigational and communications equipment was installed in the wireless room; the ship's 10,000 light bulbs were linked by 320 kilometres (200 miles) of wiring. The manufacturers were confident of the *Titanic*'s seaworthiness because inside the hull were sixteen watertight compartments separated by bulkheads, and she was designed to stay afloat even if up to four of the compartments became flooded. But there was a fatal design flaw—there was a gap above the bulkheads, which did not reach all the way to the top of the hull. This meant that if one compartment became flooded, it would overflow into the adjacent compartment, then the next, and so on until all were flooded— which is exactly what happened. It beggars belief that such an apparently obvious oversight could have remained unnoticed throughout the lengthy design and construction process.

On 3 April 1912 the *Titanic* sailed into the southern English port of Southampton to prepare for her maiden voyage. Over the next week she was stocked with provisions, including 34 tonnes of meat, 5 tonnes of fish, 40,000 eggs, 40 tonnes of potatoes, 7000 lettuces, 36,000 apples, 795 kilograms (almost 2000 pounds) of ice cream, and enormous quantities of tea, coffee, milk, cream and liquor. There were also 57,600 pieces of crockery, 44,000 pieces of cutlery, 3364 mailbags and more than 4400 tonnes of coal.

The *Titanic* sets sail for New York

Just after noon on 10 April the *Titanic* embarked on her maiden voyage to New York. The accommodation was divided into three classes. Those in first class included the world's richest man, John Jacob Astor IV, who built the Astoria Hotel in New York. But most of the passengers, many heading to the New World in the hope of starting a new life, travelled in third class under the lowest deck. As the mighty liner left her moorings, the turbulence from her huge wake caused the nearby liner *New York* to pull loose from her berth. A collision was barely avoided as the *New York* was drawn to within about a metre of the *Titanic* before being hauled off by a tugboat. After this inauspicious beginning the *Titanic* steamed across the English Channel to pick up more passengers at the French port of Cherbourg, then made a brief stop at the Irish port of Queenstown (now Cobh). As she steamed into the North Atlantic Ocean, she carried 899 crew under the command of Captain Edward Smith, and 1324 passengers.

Stars disappear

On April 14, four days into the voyage, the *Titanic*'s radio officers began receiving telegraph messages from nearby ships warning of icebergs in the vicinity. Smith made a slight southerly adjustment to the ship's course. Late that night, as stars shone brilliantly on a moonless night, ship's lookout, Frederick Fleet, was puzzled to observe that on the horizon stars were disappearing in groups of two and three. He soon realised, to his horror, that an enormous silhouette was slowly moving into the path of the great ship. Just before midnight Fleet sounded three warning gongs and telephoned the bridge with the words that all sailors dread: 'Iceberg dead ahead!' First Officer Murdoch ordered that the *Titanic* stop its engines and turn hard to port (left)—but it was too late. At 11.40 pm the iceberg sliced into the ship's right side, sending a small avalanche of ice onto the well deck, buckling the hull, and tearing a thin gash about 90 metres (almost 300 feet) long below the waterline. Water started pouring into the five forward compartments, and from this point the ship's fate was sealed. Just after midnight Captain Smith ordered that the lifeboats be prepared, and the first of many distress calls was sent.

Amazingly, the lookout officers were not provided with binoculars or a telescope, thus limiting visibility at night to about 1 kilometre (about ½ mile). Researchers have calculated that the first officer's evasive manoeuvres would have been sufficient to avoid the iceberg had he received as little as half a minute's extra warning time. And binoculars would have provided several minutes more, at least.

A few minutes later crewman Samuel Henning heard an unusual whistling noise. As he walked among the anchor chains he noticed an open hatch cover, looked down into it and felt a stiff breeze against his face and hair. He realised that the rapid air escape must be caused by

RIGHT: The Titanic *leaves Belfast for Southampton, in preparation for its maiden voyage to New York.*

displacement from water entering below. He was the first to recognise that the *Titanic* was doomed.

The wireless operators began sending Morse Code distress calls in the traditional international signal 'CQD'. They received an immediate reply from the German steamer *Frankfurt:* 'OKAY I MUST CONSULT MY CAPTAIN. STAND BY.' The British liner *Carpathia* then responded: 'DOES THE TITANIC KNOW THAT THERE ARE SOME PRIVATE MESSAGES WAITING FOR HER FROM CAPE RACE?' (the nearest land-based wireless station, in Newfoundland). The *Titanic* replied: 'WE NEED ASSISTANCE. THE TITANIC HAS STRUCK A BERG. THIS IS A CQD OLD MAN. COME AT ONCE.' The *Carpathia* immediately changed course and sped through the perilous icebergs to the *Titanic's* rescue. The *Frankfurt's* captain then sent the question: 'WHAT IS THE MATTER?' *Titanic's* graceless response was 'YOU FOOL, WE'RE BUSY HERE. STAND BY.' The *Frankfurt's* captain, understandably outraged, repeated the question, drawing the reply: 'YOU ARE JAMMING MY EQUIPMENT FOOL. STAND BY AND KEEP OUT.' The *Frankfurt's* crew became even more enraged when they overheard the following exchange between the *Titanic* and its sister ship, *Olympic,* which was about 500 kilometres (270 nautical miles) further away than the *Frankfurt:* 'WHAT IS THE MATTER?' 'WE HAVE STRUCK AN ICEBERG AND NEED ASSISTANCE.' The British were responding politely to a distant British ship, but were insulting the Germans—who were actually in a much better position to render assistance.

To the lifeboats

Soon the *Titanic* began listing to starboard as water poured into the hull. Gradually it began to dawn on the passengers that they were in great peril. They were ordered to don life jackets and make their way to the lifeboats, but many were reluctant to board them. Some of the first lifeboats, carrying women and children, were launched partially empty. As the list increased and the bow began disappearing under water, it became less difficult to fill the lifeboats. But the *Titanic's* crew had never undergone a proper lifeboat drill, such was the general confidence in the ship's indestructibility. Some of the sailors even had to be shown by passengers how to use oars, as court transcripts from the British government enquiry which immediately followed the disaster reveal:

A sailor was pushing his oar about every which way. 'Why don't you put the oar in the oarlock?' asked Mrs White. 'Do you put it in that hole?' he asked. 'Certainly', she replied. 'I never had an oar in my hand before', he explained. The men began arguing over how to manage the boat. One of them snapped at another: 'If you don't stop talkin' through that hole in yer face, there'll be one less in this boat'.

Although the boat carried insufficient lifeboats for all on board, it nonetheless carried more than were required at the time by the British Board of Regulations, whose rules were based on a ship's tonnage rather than the number of passengers on board. The last lifeboat was eventually launched just before the *Titanic* sank.

Meanwhile a light was visible on the horizon, less than an hour away. It belonged to the *Californian,* which had warned the *Titanic* (in vain) several hours earlier of the presence of icebergs in the area. But the *Californian* did not respond to the *Titanic's* distress calls because her sole wireless operator was asleep. Nor did she respond to the distress flares that the *Titanic* was by now launching regularly, perhaps because it was deemed too hazardous to travel through the icy sea; perhaps because the crew mistook the flares for maiden-voyage celebration fireworks.

The sea pours in

At 1.20 am water began to pour over the top of leaking boiler room 5 into boiler room 4. Until now, the rate of inflow had been slow, as the total surface area of the punctures in the hull was only about 1 square metre (just over 1 square yard). But as the *Titanic's* list increased, the sea began pouring through the anchor holes on the starboard side, which were now under water, doubling the rate of the inflow. Within a few minutes the starboard cargo bay doors and windows had also submerged, and the slow leaks were joined by raging torrents. Hindsight informs us that if the watertight seals between the ship's compartments had been opened, she would have sunk slowly and evenly, rather than on a slanted angle, and the original gash would have remained the only leak. The *Titanic* would have remained afloat for at least another six hours, until the rescue vessel *Carpathia* arrived.

By 2.10 am the bow was submerged up to the base of the forward smokestack. Water began pouring down ventilators, stairwells and lift shafts to the lower decks. Hundreds of passengers began instinctively clawing their way uphill toward the stern, which by now had lifted out of the water completely. No ship could possibly be designed to take such stresses—and at 2.18 am the *Titanic* broke in half. The bow section plummeted 4 kilometres (over 2 miles) to the bottom of the ocean, as the rear section momentarily regained equilibrium. Some lifeboat passengers thought the ship was miraculously righting herself, but after just two minutes the stern also sank. Imprisoned were many of the third-class immigrant families whose passage to the top deck had been barred, and the mostly French and Italian kitchen staff who had been locked into a room on E deck during the rush for the lifeboats. A massed, extended scream rent the air as hundreds of people were dumped simultaneously into the freezing water. A fortunate few managed to cling to wreckage until they were picked up by a lifeboat; anyone who remained in the water for even twenty minutes died of hypothermia. Captain Smith, having already ordered his passengers and crew to save themselves, jumped overboard just before the stern sank. He was last seen trying to assist a struggling child.

Survivors are rescued

By 3.30 am the *Carpathia* had reached the position sent by the *Titanic's* radio officer, but nothing could be seen—no lights, no lifeboats, certainly no ship. Just after 4 am, as first light dawned, one of the crew saw a green flare sent up by one of the lifeboats. Elizabeth Allen, the first passenger to be rescued, confirmed to the amazed crew of the *Carpathia* that the *Titanic* had indeed sunk. Gradually the other lifeboats approached and more and more survivors came aboard, many screaming or sobbing. By 9 am all the survivors were on board and the *Carpathia* resumed her voyage to New York. About 1500 perished in the disaster—about two-thirds of those who set out.

John Jacob Astor IV went down with the *Titanic*, but he ensured his pregnant wife, Medeleine, with her nurse and maid got into a lifeboat and were saved. The following year the first International Convention for Safety of Life at Sea was held in London. It made numerous recommendations, including that a lifeboat space be provided for each person on board ship, that lifeboat drills be held during every voyage, and that all ships maintain a 24-hour radio watch.

Discovery of the wreck

On 1 September 1985, after three search attempts over the previous five years by Texas oil billionaire Jack Grimm, the *Titanic* was discovered by a joint French–American scientific expedition. The wreck has since been explored by several manned and unmanned craft, and some small artefacts removed.

Although RMS *Titanic* sank nearly one hundred years ago and rests 3600 metres (12,000 feet) below sea level, the ship's remains continue to fascinate people around the globe. On 24 July 2007, a US Department of State media release entitled *Proposed* *Legislation to Implement Agreement to Protect RMS Titanic Wreck Site Sent to Congress* announced the government's intention to establish a protection zone around the famous wreck. By enacting this legislation and becoming a party to the agreement, the United States will become a leader in the international community in protecting perhaps the most important shipwreck in history, 'in accordance

Some of the lucky survivors—the Titanic *was fitted with only enough lifeboat space for 1200 of the 2200 on board.*

with the most current standards of underwater scientific, historic and cultural resource protection, conservation and management'.

Fiction foreshadows the *Titanic*'s fate

In 1898 Morgan Robertson published a novella titled *Futility, or the Wreck of the Titan*. It contains several eerie similarities to the fate of the *Titanic*, which had not even been designed at the time.

The *Titan* was described as the largest craft afloat, 800 feet (244 metres) long and displacing 75,000 tonnes; the *Titanic* was the world's largest liner, 882 feet (269 metres) long and displacing 53,000 tonnes. Both craft were equipped with three propellers and two masts. The *Titan* had a top speed of 25 knots, or nautical miles, per hour (46 kilometres per hour); the *Titanic* 24 knots (44 kilometres per hour). Both were travelling too fast for the prevailing treacherous conditions. The *Titan* was described as 'indestructible'; the *Titanic* was announced as 'virtually unsinkable' by its owners (only after its demise did the myth develop that the *Titanic* was considered 'completely' unsinkable). Neither carried sufficient lifeboats for all those on board—the *Titan* carried twenty-four, 'as few as the law allowed', the *Titanic* twenty, less than half the number needed for 3000 people; each ship had a maximum capacity of 3000 passengers and crew. Both set out on their maiden voyage from the English port of Southampton in April, both struck an iceberg on an April night in the North Atlantic around 650 kilometres (350 nautical miles) south of Newfoundland. More than half the 2500 on board the *Titan* drowned, their 'voices raised in agonized screams'; more than half the *Titanic's* 2200 passengers and crew died in the same gruesome fashion, according to survivors.

1914

AUSTRIAN ARCHDUKE ASSASSINATED

The assassination of the Austrian Archduke Franz Ferdinand and his wife on a visit to Sarajevo in June 1914 set in motion a series of events that led to the outbreak of World War I. Ferdinand was heir to the throne of the Austro-Hungarian Empire, and his assassin, 19-year-old Gavrilo Princip, was a Slavic nationalist. Princip believed that the death of the archduke was the key that would unlock the shackles binding his people to the Austro-Hungarian Empire, so he shot the duke and his wife as they drove in an open car through the city. What it did was lead Europe to war.

THE DEATH OF ARCHDUKE FRANZ FERDINAND: THE BUILD-UP TO WAR

I aimed at the Archduke. I'm not sure what I thought at that moment.

SERBIAN NATIONALIST AND ASSASSIN,
GAVRILO PRINCIP

Gavrilo Princip was born to impoverished parents in 1894 in the Bosnian village of Obljaj west of Sarajevo, not far from the border with Croatia. His father Petar was a postal worker who married late in life and was fourteen years older that Gavrilo's mother, Marija, who gave birth to nine children, six of whom would not survive infancy. Marija wanted to name her fourth child Spiro but, because he was born on the feast day of St Gabriel the Archangel, the local priest convinced his parents to name him Gavrilo.

At the age of thirteen he was sent by his parents to live with his older brother in Sarajevo, where it was hoped he would enlist in the army and one day become an officer. Princip, however, chose to enrol in a traditional high school in Tuzla northeast of Sarajevo and graduated in 1911. His life was a mundane and unremarkable one that most likely would have seen him continue to live in obscurity had not the Austro-Hungarian Empire annexed the Bosnian nation on 5 October 1908.

After his graduation, Princip's political convictions began to take shape at a time when anti-Austrian sentiments were rife and many students were beginning to form nationalistic associations, such as Young Bosnia and the increasingly militant Black Hand.

Nationalism in the Balkans

The Black Hand movement was created on 9 May 1911, largely in response to the Bosnian Annexation Crisis, which saw Austria-Hungary annex Bosnia and Herzegovina as a strategic buffer in the aftermath of Bulgaria's declaration of independence on 6 October 1908. Serbs now living in Austrian-controlled and administered Bosnia were denied many basic political and civil rights, but although Serbia demanded the removal of foreign troops from the region it lacked the means to do anything else but protest. The Black Hand was led by Dragutin Dimitrijevic, a rogue Serb nationalist known to his inner circle as Apis, after the mythological bull-deity of ancient Egypt. Dimitrijevic was no stranger to assassination, having participated in the killing of Serbia's King Obrenovic and Queen Draga in 1903.

The idea of a united South Slavic state— with the unification of all South Slavic-speaking peoples throughout present-day Croatia, Bosnia, Macedonia, Serbia and Montenegro—was politically popular and the Black Hand had waged a war of terror across Serbia. The organisation had no qualms about using assassination to further their nationalistic aims; nor were they averse to using impressionable, idealistic teenagers to act as their proxies.

Princip came to the attention of the Black Hand leadership through his association with Young Bosnia, whose members led austere lives free from tobacco, alcohol and the distraction of sexual relationships. The founders of Young Bosnia were heavily influenced by the political strategies of the Italian unification movement headed by Giuseppe Mazzini. Mazzini had played a key role in the unification of Italian states almost forty years earlier and was a vocal advocate of political assassination as a legitimate tool in the struggle for independence. Princip was on his way to becoming a disciplined, hardcore revolutionary, and described his zeal in a note to a friend in 1912: 'My flaming body will be a torch to light my people on their path to freedom'.

The assassins' target

In June of 1914, Archduke Franz Ferdinand, heir to the Austro-Hungarian throne, received an invitation from General Oskar Potiorek, the governor of Bosnia-Herzegovina, to review a planned military exercise in his capacity as Inspector General of the Austrian Army. It seemed an odd request. Bosnia was the most dangerous, rebellious province in the empire. And only a month before the invitation was issued, the Serbian Prime Minister Nikola Pasic had relayed a warning to the Austrian government about the likelihood of assassination attempts on its visiting dignitaries. The selection of 28 June for the review seemed to doubly tempt fate. For this was St Vitus Day, the day all

Serbia stopped to reflect on the heroism of Milos Obilic, a medieval knight who, in the aftermath of the defeat of Serb forces by the Ottoman Empire in 1389, crept into the tent of the Turkish leader Sultan Murad I and stabbed him to death. A visit by any minister representing an occupying nation, much less an archduke, on the anniversary of such a key event in Serbian history, and with the nation going through a period of resurgence after having thrown off more than five centuries of Turkish rule, must to some have seemed almost like a dare.

Archduke Ferdinand and his wife Sophie Chotek, Duchess of Hohenberg, arrived in Sarajevo by train on the morning of 28 June 1914. In high spirits after having spent the previous day in the Tyrolean resort town of Ilidza, Archduke Franz Ferdinand and Duchess Sophie climbed into the car that would take them through Sarajevo's streets. Despite coming from an aristocratic family, under Hapsburg family law Sophie was considered a commoner, a ruling that had forced her and Ferdinand to elope and marry in secret in June of 1900. On returning to Vienna, Emperor Franz Joseph forbade Sophie to be seated alongside Ferdinand in a royal carriage or vehicle. Beyond Austria's borders, however, the reins of royal protocol were often loosened, and on this day Sophie sat proudly next to her husband in their brand-new, six-seater Gräf & Stift touring car. It was a decision that was shortly to cost the duchess her life. Six Bosnian assassins, including Gavrilo Princip, were waiting at various points along the royal route for the archduke to pass, armed with hand grenades and pistols—but the crowded streets were guarded by a complacent and woefully undermanned Sarajevo police force of just one hundred and twenty, who proved more interested in watching the procession than the crowds.

The archduke and the duchess, captured on film by a Sarajevo photographer just prior to their assassination.

A royal procession

Franz Ferdinand looked every bit an archduke as the procession set off along Appel Quay. Dressed in the blue tunic and black trousers of an Austrian cavalry officer, his chest was decorated with medals and a gold-braided waistband known as a *bauchband*. The plumage on his helmet and the three stars on his buttoned collar presented an unmistakable target to the six conspirators who were waiting along Appel Quay, Sarajevo's main thoroughfare, which already enjoyed the infamous nickname 'the avenue of assassins'. Unbeknown to Ferdinand or his Bosnian hosts, there was a veritable gauntlet of potential executioners lining Appel Quay awaiting the royal motorcade, which inexplicably was not given a police escort. But Ferdinand loved the city, and made a special request to his driver to drive slowly so he could take his time and see something of its attractions.

The first in the line-up of conspirators was Mehmed Mehmedbasic, a twenty-seven-year-old carpenter waiting by the Cumuria Bridge, armed with a small bomb. He later claimed a gendarme was standing by him—and, furthermore, he couldn't get a clear shot at the archduke, and didn't want to act rashly in case one of his comrades might be better placed to strike. Mehmedbasic fled first to Montenegro and then to Serbia, and was the only one of the conspirators who managed to elude capture.

Vaso Cubrilovic, a seventeen-year-old student who didn't want to harm Duchess Sophie, was standing a few metres down from the Cumeria Bridge. Cubrilovic was once expelled from his high school in Tuzla for storming out of an assembly during the playing of the Austrian national anthem. He, like Mehmedbasic, claimed to have been poorly positioned in the crowd.

The third man was Nedeljko Cabrinovic, a twenty-year-old anarchist and high school dropout. Cabrinovic, wearing a long black coat, asked a nearby policeman in which car the Archduke was travelling; and when the policeman told him he hurled his grenade at the slow-moving vehicle. The time was 10.10 am.

Ferdinand escapes a grenade

Despite Franz Ferdinand's claim that he had knocked the bomb away with his hand, several witnesses were in agreement that it did in fact strike the car's folded-down roof-canopy of the car before bouncing off and landing underneath the following vehicle, which was carrying Count von Boos-Waldesk and the archduke's aide-de-camp, Colonel Morrizi. The grenade had an in-built ten-second delay and, when it detonated, killed two officers and wounded more than twenty bystanders. Cabrinovic then ingested a small vial of cyanide and leapt into the shallow waters of the river, but was quickly apprehended and placed under arrest. The cyanide apparently was quite old and resulted in a severe bout of vomiting, not Cabrinovic's death. The archduke's driver responded to the attack by speeding up and racing through the stunned crowd in the direction of the city hall, where Sarajevo's lord mayor, oblivious to the attack, was rehearsing the welcoming speech he had written the night before.

As the archduke's convoy sped by, the fourth man in the group, Cvjetko Popovic, later told investigators in an almost comical testimony that, because he was short-sighted, he couldn't make out which car was which and lost his nerve.

Gavrilo Princip was the fifth conspirator, positioned by the Latin Bridge. He heard Cabrinovic's bomb detonate, assumed the archduke had been killed and watched as the motorcade sped past. Waiting at the Imperial Bridge, the sixth man, Trifko Grabez, a friend of Princip's since high school, later confessed he simply could not summon the courage to perform such a heinous act and had no intention of causing harm to innocent bystanders.

In the chaos that followed the failed assassination attempt, four of the assassins, seeing that their only opportunity to strike was gone, abandoned their posts and escaped, though all were eventually arrested. Princip, meanwhile, was walking through the city's Turkish Quarter, mulling over his missed opportunity to strike a blow for Serbian nationalism.

The royal couple arrived safely at the city hall but Ferdinand was furious. 'Mr Mayor, I came here on a visit and I get bombs thrown at me. It is outrageous!' After much discussion Ferdinand then insisted, much to his wife's dismay, that rather than waiting for the arrival of troops to secure the remainder of the route through the congested streets and narrow lanes of the city's Turkish Quarter, they would instead be driven to the city's hospital so the archduke could pay his respects to those who had been injured by Cabrinovic's grenade.

A series of fatal errors

When the motorcade was leaving the hospital Franz Ferdinand's chauffeur, Leopold Lojka, became disoriented, took a wrong turn and drove into the congested streets of the Turkish Quarter. When the cars turned right at the Bascarsija intersection and entered Franz Joseph Street, General Petiorek, who was riding in the archduke's car, ordered Leopold to stop and reverse out of the street. Then, in one of the more extraordinary quirks of history, Gavrilo Princip, who had been having lunch in Moritz Schiller's Delicatessen & Café, emerged onto the pavement just metres away. As Leopold was

struggling to put the Gräf & Stift into reverse, he stalled the engine, thereby locking up its gearbox. Princip seized the moment, walked up to the car and fired two shots from his FN Model 1910 .38 Browning pistol. The first bullet hit Franz Ferdinand in the neck, severing his jugular vein. The second ricocheted off the door of the car and hit the duchess in her stomach.

The duchess immediately slumped forward in her seat. Ferdinand was heard to scream: 'Sophie, don't die! Stay alive for our children!' but she died in his arms. The archduke survived his beloved wife only by minutes. Like Cabrinovic, Princip attempted to end his life by swallowing a capsule of poison but was arrested immediately after the fatal shots were fired.

The assassins stand trial

Twenty-five men, including Princip, were tried for the murder of Franz Ferdinand and his wife. At the trial's conclusion, after all the testimonies had been heard and evidence gathered, the presiding judge asked the assembled accused to stand if they felt any contrition for what they had done. Everyone stood except Gavrilo Princip. When asked why he chose to remain seated he replied that he felt remorseful that he had unintentionally killed Duchess Sophie and that because of his actions three children were now orphaned; but he expressed not a word of regret over taking the life of the archduke. He rejected the suggestion that the group had to be encouraged by the Black Hand to strike, declaring that the idea to assassinate the archduke had come from within the group itself, despite receiving assistance from Dimitrijevic, and that the assassination was the work of men who loved their country and wanted an end to Austro-Hungarian colonialism.

Of the twenty-five accused, nine were released, eleven received terms of imprisonment ranging from three years to life, and five were hanged. Princip, too young at nineteen to be hanged under Austrian law, was sentenced to twenty years with hard labour, with the additional requirement that every year on the anniversary of the assassination his cell would be darkened and he would be refused a mattress and all meals. No evidence exists to suggest he ever questioned his decision to murder Archduke Franz Ferdinand; indeed at his trial Princip asserted: 'I am not a criminal, for I destroyed a bad man. I thought I was right'.

Cabrinovic received a twenty-year prison term and, like Princip, showed no remorse for his crimes. He died of tuberculosis in prison on 3 January 1916. Grabez, also imprisoned

for twenty years, succumbed to tuberculosis in February of 1918. Vaso Cubrilovic was sentenced to sixteen years imprisonment but was released in November 1918, moved to Belgrade, and returned to teaching. Cvjetko Popovic was also released in November 1918 and went on to become a curator in the Sarajevo museum.

Gavrilo Princip was ordered to serve his sentence in Theresienstadt, an eighteenth-century Bohemian fortress north of Prague that had been converted into a military prison, but he would not be a prisoner for long. He was kept in solitary confinement in Cell 1 and became the prison's most famous inmate; but Princip had suffered from tuberculosis since he was a child, the disease was accelerated by

Princep is arrested immediately after the assassination of the duke and duchess, his pistol wrested from his grip.

the damp confines of his cell, and he died on 28 April 1918.

The bombs and pistols distributed among the six volunteer assassins were obtained by Danilo Ilic, a former theatre usher, stonemason and teacher. Ilic became a member of the Black Hand in 1913 and was the chief organiser of the plot. He was executed on 3 February 1915.

War is declared

The death of Archduke Franz Ferdinand was one of the defining moments of the twentieth century. Europe, leading up to World War I, was a tangle of 'alliances'. There was the Dual Alliance between Germany and Austria against Russia; the Franco-Russian Alliance to protect Russia against Germany and Austria-Hungary, and so on and so on. The assassination of the archduke was all that was needed as the trigger for their enactment. A month after Franz Ferdinand's death, Austria declared war on Serbia and began a bombardment of Belgrade, the Serbian capital, which led to Russia's Tsar Nicolas II coming to the assistance of his traditional Slavic brothers. France mobilised its military. Germany honoured yet another alliance, the 1882 Triple Alliance with Austria and Italy, by coming to Austria's defence, and declared war on Russia. Germany then declared war on France and invaded Belgium, which meant that Great Britain, which had a treaty with Belgium to defend its independence, was obliged to declare war on Germany. The firing of Princip's .38 Browning pistol certainly seems deserving of the tag: 'the shot heard around the world', for it precipitated much more than simply bringing the wrath of an empire down upon Princip's tiny Balkan nation. It ignited a world war.

1917

SOLDIERS STUCK IN MUDDY HELL

The Battle of Passchendaele has come to epitomise the appalling conditions on the Western Front in World War I. It also highlighted the ineffective leadership of the Allies in particular, and both sides' costly tactic of attrition, which resulted in hundreds of thousands of deaths to gain just a few kilometres of territory. Fought between July and November 1917, the battle was launched by Field Marshal Haig in an attempt to reach the German submarine pens in Flanders. The Allied forces quickly became bogged down facing a deeply entrenched German line when the heaviest rains in thirty years began to fall. The battlefield effectively became a swamp—tanks became bogged, and many soldiers and pack animals drowned, and morale sank as the campaign became seemingly more and more futile.

THE BATTLE OF PASSCHENDAELE

... I died in Hell—(They called it Passchendaele).
My wound was slight, And I was hobbling back;
and then a shell Burst slick upon the duck-boards:
so I fell Into the bottomless mud, and lost the light.

SIEGFRIED SASSOON, 'MEMORIAL TABLET', 1918

Spring came late to northern France and Belgium in the first half of 1917. And so did summer. Instead of sunshine, unseasonable thunderstorms peppered the region throughout July. More than 125 millimetres (5 inches) of rain fell in August, more than twice the monthly average. A mercifully dry September brought some relief, but more rain fell through October and on into November. The area surrounding the town of Ypres in western Belgium was a low-lying region barely higher than sea level, with a high watertable. Much of the area was either natural or reclaimed swampland, and was transformed by the constant rains into an unrelenting, sodden world of mud. It was a miserable place to fight a war.

Field Marshal Douglas Haig, the commander of the British Expeditionary Force (BEF) from 1915 until the end of World War I, was born in Edinburgh on 19 June 1861. As a teenager he studied at Brasenose College, Oxford, before enrolling in Sandhurst's Royal Military College, from which he graduated in 1884. His first military deployment was in India in 1887; from there he went on to command the 17th Lancers in South Africa before returning to India, where he was promoted to the rank of major-general in 1904 at the age of forty-three, becoming the youngest major-general in the history of the British army. After being appointed to an administrative post in London to assist in reforms to prepare the British army for a future war in Europe, he returned to India in 1909. In 1914 he assumed the role of aide-de-camp to King George V. War was declared in Europe in August 1914, and in December 1915 Haig became Commander-in-Chief of the BEF.

The strategic importance of Ypres

As early as January 1916, Haig believed a major assault in the Flanders region of western Belgium around Ypres was the key to victory on the Western Front. But any preparations for an assault were delayed due to the German offensive at Verdun in north-eastern France, which began in February 1916 and dragged on into December, resulting in the deaths of more than three hundred thousand men.

By the spring of 1917 Ypres was the only major Belgian town still in British and Allied hands. The Ypres Salient projected into German-held territory and its occupation denied Germany access to the Channel ports of northern France. If Ypres were to fall and the salient be taken, British shipping in the English Channel would come under increased threat from German U-boats, a third of which were already operating out of Belgian ports. Haig believed that an offensive from Ypres in the direction of Roulers and Passchendaele would not only eliminate the threat of German occupation in northern France and end the U-boat threat along the Belgian coast but might even act as a springboard into the Ruhr Valley to the east, Germany's industrial heartland, and bring about an early end to the war. Haig, promoted to the rank of Field Marshal in January, was convinced the will of the German army would collapse under the weight of an Allied offensive—although this turned out to be an overly optimistic assessment of German troop strength and morale, and closely resembled the opinion Haig had entertained at the height of the Battle of the Somme a year earlier, a battle notable for unparalleled loss of life.

Prior to any advance on Passchendaele it was necessary to capture the strategic Messines-Wytschaete Ridge. The Messines Ridge offensive, meticulously planned and executed by the commander of the British Second Army, General Herbert Plumer, was one of the few World War I engagements that achieved its objectives quickly and with minimal loss of life. Eighteen months earlier, in preparation, Plumer had authorised the construction of twenty-two mine shafts that snaked their way at a depth of between 25 and 30 metres (82 and 100 feet) for a distance of over 8000 metres (5 miles) beneath the German lines. The Germans were aware of the incursion, and there were even times when their own tunnels were intersected by those being dug by the Allies, resulting in several fierce hand-to-hand encounters. But the Germans failed to grasp the extent of the tunnels that Plumer had ordered to be packed with almost 500 tonnes of explosives.

Explosives create devastation at Messines Ridge

At 3.10 am on 7 June 1917, Plumer gave the order to detonate the explosives. The effect on the German lines was devastating. In excess of ten thousand soldiers were either killed or wounded, and the noise, probably until then the loudest man-made noise in history, created a shockwave that was felt as far away as Ireland. Nine divisions of British troops then advanced toward the German lines. In just under three hours every Allied objective had been secured and the battle was over. In excess of seven thousand German prisoners were taken, and Plumer was so delighted with the results that he approached Haig and pleaded with him to bring on his assault on the Passchendaele ridge, a strategic hill between Passchendaele and Ypres. Although the ridge was not scheduled to be attacked until the end of July, Plumer saw a rare opportunity to take advantage of the demoralised German troops and of the opening he had forced in their defensive lines. Unprepared, however, for the overwhelming nature of the Messines Ridge victory and the resultant opportunity it afforded him, Haig refused.

Haig had timed his offensive in the wake of the disastrous failure of the French-inspired Nivelle Offensive in May, which despite the deployment of more than 1.2 million troops and seven thousand guns had ended in complete failure and widespread acts of mutiny throughout the French army. The failure ended the career of the offensive's originator, French Commander-in-Chief Robert Nivelle. As disastrous as this was for Nivelle it cleared the way for Haig to launch his own self-styled offensive, designed to bring an early end to the war. The strategy planned for the Third Battle of Ypres, or the Battle of Passchendaele, as it is more commonly known, involved the capture of Passchendale, a small village not far from Ypres; this would be followed by a push toward the region between the River Lys and the North Sea, ending the German occupation of the Belgian port cities and destroying their submarine pens.

Drenching rainfall immobilises advance

On 17 July Haig ordered his artillery to begin a two-week long bombardment of the German defences around Passchendaele. Unfortunately, however, not only did the estimated 4.5 million shells fired from more than three thousand artillery pieces fail to dislodge the Germans, they also destroyed much of the irrigation works in the flat plains west of the town. The barrage pulverised the clay soil, creating tens of thousands of craters that immediately filled with water—and turned the landscape into a muddy hell.

Soldiers struggle through muddy craters created by an onslaught of heavy artillery in perhaps the worst conditions of the war.

Haig gave command over the advance on Passchendaele to General Hubert Gough, and the offensive began on 31 July with the Battle of Pilckem Ridge; after just two days, despite considerable gains in territory, persistently heavy rain brought the advance to a standstill. The heaviest rainfall for more than three decades turned the pockmarked clay into a sticky, knee-high quagmire that was so thick it drowned men and horses and immobilised anything that possessed wheels or an engine. Haig postponed the offensive after just a few days. A small break in the weather saw the advance resumed on 16 August, but the terrain was deceptive. Areas that appeared to be stable were in reality little more than dry crusts over mud-filled interiors that collapsed the moment any weight was placed upon them.

On 20 September, another easing of conditions resulted in a series of carefully orchestrated Allied assaults known as 'bite and hold' advances that led to victories at the Battle of Menin Road Ridge, the Battle of Polygon Wood, and culminated on 4 October with the Battle of Broodseinde Ridge. The combined victories gave the Allied forces control of the ridge line east of Ypres and a clear view to Passchendaele. These victories, however, had come at a staggering cost. Thousands had been killed and wounded, and the view from Broodseinde Ridge was of an endless sea of mud. Heavy rain began again late on 4 October, making the bringing up of artillery to support the troops in their 'bite and hold' offensive almost impossible.

Haig orders renewed assault

On 9 October, British and Australian divisions advanced on Passchendaele village in atrocious conditions. Although little ground was gained, Haig and Gough both felt enough progress had been made to justify a further assault on 12 October. This assault, also known as the First Battle of Passchendaele (which has since gone down in history as little more than a slaughter), was led by the Australian Third Division and a division of New Zealanders, with the Australian Fourth Division in reserve. As expected, the shells from the preceding artillery bombardment that were meant to weaken the German defences exploded harmlessly in the mud as the Australian and New Zealand forces, armed only with rifles, machine-guns and grenades, were subjected to relentless heavy machine-gun fire coming from the German bunkers and 'pillboxes'.

Although several Australians managed to scramble their way to the very edges of Passchendaele, they failed to arrive in sufficient numbers to hold the position, and were soon pushed back to where the bulk of the Third Division had become mired along a small river valley. On 12 October the Third Division lost three thousand men, and the Fourth Division one thousand. New Zealand casualties were over eight hundred enlisted men and forty-five officers killed outright or lying mortally wounded in the mud—the single greatest loss of life in a single day in New Zealand history. In total there were more than thirteen thousand Allied casualties, and at this point in the campaign total casualties were approaching one hundred thousand killed and wounded. In the midst of the carnage at Passchendaele, however, poignant acts of humanity and decency shone through. Stretcher-bearers were not only avoided as targets, but were permitted free rein by the German gunners, who even guided them to their fallen comrades as they scoured the battlefield for the wounded.

Canadian troops relieve ANZACS

The failure of the Australian and New Zealand assault to capture Passchendaele saw members of Field Marshal Haig's staff approach him with requests to call off the offensive, but Haig felt, or perhaps hoped, that the German will to continue the fight was close to ebbing away. On 18 October two fresh Canadian divisions arrived to replace the exhausted, decimated divisions of the ANZACS (Australia and New Zealand Army Corps).

The Canadian troops included many who took part in the great Canadian victory at Vimy Ridge in April 1917. In just thirty minutes at dawn on Easter Monday, after a three-week artillery bombardment on entrenched German positions, the Canadian First Division, under the command of General Arthur William Currie, ignored a snowstorm and swept away the ridge's first line of entrenched German defenders and then, a mere half hour later, overran the enemy's second defensive line. At the time Vimy Ridge represented the greatest single advance since fighting on the Western Front began, and the ridge remained securely in Canadian hands until the end of the war. Four Victoria Crosses were awarded for exceptional acts of bravery, and Currie received a knighthood. These were the soldiers who were about to be thrown into what history knows as the Second Battle of Passchendaele.

On 19 October the twenty thousand men of the Third and Fourth Canadian Divisions started moving into their positions, and on 26 October the first of two offensives began. The Third Division would attack through the northern approaches to Passchendaele along the high ground of Bellevue Spur, while the Fourth Division would approach from the south following the railway line from Roulers. The Third Division, despite seizing all of its initial objectives, was forced to give ground and link up with the British Fifth Army; meanwhile, the Fourth Division, which also had reached its objectives outside the town, was forced to withdraw in the face of a vicious German counter-attack.

Second Passchendaele offensive

On 26 October the Second Battle of Passchendaele began. It had as its objectives the retaking of all ground lost in the first offensive and the capture of Crest Farm (a heavily defended farm to the south of town) as well as Meetcheele and the Goudberg area to the north. Crest Farm was taken and from there patrols were sent into the outskirts of Passchendaele itself, while the Third Canadian Division again fell short of its objectives. The Canadian Third and Fourth Divisions had suffered twelve thousand casualties for a gain of just a few hundred metres and were in desperate need of being relieved. Three days of sunshine from 3 November to 5 November provided the Allies with the opportunity to organise their evacuation and, on 6 November, the weary Canadians of the Third and Fourth Divisions were replaced by the troops of the First and Second Canadian Divisions. Despite the fact that German troops were still entrenched around Passchendaele, the Canadian First Division made a series of strong advances throughout the town and later that day, just a few hours after that final assault, Passchendaele at last fell into Allied hands.

When British and Canadian forces occupied Passchendaele on 6 November, Haig decided to call a halt to the offensive and claimed victory. But to the soldiers who had endured slogging their way through the interminable mud, stepping over the dead bodies of their comrades and horses protruding grotesquely from their muddy graves, all just to advance 8 kilometres

(5 miles)—and in the process losing over 325,000 men killed or wounded—it must have seemed like anything but victory.

A terrible victory

By the time the fighting was over, the town of Passchendaele had ceased to exist. Aerial photographs taken after the battle showed that none of the town's farms, houses or commercial buildings remained. Even the majority of its roads were pulverised, becoming at one with the monotonous, featureless, moon-like landscape. All that remained were the vague outlines of one or two more prominent roads and the gutted remains of the town centre. The patchwork of irrigated paddocks, the assemblage of the many geometric shapes that made up a typical European farming community, was gone.

Passchendaele had been 'de-urbanised'

Some months later, in the spring of 1918, the German army launched Operation Michael,

LEFT: British casualties litter the churned up battlefield during the Battle of Passchendaele.

which culminated in the Battle of the Lys and the eventual retaking of Ypres by the Germans. Virtually all the ground that Field Marshal Douglas Haig had gained at the Battle of Passchendaele was given up.

When one thinks of the waste and stupidity of war, few battles in history typify this more than Passchendaele. Haig's stubborn determination to press on regardless of the atrocious weather and the intransigence of the town's defenders is difficult to excuse. The four million artillery shells fired by the Allies into the German lines did little to dampen the German resolve but utterly destroyed the irrigation system of the region, destroying rivers and streams, wrecking the watertable and turning the very ground over which the Allies must cross into an impassable sea of mud. In the end, just over 5 square kilometres (2 square miles) of territory was gained at the cost of half a million British and Allied soldiers killed and wounded.

Field Marshall Douglas Haig survived the Battle of Passchendale—not a difficult achievement considering he never visited the front lines—and died in 1928 at the age of sixty-six. He was given a state funeral.

GANDHI AND HIS FOLLOWERS DEFY EMPIRE ON SALT MARCH

Known as Mahatma, or 'Great Soul', Gandhi was the leader of the Indian nationalist movement against British rule, and followed a doctrine of non-violent protest. On 2 March 1930, he and his followers set out on a 320-kilometre (200-mile) journey to the Arabian Ocean to harvest salt—a direct challenge to the British rulers' state-run monopoly on salt. This action formed the symbolic focal point of a campaign of peaceful civil disobedience which roused the nation and drew the attention of the world to the Indians' plight; it brought a direct challenge to British rule.

GANDHI'S SALT MARCH AND THE PATH TO INDIAN INDEPENDENCE

*If the means employed are impure, the change will
not be in the direction of progress but very likely in the opposite.
Only a change brought about in our political condition
by pure means can lead to real progress.*

MAHATMA GANDHI

There is an old Gujarat legend that says when a labourer on the salt flats of the Rann of Kutch dies, the only part of his body that survives the funeral pyre is the soles of his feet, which are baked so hard by a lifetime of walking its hot, dry saltpans that even the heat of the flames cannot make them burn.

In the aftermath of every monsoon season for the past five thousand years, salt has been harvested from the Rann of Kutch, an 18,000-square-kilometre (7000-square-miles) area of low-lying coastline in the Indian state of Gujarat. This vast desert of mudflats and salt marshes, with an average height above sea level of just 15 metres (50 feet), has been mined by generations of families. The salt it yields plays a vital role in replacing the natural salts that are taken each day from the bodies of India's labourers by the unrelenting heat and humidity of the Indian sun.

The tax on salt

Salt had been taxed in the subcontinent since the reign of the Mauryan emperor, Chandra Gupta, in the fourth century BC. In the sixteenth and seventeenth centuries the ruling Moguls placed a tax on salt in Bengal state as it passed through their territory on its journey up the River Ganges. Salt taxes under the Moguls, however, as they were throughout most of the country, were relatively light and imposed little financial hardship on the average Indian family. The taxation of salt was never a political or social issue so long as the amount at which it was taxed remained in the range of 2.5 to 5 per cent.

In 1780 the manufacture of salt and the rate at which it would be taxed was brought under the control of the British government. (India had become a colonial possession of Great Britain in 1858, and would remain part of the British Empire until independence was achieved in 1947.) Government agents were appointed and received a 10 per cent commission on the revenues from the sale of salt. In the three years starting in 1781, tax revenues from salt increased from 2.6 million rupees annually to more than 6 million rupees. In 1788 the 'fixed price policy' on salt that wholesalers had always been able to rely upon was abandoned in favour of government-run auctions. This forced up the price to the point where it became a genuine hardship for many Indian families, though arguments abounded as to just what constituted an average Indian family. It was even debated whether or not cattle should be included in calculating the needs of an average rural family. In 1880 the Madras Board of Revenue estimated that 18 pounds of salt (just over 8 kilograms) was the amount required to meet the needs of a family of six for a period of one year, and that purchasing it would take almost a month's wages from the pocket of a common labourer.

In 1885 the Indian politician and theosophist Swaminatha Iyer spoke in the National Congress against a proposed increase in the salt tax, calling it 'unjust and unrighteous' and an unnecessary imposition on the poor of India. By this time the British monopoly on salt was total. The *Salt Act* of 1882 made the individual collection of salt illegal, and punishable by a prison term of up to six months as well as the confiscation of any vehicle or animal used to transport it. What had once been an abundant and vital natural resource available to all at a reasonable price had become a revenue tool to support and sustain the British presence, with little regard for the financial strain its artificially high price was imposing on the Indian people.

Calls for Indian independence, mostly in the form of militant nationalism, began in the early years of the 1900s, but it wasn't until the early 1920s that the Indian Congress Party adopted the non-violent policies espoused by Gandhi. In December 1929, under the leadership of Jawaharlal Nehru, the Congress Party adopted a resolution demanding complete and total independence from the British Empire and called for a campaign of civil disobedience across the nation. On 26 January 1930 the Indian National Congress issued a unilateral Declaration of Independence. History was being made, and everyone looked to Mohandas Karamchand Gandhi to see what he would do next.

Gandhi develops a lifelong philosophy

Mohandas Gandhi was born on 2 October 1869 in Porbandar on the coast of Gujarat, India. Porbandar was a princely state possessing nominal sovereignty and Gandhi's father was its prime minister. In 1883 at the age of thirteen, Gandhi wed Kasturbai Makhaji, in an arranged marriage and together they had four children. In 1888 he travelled to London to study as a barrister and began to develop an interest in Christian and Hindu scriptures. In 1893 he and his wife went to live in South Africa where Gandhi became a victim of class and race discrimination for the first time in his life. He was taken off a train for refusing to travel third class despite having a first class ticket, was refused lodging at various hotels and was badly beaten by a stagecoach driver for refusing to surrender his seat to an English passenger. These events were a watershed in his personal development. He studied the effects of prejudice and pored over the principles of social justice, extending his time in South Africa to stay and fight for the rights of the country's Indian minority.

Gandhi returned to India in 1915 and in 1918–19 achieved national prominence for organising resistance in the state of Bihar to British demands that farmers grow cash crops such as indigo instead of the food crops required for day-to-day living.

Through the 1920s Gandhi became a uniting figure in the Indian National Congress, but at the same time he stayed aloof from internal politicking, preferring instead to fight the scourges of poverty and alcoholism, campaigning for the rights of the classless 'untouchables', and promoting tolerance between Hindus and Muslims. At the close of the 1920s there was no leader more respected in all of India. He had been given the title of Mahatma, or 'Great Soul', and was thought of as the Father of the Nation. If anyone could lead a protest movement to bring about the end of the British presence in India, it was he.

Gandhi plans his historic march to the sea

By February of 1930 Mahatma Gandhi had come to view the salt tax as an example of the 'heartless exploitation' of India by the ruling British and, claiming to be inspired by 'an inner voice', decided he would make the unpopular tax the focus of a symbolic non-violent protest. He would

Mahatma Gandhi during the early years of his opposition to British rule, addressing a rally in Calcutta in 1919.

orchestrate a march to the sea, from his ashram in the Ahmedabad suburb of Sabarmati to the coastal village of Dandi in Gujarat on the shores of the Arabian Sea 390 kilometres (242 miles) away. The journey would take 23 days. When he arrived in Dandi he planned to kneel, scrape up a handful of saline mud from the ground, and tell those around him to do likewise and take it home and boil it to extract the precious salt. The illegal act would symbolise India's growing rejection of British rule and, he hoped, hasten the nation along the path to independence.

On 2 March Gandhi wrote to the viceroy, Lord Irwin, to inform him of his intentions. The letter read in part:

If my letter makes no appeal to your heart, on the eleventh day of this month I shall proceed with such co-workers of the Ashram as I can take, to disregard the provisions of the Salt Laws. I regard this tax to be the most iniquitous of all from the poor man's standpoint. As the Independence movement is essentially for the poorest in the land, the beginning will be made with this evil.

Gandhi's epic march was a world-wide media phenomenon, with Ghandi issuing regular statements along the way.

Irwin's response to Gandhi was merely to warn him that if he did anything that was in breach of the law, he would be held to account. Irwin was dismissive of Gandhi's planned march and said as much in a letter he wrote to London in February: 'At present the prospect of a salt campaign does not keep me awake at night'.

Commitment to non-violent protest grows

Intent on achieving maximum publicity for his march, Gandhi announced his intentions to the media. The march would be a *satyagraha*, a synthesis of the two Sanskrit words *satya* (truth) and *agraha* (holding on to), which to Gandhi represented the sort of mix of love and firmness that comes from a commitment to non-violence as a means of personal expression and political action, and as a tool to wean one's opponents away from error—to convert your enemy rather than coerce him.

Gandhi was insistent that the march be conducted under the strict observance of the principles of *satyagraha* and according to his own rigid code of discipline, and for this reason preferred that those who would accompany him come from his own ashram and not from the Congress Party or other organisations.

On 12 March an estimated one hundred thousand people lined the streets of Ahmedabad as Gandhi and an initial seventy-eight *satyagrahis* (activists of truth and resolution) slowly made their way through the city streets. Press coverage reached saturation point. The *Bombay Chronicle* described the scene: 'so enthusiastic, magnificent, and soul-stirring that indeed they beggar description. Never was the wave of patriotism so powerful in the hearts of mankind'. The sixty-year-old Gandhi headed the procession, which soon grew to be over 4 kilometres (over 2 miles) long. He carried a stick to help him walk at a brisk and determined pace. People climbed trees and rooftops so they would be able to one day tell their grandchildren they had seen him pass. In every village and at every halting station he stopped to speak to the assembled crowds, encouraging non-cooperation with the British and inviting them to join the growing ranks of his *satyagrahis*—and to return to the spinning wheels and to wear the *khaddar*.

The *khaddar* was a simple hand-spun cotton or silk covering, the manufacture of which Gandhi had long been promoting as a step towards reducing unemployment, particularly in the rural areas of India. It had become symbolic of India's struggle for independence, and was part of the early Swadeshi Movement, which began in Bengal in 1905 and grew from a desire to boycott British-made products and to promote indigenous industries. The more the *khaddar* was made and worn, the less demand there would be for British-made textiles.

Thousands of followers join the march

The march took Gandhi through four districts and forty-eight villages. As he made his way from village to village, hundreds enrolled in the cause of civil disobedience. Many village elders resigned their posts and joined the march. Gandhi himself proclaimed he would refuse to return to his beloved ashram until the hated tax was repealed. To everyone who saw him he was an inspiration. Despite his advancing years he moved with the enthusiasm and purpose of a man half his age, an invincible juggernaut covering 19 kilometres (12 miles) a day without any obvious signs of fatigue.

The route was meticulously planned. Scouts were sent ahead to meet with the elders of every village on the route. Information on each community was relayed back to the approaching Gandhi—from the number of its 'untouchables' to each person's salt consumption, from the number of spinning wheels it possessed to the number of cows the village had, from the quality of its drinking water to the state of its health care and educational facilities.

In every village through which he passed Ghandi spoke of the need to defy the British on the collection of salt and to boycott British cloth and return to the *khaddar*. He preached religious tolerance, and encouraged those in government positions to leave their jobs and join in the Salt Satyagraha. 'Why are you afraid of such a government?' he asked in Buva village. 'What could they do if there were eighty thousand volunteers?' At Ankleshwar village he spoke mockingly of British greed: 'This government levies a duty on an item which is consumed by the poorest of the poor. We are lucky, at any rate, that there is no tax on the air we breathe!'

Twenty-three days later, on 5 April, Gandhi and his initial group of seventy-eight devotees, now swelled to several thousand, arrived at Dandi. In an interview with an Associated Press reporter on the Dandi coast, Gandhi said: 'it remains to be seen whether the [British] government will tolerate, as they have tolerated the march, the actual breach of the salt laws by countless people from tomorrow'. On the following morning, 6 April, Gandhi took a handful of mud and salt, raised his fist triumphantly into the air and declared: 'With this I am shaking the foundations of the British Empire'.

Mass defiance of the salt tax

The next day India erupted, as across the country tens of thousands of men, women and children ran to the coastline to gather salt in open violation of British law, salt which was then sold throughout cities, across the land, thus making accomplices of everyone who purchased it and swelling the ranks of the nation's passive revolutionaries almost overnight. The British responded in the only way they felt they could. Thousands were arrested and an unknown number were killed and beaten in the riots that followed.

On 4 May the District Magistrate of Surat, along with a small number of Indian officers and a squad of armed constables, came to arrest Gandhi at his small hut on Dandi beach. They had difficulty locating him amid the sea of white *khaddar*-wearing followers and had to be directed to the slight frame of the great man, who was in a deep sleep. 'We have come to arrest Mr Gandhi,' the official said. 'I am Mohandas Gandhi, and I am at your service,' said the man, and when given some time to gather his things replied that he did not need any time to do so: 'I am ready now. This is all I need.' Gandhi gathered a few personal items into a small bundle at his feet and offered no resistance. After pausing briefly to brush his teeth, he was led away to Pune's Yerwada Jail where he remained until released in January 1931.

To the more than sixty thousand *satyagrahis* who were soon in prisons all over India, Gandhi was an inspiration. He was used to being imprisoned, and because he felt the entire world was a sacred place had little difficulty in adjusting to prison life. He also knew that each new day of his eight-month incarceration brought more converts to the cause of non-violent protest and the end of the British presence in India that much closer.

1933

FDR PLEDGES 'NEW DEAL' FOR THE AMERICAN PEOPLE

In the summer of 1932, Franklin D. Roosevelt, governor of New York, was nominated as the presidential candidate of the Democratic Party. In his acceptance speech, Roosevelt addressed the problems of the Great Depression by saying, 'I pledge you, I pledge myself, to a new deal for the American people.' In the election that took place in the autumn of 1932, Roosevelt won by a landslide and swiftly set about implementing a range of social policies to drag America out of the Depression and its people back into the workforce. It was the largest program of public works in America's history, and it included banking reform laws, and emergency and huge-scale work relief programs, such as the building of the Hoover Dam.

ROOSEVELT'S PROGRAMS TO END THE DEPRESSION

When there is no vision the people perish.

PRESIDENT ROOSEVELT'S FIRST INAUGURAL SPEECH, 4 MARCH 1933

In October 1929, following a period of rapid expansion through the 1920s, a wave of panic selling swept through the financial markets of the United States. Within a week the value of all publicly listed American companies had collapsed, initiating a US-led depression that would spread across the globe and drag all the world's economies down with it. Panic selling began on 24 October, but it was on 'Black Tuesday', five days later, that investors crowding outside the New York Stock Exchange watched mutely as their life savings disappeared in front of their eyes.

The collapse was too much for some to bear, although reports of numerous suicides and people jumping out of windows would later prove to be grossly exaggerated. In early October an executive of the Earl Radio Corporation jumped to his death from the eleventh floor of a Lexington Avenue hotel. James Riordan, president of New York's County Trust Company, took a gun from a teller's drawer on 8 November, drove to his home in Manhattan's midtown, and shot himself in the head. These were, however, isolated though very public examples. Mostly the pain fell on ordinary Americans, and the fear in people's eyes was clearly evident. In New York, as evidence of plummeting stock values came out over the tickertape machines, many openly wept.

Collapse of the American economy

In just three years, from 1929 to 1932, the American economy went from relative prosperity to being on life support. Unemployment rose from 3 per cent to 25 per cent, which represented more than 13 million people, and the average family income fell by almost half. Farm foreclosures were being counted in the hundreds of thousands. In mining states such as Pennsylvania and West Virginia, two of the poorest states going into the Depression years, more than three out of four schoolchildren were reported as malnourished. Corporate profits across the nation fell by 90 per cent, from $10 billion in 1929 to $1 billion in 1932. The number of new homes under construction fell by 80 per cent and, by 1932, two in three Americans were classified as 'poor' by federal government agencies. By 1932, five thousand American banks had gone out of business. It was an economic holocaust that seemed to have no end. One Manhattan-based Soviet trading company was receiving almost four hundred approaches every day from ordinary Americans enquiring after work in the USSR.

In the presidential elections of 1932, voters took out their anger and frustration on President Herbert Hoover, the Republican from Iowa who was the first occupant of the White House to be born west of the Mississippi. Unlucky enough to have won the 1928 presidential election, Hoover's name became synonymous with the crash and the Depression that followed. The thousands of slums that appeared almost overnight, it seemed, were nicknamed Hoovervilles, and he was lampooned in the press as a 'do nothing' president. In fact Hoover did intervene, but the actions he took, particularly the raising of tariffs in a vain attempt to protect the economy, lengthened the Great Depression's impact.

The need for a 'new deal'

Franklin Roosevelt first mentioned the need for a 'new deal' for the American people when he accepted the Democratic Party's nomination for the presidency in Chicago in July 1932:

Washington has alternated between putting its head in the sand and saying there is no large number of destitute people who need food and clothing, and then saying the States should take care of them if there are. Throughout the nation men and women, forgotten in the political philosophy of the government, look to us here for guidance and for a more equitable opportunity to share in the distribution of national wealth … I pledge myself to a 'new deal' for the American people. This is more than a political campaign. It is a call to arms.

Roosevelt's subsequent election ended twelve years of Republican domination in Washington with a landslide victory, carrying forty-two states to Hoover's six (Hawaii and Alaska not yet having been admitted to the Union) and winning 57.4 per cent of the popular vote.

Few presidents had entered the White House bringing with them such a wealth of experience and tenure in public service. Elected to the New York State Senate in 1910, Roosevelt became assistant secretary of the Navy in 1913 and played a key role in establishing the United States Navy Reserve. In 1920 he ran as the Democratic Party's vice-presidential candidate alongside the party's candidate for president, Governor James Cox of Ohio, who was defeated by Republican Warren Harding. In 1921 Roosevelt contracted polio while holidaying at the family home on Campobello Island, New Brunswick. The disease left him paralysed from the waist down.

Throughout the 1920s, Roosevelt never lost touch with his beloved Democratic Party, and in 1928 was persuaded to return to the political arena. He was narrowly elected governor of New York. During his second term as governor that he took on the corrupt might of Tammany Hall (New York headquatres of the Democratic Party)—initiating in 1930 an investigation into its suspect system of appointments, which led to New York's notorious Mayor Jimmy Walker leaving the country to escape being indicted. Chosen in 1932 by the Democratic Party as its presidential candidate, Roosevelt's response to the raft of social and economic challenges he now faced would define a generation.

In his inaugural speech on 4 March 1933 as the thirty-second president of the United States, Roosevelt demonstrated he knew full well that the public's fear of putting their hard-earned savings back into the fractured banking sector was badly affecting the country's ability to recover. Roosevelt recognised that this fear had to be met head on and he wasted no time in firing the first shot at restoring confidence in the country's financial markets:

So first of all, let me assert my firm belief that the only thing we have to fear, is fear itself, nameless, unreasoning, unjustified terror, which paralyses needed efforts to convert retreat into advance …

Roosevelt shakes hands with embattled farmers during his election campaign in 1932.

On 6 March, just forty-eight hours after assuming office, Roosevelt declared a mandatory five-day bank holiday to prevent panicked investors from withdrawing their savings, at the end of which the *Emergency Banking Relief Act* (passed in record time by a newly elected Democratic Congress) gave him the power to regulate and oversee all banking transactions. It was hoped this would bring to an end the horrific rate of bank closures (which had averaged almost fifteen hundred a year in the final two years of the Hoover presidency) and restore public faith in the financial sector. Then on 12 March

Roosevelt spoke directly to an audience of fifty million for the first time in a series of live, reassuring 'fireside chats' over the radio, laced with the optimism that would go on to become one of the defining hallmarks of his presidency.

The New Deal—first steps to recovery

The New Deal that Roosevelt had first spoken of in his acceptance speech at the Democratic National Convention in July 1932 was to come in two stages. The First New Deal (1933–34), which began with the passage of the *Economy*

Act on 20 March 1933, slashed the salaries of public servants and reduced veterans pensions in an effort to limit the size of the budget deficit. But it only succeeded in reducing the deficit by only $243 million—barely half the reduction the president was hoping for—and in the end had a negligible impact on either the size of the deficit or the economy. Roosevelt was a keen student of the economist John Maynard Keynes, who believed government spending should, in theory, 'kick-start' a stagnant economy. He realised that, to stimulate growth in the absence of any meaningful investment from the private sector, massive injections of government money would be required. This put an end to any thoughts of returning the budget to surplus. The *Economy Act* was followed in May with the establishment of the Federal Emergency Relief Administration (FERA), whose job was to alleviate the debt incurred by the country's state and local authorities.

FERA was one of the many so-called 'alphabet agencies' that Roosevelt created in the frenetic legislative agenda that characterised his first few months in office and which collectively would be given the responsibility of implementing the policies of recovery. Such reforms and agencies included the Agricultural Adjustment Administration (AAA), the Civil Works Administration (CWA) and the Civilian Conservation Corps (CCC). The CCC took unemployed young people, paid them a wage of thirty dollars a month, and sent them to work on conservation and forestation projects around the country. During the CCC's nine-year existence it employed close to three million people. Other agencies, such as the Tennessee Valley Authority (TVA), were created by Congress to provide jobs for those regions that needed it most. In the Tennessee Valley for instance, where one in three people suffered from malaria,

generations of destructive farming practices had resulted in poor crop yields and unproductive soils. Farm incomes had been decimated, and its poorer communities were enduring living conditions typical of the developing countries of Latin America. The TVA was tasked with raising the living standards of the valley's residents, advising them on improved methods of crop rotation and new fertilisers.

Meanwhile reforms in the banking sector continued apace. On 16 June 1933 the second *Glass–Steagall Act* created for the first time a distinction between commercial and investment banks, made it illegal for banks to invest in the stock market and paved the way for the creation of the Federal Deposit Insurance Corporation (FDIC) which insured the deposits of ordinary investors to the value of $5000.

Unprecedented government intervention

In June Roosevelt established the National Recovery Administration (NRA), an agency that was fundamental in implementing many of the early initiatives of the new government, including the building of soup kitchens and shelters across the country to feed and house America's new underclass. The NRA also had the power to exempt businesses from anti-trust laws if they complied with new government guidelines on working conditions and wage and price restraint. Throughout 1933, federal government programs would usher in an era of government intervention on a hitherto unprecedented scale, designed to stimulate recovery in the industrial sector and to provide assistance to the millions of Americans whose livelihoods had been stripped from them. June 1933 also saw the creation of the Public Works Administration (PWA), whose job it was to oversee the appropriation and allocation of funds for large-scale building programs, including highways and schools, and naval vessels from landing craft to aircraft carriers.

In 1934, in an attempt to control the sort of bad lending practices and rampant speculation that contributed to the 1929 stock market crash, the *Securities Exchange Act* saw the creation of the Securities and Exchange Commission (SEC)—in the hope the new agency would restore the public's faith in the banking system.

The Second New Deal (1935–38) was characterised by the passage of the *National Labor Relations Act*, essentially a workplace reform act designed to limit employer interference in the creation of labor unions and assist efforts by employees in the pursuit of collective bargaining and in the selection of representatives of their own choosing.

Burgeoning opposition to New Deal policies

The Second New Deal saw a far heavier reliance on the deficit-spending theories of John Maynard Keynes. As the Democrats' deficit spending soared, opposition to the New Deal from both the socialist left and the conservative right began to grow. The radical Senator Huey Long (Democrat, Louisiana) attacked Roosevelt for not providing enough assistance—although his own Share The Wealth plan, which would see the confiscation of any personal fortune over the amount of $3 million dollars redistributed to the poor, would surely have ushered in a new American Revolution if actively pursued. Father Charles Coughlin, an anti-Semitic Roman Catholic priest with a national radio audience of over forty million, also became a thorn in Roosevelt's side. Coughlin, sometimes referred to as the 'father of hate radio', referred to Judaism as 'that synagogue of Satan' and to

Roosevelt's New Deal as 'the stinking cesspool of pagan autocracy'.

Undaunted by the criticism, Roosevelt ploughed on. The first major legislative accomplishment of the Second New Deal was the Works Progress Administration (WPA), a body similar to the Public Works Administration (PWA) of the First New Deal in every respect except its scale—the WPA would eventually employ more then ten million Americans on new infrastructure projects across the country in a torrent of spending that saw Congress channel more than $10 billion into the scheme in ten years.

Roosevelt re-elected

On 14 August the *Social Security Act* of 1935 was passed, establishing a pension system for workers and introducing compensation for the victims of industrial accidents. The bill also included funds for vocational training to enable more people to enter the workforce, and assistance for the blind as well as for dependent and disabled children. Farmers benefited greatly from the *Soil Conservation and Domestic Allotment Act*, which paid subsides to farmers to limit overproduction and provided financial incentives to plant soil-enriching crops. There was barely a corner of American society that Roosevelt had not reached into with reforms and assistance, and in the presidential election of 1936 he was re-elected in the greatest landslide since the two-party system of government was established in 1850, winning over 60 per cent of the vote and carrying every state in the union with the exception of Maine and Vermont. In fact, Roosevelt and the Democratic Party had become so synonymous with what was best for America that in the days after the election, on a highway as it crossed the border into Vermont, a prankster erected a sign that read: 'You are now leaving the United States'.

The construction of the Hoover Dam—one of the massive public works ordered by Roosevelt as part of the New Deal.

The final deal

In 1937 Roosevelt scaled back deficit spending. The economy, despite growing steadily since 1933, had not been strengthened sufficiently to continue prospering in the absence of any external stimulus and slipped back into a period of negative growth that opponents labelled the Roosevelt Recession. Mid-term congressional elections in 1938 saw the Republicans claw back some representation and, although the Democrats still retained a two-thirds majority, the Republican resurgence spelled the end of the era of New Deal politics. In his State of the Union address in January 1939 Roosevelt offered no new domestic reform legislation, instead focusing on the prospect of war in Europe, a war that would see the United States return to a war economy footing, which would in turn erase the last vestiges of the Great Depression.

Not merely a response to difficult economic times, Roosevelt's New Deal also left a lasting legacy. It helped create a climate where those Americans striving for social justice could challenge more openly the notion of white supremacy. African Americans began to believe the New Deal rhetoric that economic security was for *all* Americans. For Native Americans, gone were the days of cultural 'assimilation' for the Indian New Deal of 1934 fostered the creation of tribal self-government. The foundation for America's post–World War II economic growth was laid in the New Deal's $6.5 billion public works projects that saw the creation of water projects, dams, sewerage plants, bridges, tunnels, schools and highways. Many New Deal programs still exist today, including the Tennessee Valley Authority (TVA), the Federal Housing Administration (FHA), the Securities and Exchange Commission (SEC) and, of course, the nation's social security system, which gave Americans a system of welfare that brought the country closer to the true spirit of its own Constitution than it had ever been before, and changed forever the relationship between its people and their government.

1934

RED ARMY UNDERTAKES MAMMOTH MARCH

The Long March was actually a series of military retreats undertaken by the Red Army, led by Mao Zedong, to evade the pursuit of the Kuomintang. The best known of these moves was the march from Jiangxi province to Guizhou, which began with 90,000 men and women. Starting in October 1934, the Red Army covered 9600 kilometres (6000 miles) in 370 days, passing through some of the most difficult terrain of western China under constant assault from the Nationalists. When the marchers finally arrived at the Red Army's new base in northern China, less than half of the original contingent remained. Despite the heavy losses, the Long March came to symbolise the struggle of the Communist Party and the rise of the mythology of Mao.

THE LONG MARCH: THE RISE OF MAO ZEDONG

The Red Army is not afraid of hardship on the march, the long march. Ten thousand waters and a thousand mountains are nothing ... The far snows of Minshan only make us happy and when the army pushes through, we all laugh.

MAO ZEDONG, 'THE LONG MARCH', OCTOBER 1935

Kang Keqing was born in Jiangxi Province, China, in 1912 in the rear of a small fishing boat on the Gan River. Her parents were peasants and, because her father was barely able to feed the three sons he already had, he gave Kang away, as he had the six girl babies before her. She grew up with foster parents in a mud brick house in the nearby village of Luotangwan and played with the other children of the village on the stone steps that led from her street to the river below. Her prospects were poor, with little to look forward to beyond a lifetime of childbearing and endless toil.

Kang's story

Kang was fifteen when an official from the local Communist Party visited Luotangwan and convinced her that communism would free her from poverty and oppression. In the 1920s, 80 per cent of China's population were rural peasants, barely half of whom possessed even a tiny plot of land from which they could derive a small income. In 1928, at the age of sixteen, Kang joined the Red Army, which at the time was not much more than a collection of untrained and ill-equipped peasantry with little ideological commitment to the core values of communism. A few months later, while serving as a party organiser in the neighbouring province of Suichuan, she met Commander Zhu De, the diminutive commander of the Fourth Red Army and second only to Mao Zedong himself. After meeting Kang just a few times and exchanging nothing more than polite conversation, the forty-three-year-old Zhu asked her to marry him. She was paralysed with fear and unable to respond—Zhu De took her silence as a 'yes' and they were married in late 1929. Kang later enrolled in the Red Military Academy and graduated second in her class.

In October 1934 Kang, Zhu and 86,000 Red Army soldiers embarked on the Long March, the euphemism given to their tactical retreat from Jiangxi Province in a desperate attempt to avoid encirclement by the pursuing Kuomintang (KMT or Chinese Nationalist Party) army. In the first few days of the march, during a routine inspection tour of a three-hundred-strong contingent deep in the rear of her army column, soldiers of the KMT appeared from nowhere and a small but intense battle ensued. In the midst of the fighting the three hundred men elected Kang, the only woman present, as their commander. The shooting lasted for more than two hours, at the end of which the KMT troops were forced to retreat after suffering heavy casualties. It was an exhilarating encounter for Kang, who later confessed she was unable to confirm whether she had actually killed or injured anyone despite being an excellent marksman. Her leadership, however, was proved beyond question and, from that moment, the now twenty-three-year-old Kang Keqing, whose last name meant 'to vanquish', became known to the soldiers of the Red Army by her new nickname: the Girl Commander.

Kang was later to confide to her biographer that the Long March 'was as easy for me as taking a stroll every day'. Feeling she should set an example as the wife of a Red Army commander she carried her belongings on her own back, which included as many as three or four firearms, as well as stopping often to help others alongside her who were struggling. In one month she walked 300 kilometres (186 miles). When passing through the Yuecheng Mountains on the Guangxi-Hunan border and with the KMT following closely behind, the First Red Army, of which she was a part, was ordered to discard their packs so they could move faster through the forest and put some distance between themselves and their pursuers. Without complaint Kang gave away her quilt, all her excess clothing and mosquito net to Yao villagers, the ethnic minority who had inhabited the Yuecheng Mountains for more than two thousand years. They marched in bare feet—and at night. Violent storms caused many marchers to fall down ravines into the blackness, never to be seen again. Window shutters were borrowed as makeshift beds and carefully replaced the following morning before the marchers moved on. Sleet and snow made sleeping in the open difficult. In one extraordinary demonstration

of determination and courage, 300 kilometres (186 miles) were traversed in just ten days. For the young peasant girl from the village of Luotangwan, and for thousands of others lifted out of their mundane existences, this was not just a military retreat. It was a glorious victory on the road to nationhood, an achievement of mythic proportions that would later become a propagandist's dream in the unfolding history of the Chinese Communist Party (CCP), and a grand adventure beyond anything Kang, as a young girl, could possibly have hoped for.

Setting out from Jiangxi Province

Only thirty-five women marched among the approximately one hundred thousand communist soldiers and more than fifteen thousand government officials and party leaders who set out from Jiangxi Province in October 1934. As for children, it had been decided that only those old enough to march long distances each day would be permitted to go, which meant that the two young sons of Mao Zedong and his wife Zizhen would have to be left behind. They would never see them again.

The journey would be an epic one. The circuitous route took those strong and determined enough to survive it on a 9600-kilometre (6000-mile) journey through eleven Chinese provinces, over almost twenty mountain ranges and across two dozen rivers. Its participants would one day go on to form the core of China's People's Liberation Army and, on the way, Mao Zedong began his methodical ascent to power, successfully outmanoeuvring his rivals within the fledgling group of revolutionaries to eventually assume complete control of the CCP.

In late 1933 the five hundred thousand troops of the KMT operated under the tactical gaze of a German. General Hans von Seeckt, famous for organising the *Reichswehr* (German Army) during the years of the Weimar Republic, had slowly been tightening the noose about the Red Army's neck, advancing relentlessly but purposefully, building thousands of concrete pillboxes and blockhouses as he went, and pushing the communists into an ever-decreasing pocket of resistance. If the Red Army didn't act quickly, it would be encircled and mercilessly annihilated.

The idea for the Long March came not from Mao Zedong, Zhu De or any other Chinese revolutionary, but from another German, a communist of limited tactical ability named Otto Braun. A graduate of Russia's Frunze Military Academy, Braun was sent to China by Joseph Stalin to oversee the Red Army, and the following of his orders was a condition of continued Soviet assistance. Braun preferred frontal assaults on the KMT and was able to convince the Red Army leadership that Mao's strategy of smaller, guerilla-style assaults would prove fruitless. Braun's decision, however, would prove costly—the ensuing frontal assaults on heavily entrenched KMT lines (built around concrete blockhouses that all but encircled Jiangxi) led to heavy communist losses. Mao, who at this point was not high enough in the military hierarchy to have any real influence in decision making, wanted to break out through the KMT lines and then wheel around and attack the enemy from the rear. Braun was also in favour of a breakout, but not in order to mount an attack. He argued instead for a retreat in the general direction of Hunan to the southwest, where the Red Army could take time to consolidate itself and form a stable power base. Braun's opinion, strengthened of course by his political backers in Moscow, carried the day, and 87,000 soldiers, carrying more than 30,000 guns and two million rounds of ammunition began to extricate themselves from the trenches and blockhouses of the KMT that surrounded them.

History is blurred on the subject of whether what was to follow was one of the great military retreats or little more than a series of strategic blunders, but what is not in dispute is the phenomenal scale of the accomplishment in human terms. To have moved as many people as far as they did, under the conditions they did, was one of the twentieth century's most heroic tales of survival.

KMT forces crush the Red Army

The first military engagement of the Long March was a disaster bordering on a debacle for the Red Army. On the banks of the Xiangjiang River on 25 November they encountered forces of the KMT, and for seven days and nights fought a pitched battle that resulted in fifteen thousand communists killed and as many again lost to desertion. Many of the civilian porters who had been charged with the task of transporting the furniture, printing presses, typewriters and documents that represented almost the entirety of the bureaucratic infrastructure of the Communist Party also fled the killing. Chiang Kai-Shek and the Nationalists had accurately predicted the communist escape route and had brought overwhelming forces to bear, outnumbering their enemy by something like six to one. The defeat at the Xiangjiang River had a devastating effect on morale, which wasn't helped by the fact that during this early stage of the march no precise destination had been decided on and no clearly defined purpose or sense of direction had been articulated. After the battle, Mao argued that they should head in a southwest direction into Guizhou Province where the Nationalist presence was low.

The leadership of the Communist Party began to swing Mao's way. In mid-January 1935, a secret meeting took place in Zunyi (a city the Red Army captured after entering it

The soldiers of the Red Army were joined by many poor peasant farmers on their Long March.

posing as Nationalist troops) between Mao and his supporters and the military leadership of General Secretary Bo Gu and Otto Braun, who had presided over the Red Army's catastrophic crossing of the Xiangjiang River. The Zunyi Conference saw Bo and Braun accused of failing to initiate a more mobile attacking strategy in Jiangxi and they were both demoted. Despite the position of General Secretary going to Zhang Wentian, Mao Zedong's rising status unquestioned. From now on battles would be fought his way. Selective assaults would be preferred to large-scale fights, or avoided altogether if victory could not be guaranteed. Soldiers would be told in detail about objectives, and the reasons behind military decisions. And with the banishment of Otto Braun, the Chinese revolution had finally emerged from Moscow's distant shadow.

Horrors of the Long March

Heading north, Mao's troops entered Sichuan Province and in the summer of 1935 came face to face with the Great Snow Mountains. Lacking

Mao Zedong during the Long March.

winter clothing and in no way welcomed by the region's Fan minority (who rolled boulders down onto their thinning ranks), the marchers scaled the range, daunting at approximately 4880 metres (16,000 feet) in height. Constant mist and rain soaked through their clothing and hundreds were lost to exposure. There were no paddy fields to provide them with rice and the locally grown corn did not agree with the soldiers' southern stomachs.

The twenty days spent crossing the grasslands on the high plateaus along the Shensi border were one of the chief horrors of the Long March. The grassy plains of Gansu Province may have looked benign but they hid deep bogs that could swallow men and even horses, so easily that the soldiers were encouraged to follow those in front of them and not to go their own way. The local Man minority, long hostile towards the Chinese, also refused to assist them—with the Man queen promising to boil alive anyone caught providing the communists with assistance. The conditions had become intolerable. Food became so scarce that even the hair from the skin of slaughtered cattle was burned off so the skin could be eaten. Grass, roots and leaves were boiled and eaten. Dog meat became a delicacy. Salt and water were mixed together with grass and boiled to produce a rudimentary broth, and when water became scarce the urine from their horses was harvested and drunk. Those who fell behind were left to the elements. Many of the sick and wounded simply sat down and died. The Nationalist Army, which had followed the communists into the grasslands, suffered equally great losses, and made the decision to end the pursuit.

After leaving the grasslands, an ongoing difference of opinion between Mao and Zhang Guotao over what the Long March was supposed to accomplish resulted in the splitting up of the army. Mao, with his ten-thousand-strong First Red Army continued to push northwards towards Shaanxi Province while Zhang and the Fourth Red Army returned south with the majority of the supplies in an attempt to re-establish a communist presence there. The split gave Mao the breathing space he needed as the Nationalist Army focused on the larger threat that Zhang's forces represented.

Assault on the Lazikou Pass

In September 1935 Mao's troops reached the border with Shaanxi Province to confront one of the last natural obstacles to their progress: the Lazikou Pass. The narrow pass had a vertical 305-metre (1000-foot) high cliff on one side and another high cliff on the other side—and it was defended from above by Nationalist troops in sturdy blockhouses. The choice facing Mao was a stark one. Either they capture the pass and continue on to Shaanxi, or retreat across the dreaded grasslands. The decision was made to take the pass.

Mao's troops mounted a series of night assaults and suffered heavy casualties. Little progress was made and Mao turned to a group of experienced mountaineers, who scaled one wall of the canyon. On reaching the top they hurled grenades onto the entrenched Nationalists—but only succeed in removing them when an unknown soldier strapped explosives to his waist and threw himself into their midst.

On 20 October 1935, after 368 days of relentless hardship, just six thousand troops—10 per cent of those who had set out with him from Jiangxi twelve months earlier—entered Shaanxi Province, to be greeted by Xu Haidong, a local communist organiser. Mao Zedong walked up to him and said, simply: 'Thank you for taking so much trouble to come and meet us.' Their time in Shaanxi would provide them with the isolation required to gather a new army and mount fresh challenges. That night Mao slept in safety in a cave, beneath a rocky overhang.

Military defeat ... or a powerful legend?

Although the Long March was unquestionably a military defeat, if not a debacle, the political mileage and the foundation it laid for the later growth of the party was undeniable. The communists had passed through eleven provinces that represented two hundred million ordinary Chinese, winning thousands of converts as they went and creating lasting goodwill and a potent mythology. It was just as well. Warlords in Yunnan and Guizhou provinces, who knew their terrain and were well armed, could have annihilated Mao's sick and weary troops had they wanted to.

The Long March transformed the communists from a sectarian power largely irrelevant to those living in the far reaches of the country's endless horizons to a patriotic force that represented China's future to millions of peasants, potential revolutionaries all of them, who were mostly illiterate and who had never heard of Marx and Lenin. The march also brought cohesion and mutual trust to the CCP leadership and transformed Mao from a regional and largely unknown leader into a heroic figure of national importance.

Kang Keqing, the peasant girl from Jiangxi Province who rose from obscurity to become the wife of Zhu De and for whom the Long March felt like 'taking a stroll', went on to become Vice Chairman of the fifth Chinese People's Political Consultative Conference (CPPCC) and an influential member of the All-China Women's Federation. She died in Beijing in 1992.

1934

HITLER UNLEASHES HIT MEN IN NIGHT OF CARNAGE

The events known as the Night of the Long Knives took place in Germany between 30 June and 2 July 1934, when the Nazi regime executed at least 85 people for political reasons. Most of those killed were members of the SA, a Nazi paramilitary organisation led by Ernst Röhm, a group that Hitler saw as a direct threat to his leadership. The purge represented a triumph for Hitler, and a turning point for the German government. It established Hitler as the undisputed ruler of Germany, garnered the support of the army and parliament, eliminated threats within the SA, empowered the SS and secured the Nazi totalitarian state.

THE NIGHT OF THE LONG KNIVES

Let the nation know that its existence—which depends on its internal order and security—cannot be threatened with impunity by anyone! And let it be known for all time to come that if anyone raises his hand to strike the State, then certain death is his lot.

ADOLF HITLER, NATIONALLY BROADCAST SPEECH
TO THE REICHSTAG, 13 JULY 1934

The phrase Night of the Long Knives was first used in the fifth century to describe a treacherous massacre—albeit quite likely an apocryphal one—in which a group of Celtic Britons were slaughtered by Anglo-Saxon soldiers while attending peace negotiations on Salisbury Plain in the south of England. Fourteen hundred years later, in November 1841, the phrase surfaced again, this time used to describe the assassination of Alexander Burnes, the great British explorer of the Indian subcontinent, in Kabul, Afghanistan. However, despite existing in literature for 1500 years, it wasn't until the bloody events that took place in Bavaria, Germany, in mid 1934, that the phrase at last found its terrifyingly appropriate place in history.

Hitler comes to office

Adolf Hitler was sworn in as German Chancellor in the presidential offices of Field Marshal Paul von Hindenburg, the German head of state and guardian of the constitution, at midday on 30 January 1933. His inauguration marked the end of Germany's brief, fourteen-year flirtation with democracy known as the Weimar Republic. It was the culmination of a period of political and racial intimidation orchestrated by Hitler and achieved using his loyal *Sturmabteilung* (SA) or 'assault detachment', a pseudo-military organisation created in the early 1920s to intimidate and coerce his political opponents.

The SA had its genesis in the German Worker's Party (*Deutsche Arbeiterpartei*, or DAP), which was founded in January 1919 and which Hitler himself joined later that same year. Hitler's skills as a stirring, almost hypnotic orator saw him rise quickly through the party's ranks; and, in public meetings as early as 1921, whenever Hitler was subject to heckling from his audiences, armed party members would storm the crowd and throw the often bloodied and bruised hecklers into the street. These 'stormtroopers' represented the beginnings of what would one day become the SA, Hitler's chief instrument of Nazi political persuasion.

The rise of Röhm and the SA

Banned by the German government in the wake of the Beer Hall Putsch in 1923 (a failed Nazi coup led by Hitler), the SA was reorganised in April 1924 by the fanatical Ernst Röhm and renamed the *Frontbann*. Composed essentially of those who formerly made up the SA, membership in the *Frontbann* grew to more than 30,000. In February 1925, when the ban on the Nazi Party was lifted, the *Frontbann* assumed its old title, *Sturmabteilung*, and new SA groups began to spring up right across the country and continued to grow in strength and numbers—until Hitler removed Röhm as its head and assumed personal control of the organisation in September 1930.

Though Hitler was now in place at the head of the SA, it was Röhm who continued to enjoy the loyalty of his troops. Known collectively as the 'brownshirts', the SA by 1930 had grown into a powerful political and military unit with well over a million members. In 1925, however, its original function of protecting the party's leaders had been taken from the SA and given to the newly formed *Schutzstaffel* (SS), an organisation formed initially in 1925 to be Hitler's personal bodyguard. The SS demonstrated an unwavering and fanatical loyalty to Hitler and by 1941, under the command of Heinrich Himmler, had grown to over a million men and exerted as much influence within the Third Reich as the German armed forces themselves. The SA, with Röhm as its chief of staff at Hitler's personal request, continued in its role as the party's enforcer in its running campaign against its real and imagined communist and Jewish opposition, pursuing increasingly violent street confrontations with the Communist Red Front, and terrorising Jewish businesses and indeed anyone who demonstrated opposition to Nazi principles and ideals. Even among ordinary Germans there was a growing revulsion towards the tactics pursued by the SA.

Despite Röhm's demotion he retained the loyalty of the SA and had grown in stature to become one of the most powerful figures in the Nazi Party and, many thought, with enough of a following to become a threat to the leadership of Hitler himself. Nevertheless Hitler and Röhm had become close friends. Röhm was one of the elite group of Nazis (including Hermann Göring and Joseph Goebbels) who were able to address Hitler using the familiar and personal form of *du*, and one of the very few able to call him by his Christian name.

Upon Hitler's election as Chancellor, however, a rift began to emerge between the SA and the regular army. The SA was instrumental in consolidating the Nazi Party's grip on power in the wake of the 1933 elections and saw themselves as the vanguard in the coming National Socialist revolution. With its burgeoning number of recruits the SA also began to harbour thoughts of replacing the German Army (*Reichswehr*) itself. By early 1934 almost one in five of all German males over the age of fifteen were SA members, four million in all, and its potential to indoctrinate and coerce German society was second to none. With the Nazi Party now in power, all the restraints that kept the excesses of the SA in check were removed.

SA popularity threatens Nazi dominance

Hermann Göring, with Heinrich Himmler (whom Hitler had made chief of the secret police, the Gestapo, in Prussia in April 1934), began to counsel Hitler that he must make a determined move against the SA before Röhm struck first. Himmler considered Röhm and the SA to be a threat to his own SS and wanted the power of the SA brought under control in order to prevent a leadership struggle that he

FOLLOWING PAGES: SA Commander Ernst Röhm inspects his troops in Berlin in 1933.

felt had the potential to rip the party apart. The German High Command, which viewed the SA brownshirts as little more than vulgar, bloodthirsty thugs, also wanted Röhm and the SA leadership removed, especially in light of Röhm's publicly stated desire that a loyal, 'nazified' SA should merge with the conservative and 'ideologically suspect' *Reichswehr* and its class-ridden High Command. Even the country's conservative Vice-Chancellor Franz von Pappen urged Hitler to act. Although the SA was at the peak of its power, Röhm's stubborn independence had helped draw together some very powerful enemies.

Acting on the excuse that SA-led uprisings against the Nazi leadership in Berlin and the Bavarian capital of Munich were imminent, in the early hours of 30 June 1934 Hitler flew to Munich. With his entourage, he drove directly to the Bavarian Interior Ministry, where he ripped the epaulettes off the shoulders of Munich's chief of police, Obergruppenführer Schneidhuber, for failing to maintain order during an SA rampage through the city's streets the night before. After a group of SA stormtroopers were arrested and imprisoned on Hitler's orders, Hitler and a group of loyal SS members and a contingent of the Munich police drove to the Hotel Hanselbauer in the Bavarian spa town of Bad Wiessee where Röhm and the SA leadership were staying. The SA leadership consisted of far more than the stereotypical collection of street thugs and ideological misfits. Those who had risen to the top of the SA were often of high military standing and had trained and served in the old Imperial Army of Kaiser Wilhelm. One in three were professional soldiers whose years of service predated World War I, while two-thirds were decorated combat veterans of the war itself. They survived the brief communist revolution of 1918 that saw the overthrow of Kaiser Wilhelm, and in the early 1920s joined the fledgling SA movement because they possessed the leadership skills and military experience the SA was looking for. Hitler was of course well aware of the legacy of service to the nation the SA's leadership represented, but decided to move against it anyway, demonstrating to his rivals and to the world his ruthless treatment of anyone who opposed his autocratic rule, regardless of how good and loyal a German they might be.

Hitler's chauffeur, Erich Kempka, had flown with him to Munich and drove Hitler, at the head of a three-car motorcade, first to the Interior Ministry and then to Bad Wiessee to confront Röhm. The propaganda minister, Josef Goebbels, and the man Hitler has chosen to replace Röhm, Viktor Lutze, were sitting behind. Lutze had been involved in compiling the list of those SA leaders to be shot, but was not universally liked within the party. Goebbels himself once described him as possessing 'unlimited stupidity'. In an interview given in 1954, Kempka described what happened next.

Hitler confronts Röhm

Hitler asked Kempka to ignore any SA guards that might be placed around the hotel's perimeter and to drive straight to the entrance. Kempka was then told the reason for coming to Munich was that Röhm was planning a coup and that he and the SA leadership had to be 'removed'. Kempka could hardly believe his ears but barely had time to comprehend what was happening before he found himself rushing into the foyer alongside detectives from the Munich police force who had been following in the cars behind. Röhm's staff guard, Standartenführer Julius Uhl, was the first to be arrested and was locked away in the laundry room. Hitler himself, accompanied by two detectives with pistols drawn, went upstairs in search of Röhm, bursting into his room yelling: 'Röhm, you are under arrest'. Röhm, still in bed, pleaded his innocence but Hitler would have none of it. Röhm was spared incarceration in the laundry room. Instead he was taken down to the foyer, where he slumped into a large armchair and immediately ordered a black coffee. If, instead of a coffee, Röhm had decided to test the loyalty of his SA troops and ordered them to oppose their arrest, the history of Europe and of the world could have been very different.

SA leaders began emerging from their rooms and each was asked, individually, if they were participants in or had any knowledge of Röhm's supposed 'coup'. One by one, they denied any knowledge of it, but their protestations had little effect. The laundry room filled up with the accused. One of Röhm's most senior officers, Edmund Heines, was found to be in bed with another SA officer and both were executed on Hitler's orders. Homosexuality had long been a part of SA practice, and Röhm himself was openly acknowledged to be a homosexual.

A bus was ordered to take those arrested back to Munich. Remarkably there was no resistance. Then a group of armed SA men arrived in a lorry and Kempka recalled at that point feeling certain that the operation would erupt in gunfire. As Kempka moved his hand slowly towards his sidearm, to his astonishment Hitler strode up to the armed group, negotiated with its leader, then ordered him to take his men and return to Munich—and, what's more, if they encountered the SS on the way were to permit themselves to be disarmed.

The arrested SA officers were then led from the laundry room to a bus, followed by Röhm himself, who offered no resistance and barely acknowledged Hitler's presence as he was marched past him, head bowed in an acceptance of whatever fate awaited him. Hitler then asked Kempka to return to their car, and again at the head of a column that had by now grown to include more than twenty vehicles, began to head back towards Munich.

Not all were similarly treated, however. When Ernst Röhm's personal doctor, SA Gruppenführer Ketterer, and his wife, walked from their room Hitler approached them and, after greeting them both cordially, advised them to leave the hotel immediately and not return.

The murders begin

Over the following two days more than eighty-five of the SA hierarchy were murdered, although the actual number has been put as high as two hundred. Hitler also used the occasion to remove other selected opponents of the Nazi regime, including the man who preceded him as chancellor, Kurt von Schleicher, and Gregor Strasser, a former Nazi who had resigned from the party in 1932 after a dispute with Hitler over the political direction of the party. Strasser, a World War I veteran and Iron Cross recipient, was murdered in a prison cell in the basement of the Gestapo headquarters in Berlin, shot several times in the back of the head.

Ernst Röhm, the faithful Nazi who had stood by Hitler from the very beginning and against whom no charges or accusations of treason were ever proved, was taken to Munich's Stadelheim Prison, one of the country's largest gaols. Röhm was placed in cell 70, a celebrated address of sorts, whose previous occupants included the organiser of the overthrow of the Bavarian Wittelsbach monarchy in 1918, Kurt Eisner, and later Eisner's assassin, Anton Graf von Arco auf Valley, who was in turn moved to make room for Adolf Hitler, who called Stadelheim home for a month in 1922. Hitler was anything

Adolf Hitler addresses the nation in a public broadcast a few months after the assassinations.

but eager to kill his old comrade, but was unable to imprison him indefinitely and felt him too dangerous and knowledgeable about the workings of the party to send him into exile. On 2 July, at the personal request of Hitler, SS Brigadeführer Theodor Eicke, the commander of the Dachau concentration camp, and an SS officer, Michel Lippert, confronted Röhm in his cell and left behind a loaded Browning pistol with the instructions that he had ten minutes in which to shoot himself; if he didn't they would return and shoot him themselves. When ten minutes were up, Eiske and Lippert returned to the cell to find Röhm still alive. Lippert picked up the pistol and shot the former head of the SA at point blank range. Röhm slumped to the floor, dead.

In a speech before the German parliament, the Reichstag, on 13 July 1934, Hitler announced the purge to the nation, claiming that Röhm and his other 'conspirators' had come dangerously close to attempting to overthrow the government. His speech read in part:

In this hour I was responsible for the fate of the German people. I gave the order to shoot the ringleaders in this treason, and I further gave the order to cauterize down to the raw flesh the ulcers of this poisoning of the wells of our domestic life.

All rivals vanquished

Then, to ensure the legality of the massacre, retrospective legislation drafted by the former Bavarian and now German minister of justice Franz Gürtner was approved by cabinet on 3 July. It made clear that the suppression of treasonous acts with deadly force was a legal and acceptable response in the safeguarding of the state. There was little open dissent. The German high command applauded the action that effectively ended the political and military aspirations of their SA rival, and even the ailing Hindenburg sent Hitler a telegram— whether coerced or not it is impossible to say— congratulating him for his expeditious handling of the matter.

Hitler ordered the new commander of the SA, Viktor Lutze, to clamp down on the drunken excesses, the homosexuality and the extravagant lifestyle that had become synonymous within the upper echelons of the SA leadership.

The night of the long knives was a turning point both for the Nazi Party and for Adolf Hitler personally. From the night of the long knives onwards, Germany was under the leadership of a despot who in every respect was above the law, able to do and say whatever he pleased in the absence of any organised opposition that might have dared to stand in his way.

1942–43

1.5 MILLION LOST IN HISTORY'S BLOODIEST BATTLE

The Battle of Stalingrad is often considered the turning point of World War II in Europe. It was arguably the bloodiest battle in human history—with both Hitler and Stalin refusing to back down. With combined casualties estimated at more than 1.5 million, the battle was marked by brutality and disregard for military and civilian casualties on both sides. The battle was fought during the winter of 1942–43 and turned into a siege, with soldiers often fighting in hand-to-hand combat in a city reduced to rubble. Areas captured by the Germans during the day were re-taken by the Russians at night, and the stalemate in the bitter Russian winter led to starvation, frostbite, dysentery and typhus. Ultimately the battle at Stalingrad bled the German army in Russia dry.

THE BATTLE OF STALINGRAD

Die, but do not retreat.

JOSEPH STALIN, WAR SLOGAN

On 23 August 1942, a warm Sunday afternoon, as families picnicked on the hills overlooking their modern, showcase Soviet city, World War II came to Stalingrad. In previous weeks, as the German Nazi war machine had closed in, air-raid sirens had frequently sounded false alarms, so few citizens were prepared for the Luftwaffe's onslaught. Two days of carpet bombing began, creating a firestorm 56 kilometres (35 miles) long that incinerated the small wooden houses of the suburbs and gutted city buildings, claiming the lives of tens of thousands. Massive fuel tanks along the River Volga were hit, sending volcano-like columns of flame more than half a kilometre into the air. The Luftwaffe commander responsible for this carnage, General Wolfram von Richthofen (a distant cousin of World War I flying ace the Red Baron), surveyed his handiwork from the air when the bombardment was over. He wrote that Stalingrad had been 'destroyed and [was] now without any further worthwhile military targets'. As the elite German Sixth Army raced in to mop up what was left of the Soviet forces, it seemed to most that the fight for Stalingrad was all but over. But one of the bloodiest battles in history was only just beginning.

Hitler sets his sights on Stalingrad

The city of Stalingrad lay over 3200 kilometres (2000 miles) from the German border. What propelled the armies of the Axis powers (Germany and her European allies, Italy, Hungary and Romania) to that spot was 'the limitless character of Nazi aims', as one of Adolf Hitler's henchmen later said during the Nuremberg war crime trials. Not only were oil, land and minerals abundant, but Hitler also considered Russia to be Germany's ultimate enemy—the headquarters of both communism and the 'Jewish world-conspiracy'.

During the first two years of the war, Hitler maintained a non-aggression pact with Soviet leader Joseph Stalin while he conquered most of Europe and reached a stalemate in his struggle against Britain. In June 1941 he was at last ready to invade the Union of Soviet Socialist Republics (USSR). In what was possibly the most costly military mistake in history, he launched four and a half million soldiers across the border in an invasion that took the Soviets by surprise, largely because Stalin had dismissed all warnings (and obvious signs), thinking that the Allies were trying trick him into fighting the Nazis. The opening months saw millions of Soviet soldiers captured, along with the most fertile and developed western regions of the Soviet Union. The Axis forces came very close to taking Moscow, only to be repelled on the outskirts by massive counter-attacks. In the closing stages of that battle, winter descended with full force, almost literally freezing the invasion in its tracks for the next five months.

When campaigning resumed in the following spring of 1942, the focus was no longer Moscow but the oilfields near the Caspian Sea and the Volga that flowed into it. The river was Russia's main supply line, and Hitler planned to capture or destroy Stalingrad, the main city on the Volga, in order to cut this key artery and prevent the Soviets from defending their southern regions.

Hitler entrusted General Friedrich Paulus with the task of taking Stalingrad. Paulus was a former staff officer—a polite, impeccably well-groomed social climber with a passion for war games, whose hobby was making detailed maps of Napoleon's Russian campaigns. The general had proved to be an effective commander in recent battles on the vast Russian prairies and now, as the tattered Soviet armies pulled back towards Stalingrad, he advanced with over two hundred thousand highly skilled, well-equipped veterans at his command, along with the Fourth Panzer Army and the Fourth Air Fleet.

Stalin orders: 'cowards should be exterminated'

Ranged against him were fifty thousand Red Army personnel, a mixture of raw recruits and soldiers cobbled together from various shattered armies. They had to defend a city 56 kilometres (35 miles) long and 8.5 kilometres (5 miles) wide, spread along the west bank of a broad river. Desperate measures were enacted to halt the endless retreats. Stalin's Order 227 declared: 'Not one step back! ... It is necessary to defend every position, every metre of our territory, up to the last drop of blood ... cowards should be exterminated'. Accordingly, machine-gun battalions were placed behind the front lines, ready to mow down anyone who broke and ran from the Germans, while the Soviet secret police, the NKVD, executed more than thirteen thousand soldiers for disciplinary offences during the course of the battle.

As the Luftwaffe struck, turning the city into an inferno, the citizens were mobilised. The Stalingrad Defence Committee organised students, and most of the workers, into militias, urging the populace to turn 'each street, each house into an unassailable fortress'. With brutal logic, Stalin forbade the civilian evacuation of the city early in the battle, calculating that the militias would fight even harder knowing that their loved ones were trapped there.

What the militias lacked in weapons, uniforms and training, they often made up for with suicidal determination, and their sacrifices bought the Red Army precious time to assemble in the city behind them. The first units to resist the Germans were made up of women, who operated dozens of anti-aircraft batteries at Gumrak, on the western outskirts of the city. As the panzer tanks charged across the plain towards them, the women levelled their anti-aircraft flak guns at them, destroying many and forcing the panzers to call in air support. The flak crews had never been trained to fire at ground targets, but they stayed at their posts for days until their ammunition ran out and they were overrun. The Germans were horrified and embarrassed to discover that they had been fighting women.

The layout of the city prevented the typical German tactics from being deployed. Denied the option of surrounding the Soviets, Paulus planned to drive several large wedges into Stalingrad, pushing through to the river bank and then systematically mopping up the isolated units. Panzers raced through farmland and orchards on the edges of Stalingrad to reach the Volga, where they shelled the river traffic and fought off heavy counter-attacks. On 10 September, the Russian 62nd Army, ordered to hold the ruined city, found itself cut off from the other Soviet armies adjacent to Stalingrad, its only lifeline a river filling up with burning oil and bombed-out ships.

General Chuikov directs new tactics

Many on the Soviet side felt defeat was inevitable, including General Lopatin, commander of the 62nd Army. He was replaced by General Vasilii Chuikov, a rugged, crude and outspoken street-fighter from dirt-poor peasant stock. He had a broad, pockmarked face with a mouth full of glittering, gold-capped teeth and a deep booming laugh, and was so unkempt that he was frequently mistaken for a private. Chuikov crossed the river into the burning city, moving through the refugees and deserters crowding the river bank as he sought his headquarters on the Mamaev Kurgan—the ancient Tartar burial mound that formed a hill which overlooked the city.

On 13 September, Chuikov had barely settled in to his HQ when Paulus launched a massive, coordinated assault on the heart of the city. Intense air and artillery bombardment came first, forcing Chuikov to abandon the Mamaev Kurgan, which was overrun by German infantry later in the day. Chuikov was now in great danger, because the hill would allow German artillery to control the river crossing and strangle his army. Just in time, the ten thousand men of the elite Soviet 13th Guards Rifle Division—veterans of the Spanish Civil War—arrived. They scrambled up the river bank, overcoming German units which had reached the river but had not yet dug in. The guards made frantic assaults to retake the Mamaev Kurgan and several other key points, and they succeeded, saving the day. But almost a third of them were dead or badly wounded within twenty-four hours of arriving in Stalingrad.

Chuikov had to think on his feet and direct an army reduced to twenty thousand men to defend positions he had never seen, against a very determined foe.

He also had to do something about the Luftwaffe's overwhelming air superiority, as the Red Army planes were fewer, slower and piloted by inexperienced crews. Chuikov directed all Soviet frontlines to be no further than grenade-throwing distance from the Germans, which meant that the Luftwaffe could not drop bombs without hitting their own. He also favoured night attacks because, again, the Luftwaffe could not respond—and he wanted to heighten their terror.

Chuikov knew that the Germans were very efficient out in the open, where they could maintain their discipline and organisation and draw upon the support of tanks and planes, so he encouraged his men to form small squads and fight vicious hand-to-hand battles, armed with grenades, light machine-guns, and even knives and sharpened shovels.

Soviet lines ran right through the city, through parks, yards and squares, and were anchored by strong points—usually four- or five-storey buildings. As the German attackers moved around these strong points, aiming to encircle them, they would enter minefields and take fire from camouflaged Russian tanks, or suffer sudden ambushes from small assault squads.

In late September the focus of the battle shifted to the factory complexes in the north of the city. During this assault, many Soviet units were surrounded for days and even weeks, the most famous being Sergeant Pavlov's twenty-five soldiers, who fortified an apartment block in the middle of the city and successfully held out against daily attacks for fifty-eight days.

In November of 1942, temperatures fell to −40°C (−40°F). The climax of the battle was drawing near; Paulus knew that his air support would be drastically reduced in the worsening weather, and his men would have to prepare winter quarters. For now, though, as the Volga froze, the weather gave the German forces an advantage. Large ice floes made the river crossing increasingly treacherous for Soviet reinforcements. Paulus' final offensive began on 11 November. German soldiers fought their way through enemy lines down to the river bank behind the Red October factory, but many of the surrounded Soviets preferred to die rather than surrender.

Zhukov launches Operation Uranus

Well over 90 per cent of the city now lay in German hands, but the remaining defenders clung to the buildings along the river bank as this final assault lost its momentum. Soon it was broken off altogether, for an excellent reason. Operation Uranus (also known as Operation Uran), the great Soviet counter-attack, had begun.

On 18 November the new German chief of staff, Kurt Zeitzler, convinced the Red Army was on its last legs, declared, 'The Russians no longer have any reserves worth mentioning and are not capable of launching a large-scale offensive'. But the next day, roughly a million Soviet soldiers plunged into the overextended and undermanned German lines far to the west and south of Stalingrad. Hitler had driven Paulus so hard to win the battle that the latter had been forced to commit most of the available German tanks and troops in the area to take the city, leaving their less-trained, under-equipped Italian and Romanian allies to hold the long front out on the frozen plains. Russia's greatest general, Georgy Zhukov, planned the counter-attack and kept the scale of it a secret from almost everyone until the moment it was unleashed. Paulus ordered his panzer tank crews to beat back the attacks, but the tanks

held in reserve had been sitting idle in the snow, and most were now useless because rats and mice had eaten the insulation around the wiring in the engines. Three days after they began, the two great Soviet thrusts met up at the town of Kalach, and roughly three hundred thousand enemy soldiers were now caught in a vast pincer trap.

The besiegers had now become the besieged, caught in what the Germans called the *Kessel*, or cauldron. Paulus repeatedly requested permission from Hitler to break out of the Kessel, but this was never granted. Hitler had already made speeches declaring 'No one will shift us from the Volga', and Göring, commander of the Luftwaffe, ignored the doubts of his own staff and assured Hitler that the Sixth Army could be supplied by an airlift for as long as necessary. Luftwaffe crews desperately tried to carry out this task, but far too few planes made it through the blizzards, the anti-aircraft guns, and the rapidly improving Soviet air fleet. Trapped in the Kessel throughout the Russian winter, and running out of food, clothing, medical supplies and ammunition, the suffering of the German troops and their allies was extreme. Starvation, typhus, dysentery and frostbite claimed tens of thousands of lives, as did the constant attacks designed to force them to use up their ammunition and deny them any chance to rest. Additionally, the gun oil in German weapons froze, rendering most of them useless. The Russians—more experienced in low-temperature warfare—mixed petrol in with their gun oil to lower its freezing point, thus preserving the effectiveness of their weapons.

Dead on their feet, the Germans were soon too weak to break out, even if they had been given the order. In any case, they would have had to fight through chest-high snow for 64 kilometres (40 miles), in ragged clothing and carrying all their equipment.

Deserters started to cross over to Soviet lines in ever larger numbers, and around the airfields riots broke out as men tried to clamber onto outgoing aircraft, which were reserved for specialists and the wounded. Men sought to escape the Kessel by wounding themselves, or poking their hands up over the trenches to get the Soviets to do the job. But the military police guarding the airfields were aware of this ploy, and many soldiers grew even more desperate, shooting themselves (or each other) in the chest or abdomen instead.

German prisoners of war marching out from the Red October factory amidst the ruins of war-torn Stalingrad.

Surrender ... and a horrific toll

When Paulus requested permission to surrender in late January, Hitler told him, 'Capitulation is impossible. The Sixth Army will do its duty to the last man'. In an attempt to bribe Paulus to accept certain death, Hitler promoted him to field marshal, knowing that no German field marshal had ever surrendered. To his generals, Paulus remarked, 'I have no intention of shooting myself for that Bohemian corporal'. The next day, 31 January 1943, he surrendered, along with 23 generals, some 90,000 soldiers, 60,000 vehicles, 1500 tanks and 6000 artillery pieces. The toll had been horrific, almost too high to measure. Common estimates are that well over half a million casualties were suffered by the Germans and their allies, along with over a million Red Army casualties. No one knows how many civilians were killed, or how many escaped to safety, but the death toll certainly numbered in the hundreds of thousands, mostly as a result of indiscriminate Luftwaffe bombing. Stalingrad's population had been roughly 850,000 before the war; a 1945 census found only 1500 people in the city.

The battle was the turning point of World War II. The Germans never did return to the Volga or seize the oilfields they had coveted. Germany had never experienced a defeat like this, and it was now clear how the war would end. Germany's European allies—Italy, Hungary and Romania—had each lost almost an entire army in the battle, and they quietly began peace negotiations with the Soviets and the other Allies. And, on 2 May 1945, the Soviet Army would capture Berlin.

LEFT: Newly promoted Field Marshal Paulus walks to the Russian command to surrender, 1 February 1943.

THE MODERN TIMES

*LEFT: Nelson Mandela raises his fist
in triumph as he addresses a crowded
stadium in Soweto following his
release from prison in February 1990.*

1961

KENNEDY INVADES CUBA

The Bay of Pigs invasion was an unsuccessful attempt by US-backed Cuban exiles to overthrow the government of the Cuban dictator Fidel Castro. Increasing friction between the US government and Castro's leftist regime led President Dwight D. Eisenhower to break off diplomatic relations with Cuba in January 1961. The invasion plan was approved by Eisenhower's successor, John F. Kennedy. On 17 April 1961, about 1300 exiles, armed with US weapons, landed at the Bay of Pigs on the southern coast of Cuba. When it became evident that the operation was failing, Kennedy decided against backing it up with the air force. By the time the fighting ended on 19 April, ninety exiles had been killed and the rest had been taken as prisoners. The result was a complete deterioration in US–Cuban relations.

THE BAY OF PIGS INVASION

The evidence is clear—and the hour is late ...
Together we must build a hemisphere where freedom can
flourish; and where any free nation under outside attack
of any kind can be assured that all of our resources stand
ready to respond to any request for assistance.

PRESIDENT KENNEDY, PUBLIC ADDRESS, 20 APRIL 1961

The Bay of Pigs is a translation of the Spanish Bahiia de Cochinos and is the name given to a small bay in the Gulf of Cazones on the southern coastline of Cuba. Just 150 kilometres (93 miles) south of the Cuban capital of Havana, the Bay of Pigs is an insignificant stretch of sand, with coral reefs dominating its western approaches along the Zapata Swamp, with extensive mangroves and swampland to the east. In many ways it is a typical coastal inlet, no different from hundreds of others, and in 1961 few outside of the tiny village of Buena Ventura at the bay's northern end had ever heard of it. Events that spanned 14–20 April 1961, however, would soon put the name Bay of Pigs on the front pages of newspapers around the world and help to lay the political foundations for the later Cuban Missile Crisis.

In 1953 a little-known revolutionary and former lawyer named Fidel Castro led an assault on a government army barracks at Moncada, Cuba. The attack was a disaster and sixty of the one hundred and thirty-five men under his command were killed. Castro and many of those who survived, including his brother Raúl, were captured and tried. Almost all of those captured were later executed by the Batista regime, though in a stroke of good fortune a former university classmate who was an officer in the Cuban army had recognised Castro. Instead of being shot, Castro and his brother were given lenient sentences of fifteen years—and released after serving just two. The attack, in hindsight, marked the beginning of the Cuban Revolution and the eventual overthrow of the regime of the strongman Fulgencio Batista. Batista ran a corrupt and autocratic regime throughout the 1950s. He opened up Cuba to the Mafia and profited enormously from kickbacks from the Mob, for whom he provided unfettered access to his nation's racetracks and casinos. In a speech on 6 October 1960, US President John F. Kennedy accused Batista of murdering twenty thousand Cubans over a seven-year period. Cuba, it seemed, was ripe for revolution.

Cuban Revolution installs a socialist government

Upon his release Castro fled to Mexico where he met avowed Marxist, Argentinian revolutionary Ernesto 'Che' Guevara, and other Cuban exiles. As a response to the oppressive Batista regime they formed the 26th of July Movement and over

263

the next seven days sailed back to Cuba on the diesel-powered yacht *Granma*, arriving there on 2 December 1956. Named after the date of the failed assault on the Moncada Barracks, the 26th of July Movement grew to include some three hundred fighters who repeatedly were able to withstand the largely ineffective offensives of the numerically superior Cuban army. Che Guevara rose to become the organisation's second-in-command, assisted in training the insurgents and played a key role in the two-year campaign that would eventually see the end of the Batista regime. A series of victories over Batista's forces through 1958 saw Castro's revolutionaries grow in number and emerge from their stronghold in the Sierra Maestra Mountains to march towards the capital, Havana. Castro's forces took Havana and overthrew Batista on 1 January 1959.

The Cold War climate that prevailed at the time of Castro's socialist revolution—occurring as it did in a country just 150 kilometres (93 miles) from the Florida coast—ensured that it would be viewed as an unacceptable development by American strategists and the intelligence community. The US mood towards Cuba was summed up by no less than President Dwight D. Eisenhower, who warned: 'if the United States does not conduct itself in precisely the right way vis-à-vis Cuba, we could lose all of South America'. Eisenhower was also concerned that revolutionaries in Mexico would take heart from events in Havana and begin an uprising of their own. Speaking of Mexico, Eisenhower added: 'if we were to see the Communists come to power there, in all likelihood we would have to go to war'. In this era of Cold War paranoia, the US government was seeing communist threats not only in eastern Europe or Vietnam, but in places uncomfortably close to home.

US government campaigns to overthrow Castro

On 17 March 1960 Eisenhower authorised the Central Intelligence Agency (CIA) to initiate the covert training of an initial three hundred Cuban exiles as well as the establishment of an anti-Castro political coalition, the support of anti-establishment activities within Cuba itself, and the creation of an extensive propaganda campaign. The US government also engaged in attempts to subvert the Cuban economy and to isolate it diplomatically, particularly from the governments of Latin America.

The broadcasting of propaganda began from a CIA transmission tower on a small island off the Honduran coast on 17 May. Within the CIA, discussion had begun on not merely how best to overthrow Castro—but how best to kill him. CIA plotters initiated scheme after scheme for either killing or neutralising the Cuban leader, with each plot more fanciful and comic than the last. One approach was to attack his masculinity by somehow sprinkling thallium salts on his shoes, in the hope the salt's depilatory compounds would cause his beard to fall out and so erode his credibility with the Cuban people. Another CIA operative wanted to plant a device in the Castro's favourite dive spot, and detonate it by remote control as he swam by. All of these strategies beg the question: if a CIA operative could get close enough to sprinkle salts on Castro's shoes or plant an exploding seashell in his favorite dive spot, why not simply point a gun at his head and pull the trigger?

In August 1960 Eisenhower approved additional expenditure of $13 million for the anti-Castro campaign. The number of Cuban exiles had grown to a force of approximately fourteen hundred; however, Eisenhower was becoming frustrated at the CIA's inability to unite the anti-Castro factions both at home and

Fidel Castro and fellow revolutionaries in the Sierra Maestro Mountains in 1957.

in Cuba. In the 1960 presidential campaign, fought between Senator John Kennedy and Vice President Richard Nixon, Kennedy frequently argued that the Republicans had 'lost Cuba to Communism'. Any instability in the region, such as political upheaval in Guatemala in which a group of junior military officers fled to Cuba after failing to overthrow their pro-US leader, had the US immediately suspicious of Cuban involvement. In November, John Kennedy defeated Richard Nixon by the narrowest margin in US history; and by the time he assumed the presidency on 20 January 1961, the push to remove Castro had already long been the subject of intense organisation and considerable expenditure.

Planning confidently proceeds

That the US government once seemed to believe that landing a group of fourteen hundred trained Cuban exiles in the Bay of Pigs would end in regime change (when Castro had a standing army of twenty to thirty thousand to call upon and between four thousand and five thousand armed police) seems barely credible. Speculation that if Eisenhower had been president, his years of military experience would likely have resulted in his cancelling the entire mission, may seem a moot point. Nevertheless, Kennedy was desperate to gain an early foreign policy victory and demonstrate his credentials as being as tough on communism as his predecessors. The fact that British intelligence reports at the time made it clear that Castro enjoyed great support, particularly among Cuba's rural population, and that any invasion was most unlikely to result in a counter-revolution, also highlights the considerably over-optimistic assessment of the invasion's chances of success.

If sufficient forces had landed there in the first place, the Bay of Pigs would have made an ideal choice as a landing site and afforded every possibility of success. The bay was at the northernmost end of a 33-kilometre (20-mile) inlet that projected into the midst of the Cuban hinterland and was protected by extensive swamplands that would have made it difficult for Castro to mobilise and deploy his motorised divisions. Nevertheless, on 14 April the fourteen hundred Cubans left their training base in Guatemala and crossed the border into Honduras where they boarded a small flotilla of vessels that would take them east across the Caribbean to Cuba. On 15 April the first of three planned air raids took place. Obsolete World War II–era B-26 bombers, crewed by former Cuban pilots and disguised to look like Cuban aircraft, attacked three airfields in the hope of neutralising the Cuban air force—but the attack inflicted only minimal damage and left Cuba's air force almost wholly intact. Kennedy had halved the number of planes that would take part from sixteen to eight; he had also cancelled two subsequent air strikes (to be launched from the deck of the aircraft carrier USS *Essex* stationed nearby), possibly in response to bellicose threats of an escalation of the conflict from Soviet Premier Nikita Khrushchev. These decisions would later be given as a primary reason for the failure of the operation. After the first assault Castro ordered his pilots to sleep beneath the wings of their aircraft and be ready to take to the air at a moment's notice.

Invasion fleet lands at Playa Larga

Finally, on 16 April, after two unsuccessful diversionary landings the day before, the invasion fleet comprising five armed freighters and two landing craft (LCIs) was escorted to a point 65 kilometres (40 miles) south of the Bay of Pigs by a veritable bevy of US destroyers. At midnight on 17 April the two LCIs, together with four transport ships carrying tanks and various other armoured vehicles, cruised up the Bay of Pigs. The initial landing by the Cuban Expeditionary Force (CEF), also known as Brigade 2506, was a success even though the landing craft foundered on their way through the coral reefs and lost the element of surprise. Nevertheless the token militia forces defending the head of the bay were easily overrun, although it quickly became apparent that the hoped-for support from the local Cuban population would not be forthcoming, as the earlier reports from British intelligence had warned. (The area had done particularly well under Castro's revolution, with the construction of several new roads, a successful literacy campaign and the development of small-scale tourist infrastructure that brought some belated and much needed employment to the region.)

At 3.15 am Castro was woken from his sleep and told an enemy force was landing at Playa Larga (Red Beach). He ordered several platoons of armed militia, a contingent of nine hundred men stationed by a nearby sugar mill, three mortar batteries and several battalions from nearby Las Villas Province to intercept the invaders.

Cuban Air Force strike hits US ships

At daybreak on 17 April two T-33 jets and three Sea Furies belonging to the Cuban air force appeared overhead and attacked the transport *Houston* as it was in the process of unloading its men and equipment. The *Houston*'s captain, Luis Morse, beached the ship on the western shoreline of the Bay of Pigs. One hundred exiles on board the *Houston* were killed while the remaining one hundred and seventy-five had their supplies and guns destroyed and were forced to return to their destroyer escorts. The *Rio Escondido*, a freighter with almost two weeks'

supply of gasoline and 145 tons of ammunition and provisions, was hit amidships and exploded in a massive fireball. The loss of the *Houston* and the *Rio Escondido* and their cargoes all but doomed the invasion then and there. Signalling equipment aboard the *Rio Escondido* was lost in the attack, which hampered ground contact with Washington by those troops able to get ashore. In the absence of any air support, the remaining vessels abandoned their landing operations and put to sea for safety. Meanwhile Castro's Matanzas Cadet Battalion retook the nearby town of Palpite, prompting Castro to declare: 'We've already won the war!' By the morning of 18 April, the situation was grim and not getting any better.

An attempt to land the one hundred and seventy-seven men of Brigade 2506's parachute regiment on the road to Palpite also met with disaster, when most of their heavy equipment landed in swampland and couldn't be retrieved. Other attempts to land troops at critical road junctions were more successful. Drops at San Blas and Horquitas saw Brigade 2506 troops hold their positions for two days until the fighting finally came to an end on 19 April.

Meanwhile, elements of the Cuban armed forces, supported by Russian T-34 tanks, continued to advance on other fronts towards the bay, steadily pushing the invaders back towards the water. Cuban reserves continued to arrive throughout 17 April, bringing with them 122-millimetre howitzers and various light artillery that, when combined with the air cover provided by Cuba's T-33 Lockheed fighters, proved to be more than enough firepower to doom any hope the CEF may have had of being able to organise an effective retreat. On 19 April, with no air support and facing an increasing barrage from Cuban artillery and ground troops, the remaining men of Brigade 2506 surrendered.

Castro triumph a humiliation for Kennedy

Total Cuban losses, including militia and various armed civilians, were estimated at two thousand two hundred killed with as many as three thousand wounded and missing. Ninety Cuban exiles had been killed and approximately twelve hundred taken prisoner. Some died from asphyxiation while being transported to Havana in a closed, airtight van, and five were eventually executed after being tried and found guilty of murder and various other

President Kennedy faces the media at a press conference on 21 April about the attempted invasion of Cuba.

capital crimes. The majority of the prisoners, however, were released twenty months later after intensive negotiations—which opened with an offer by Castro to return the prisoners in exchange for more than five hundred farm tractors and which grew to eventually see the US provide Cuba with $53 million worth of food and pharmaceutical supplies.

In the end, President Kennedy took full blame for the Bay of Pigs fiasco, as propriety and his high office suggested he should. Privately, however, he seethed with anger towards the CIA and fired the three executives responsible for planning the attack: Director Allen Dulles, Deputy Director General Charles Pearre Cabell and Deputy Director of Operations Richard Bissell. Kennedy also began to make plans to take the responsibility for the planning of military operations away from the CIA.

In the end the Bay of Pigs invasion was a disaster for the new Kennedy administration and a triumph for Castro. Kennedy was humiliated whereas Castro's oft-foretold invasion of Cuba by the United States had not come to pass—and his popularity with the Cuban people reached new heights. Castro also used the invasion as a pretext for eliminating any remaining vestiges of political opposition and arrested an estimated three hundred thousand suspected political opponents. With Castro's position strengthened, the increased likelihood that his revolution would now succeed also convinced the Soviet Union that they could exploit the perceived weakness of the new American president and form an alliance with Cuba that would ultimately lead, in October 1962, to the Cuban Missile Crisis, described by some as the closest the world ever came to nuclear war.

1972

MASSACRE AT THE GAMES

In 1972 the Olympics were held in Germany for the first time since 1936, intended to present a new, democratic and optimistic Germany to the world, as shown by the official motto of the Happy Games. However, on the morning of 5 September, with six days of competition left, eight Palestinian terrorists broke into the Olympic village and raided the Israeli athletes' rooms. Two Israeli athletes were killed and nine more were seized as hostages. After a day of unsuccessful negotiations, the terrorists took the hostages to the airport and demanded a plane. German sharpshooters opened fire, killing three of the Palestinians. A horrifying gun battle ensued, claiming the lives of all nine of the hostages, along with one policeman and two terrorists.

THE MUNICH OLYMPICS TERRORIST ATTACK

When I was a kid my father used to say 'Our greatest hopes and our worst fears are seldom realised'. Our worst fears have been realized tonight. They have now said there were eleven hostages; two were killed in their rooms yesterday morning, nine were killed at the airport tonight. They're all gone.

JIM MCKAY, ABC NEWS AMERICA, 6 SEPTEMEBER 1972

At 9 pm on the evening of 4 September 1972 nine men assembled at a restaurant in Munich's central railway station. Eight of them had arrived in the German city of Munich in pairs, shortly after the commencement of the Games of the twentieth Olympiad. A ninth, Abu Daoud, a Palestinian Liberation Organisation (PLO) militia leader and member of the militant group Black September, had helped plan the assault that would soon take place and was now in Munich to give his assassins one last, final briefing.

The men selected for their 'unspecified mission' were mostly young Palestinians known as *shababs*, recruited from various refugee camps throughout Lebanon and flown to Libya in North Africa where they trained in hand-to-hand combat. Daoud had spent the earlier part of the evening stuffing eight bags, each with the Olympic logo clearly visible, with weaponry including Russian-made AK-47 Kalashnikov assault rifles and hand grenades, food, nylon stockings to disguise their identities, lengths of pre-cut rope for binding their victims and first-aid kits.

Two days prior to the opening ceremonies, Daoud and Luttif Afif (also known as 'Issa'), the Palestinian commander, had lied their way into the village, pretending to be Brazilians with a lifelong dream to one day visit the Jewish nation—and were shown around the Israeli apartments by an unsuspecting member of the Israeli delegation. They took note of the configuration of the apartments, the location of stairwells, telephones, windows, and the various exit and entry points of the complex, and when they were finished were given a handful of miniature Israeli flags to take back to Brazil. That night in the railway restaurant, Daoud and Issa told the young Palestinian *shababs* that from that moment onwards they should consider themselves to be dead—killed pursuing the PLO's objective of establishing a Palestinian state in Israel. They were each given a duffel bag and a track suit, on the back of which was printed the name of an Arab nation; they gave Abu Daoud their passports and, some time after 3 am, left the restaurant in taxis bound for the Olympic Village.

The Israeli team arrives

When the Israeli Olympic team boarded their flight in Israel bound for the Munich Olympics, twenty-seven years had passed since the end of World War II. Israeli participation in the

German games was significant. Several of the twenty-three Israeli athletes and officials had lost family members in the Holocaust. The horrors perpetrated by the Nazi regime were still fresh and vivid, and the West German government was keen for the world to see their divided nation as having come to terms with its past and facing the future with optimism and hope.

When the Israeli team arrived there was a joyful and almost cavalier atmosphere throughout the Olympic Village. Security was deliberately lax and passes were often ignored. Some athletes were even seen scaling the village's 1.8-metre- (6-foot-) high perimeter fencing to bypass the official checkpoints. In addition, as if to emphasise the fact that the nation had moved away from its militaristic past, there was not a single armed guard to be seen anywhere. Adding to the concerns of Shmuel Lalkin, the head of the Israeli delegation, the Israeli team would be housed in 31 Connollystrasse, a small building near an access gate in an isolated part of the village that would be difficult to defend in the unlikely event of an assault. Not entirely oblivious to the likelihood of a breach of security, the German authorities had drawn up a list of twenty-six possible threat scenarios, of which Scenario 21 eerily paralleled the shocking events that were to come—but it was dismissed by security analysts as simply too unlikely to be taken seriously.

On the evening of 4 September the Israeli team returned to their rooms late, after attending a performance of the musical *Fiddler On The Roof* and, later, posing for a group photograph.

The terrorists gain entry to the village

Just after 4 am in the morning on 5 September, five Palestinians belonging to the Black September terrorist organisation scaled the chain wire fence that surrounded the Olympic Village and rendezvoused with three accomplices who had already gained access. The five men had concealed their weapons in athletic bags and, although several witnesses watched as they climbed over, there seemed nothing overtly suspicious or out of place, as athletes had been routinely scaling the makeshift fence since day one of the games without incident. The eight men then used stolen keys to gain access to the apartments that housed the Israeli team.

At just after 4.30 am in apartment 1 the team's wrestling official, Yossef Gutfreund, heard a series of scratches at the door and went to investigate. To his horror he was confronted by three masked gunmen. He immediately used his 135-kilogram (300-pound) bulk to keep the door closed long enough to shout out to his teammates to get out any way that they could. Weightlifting coach Tuvia Sokolovsky leaped from the balcony to safety, thanks to Gutfreund's heroic efforts to keep the terrorists at bay. After ten seconds or so of stubborn resistance they were able with their Kalashnikov assault weapons to pry open the door and force Gutfreund to the floor—but Gutfreund had been able to hold the door closed long enough to allow Sokolovsky to run across an open patch of lawn and take refuge behind a garden bed. Sokolovsky later recalled how he could hear the 'whizzing' of bullets flying past his ears as he fled.

Chaos and horror in apartment 1

Chaos erupted throughout the apartment. Amitzur Shapira, Israel's premier track and field coach and father of four children, was hauled from his bed, as was Kehat Shorr, a Romanian who had fought against the Nazis and lost his wife and daughter in the Holocaust. In 1963 Shorr emigrated to Israel and became the coach of its national shooting team. When the terrorist group's commander Luttif Afif (soon to be known the world over as 'the man in the white hat') burst into the bedroom of burly wrestling coach Moshe Weinberg, Weinberg responded swiftly. He grabbed a knife from his bedside table and lunged at Afif, slicing open the breast pocket of his jacket and wrestling him to the floor. As the

two were struggling another terrorist entered the room and shot Weinberg through the mouth.

The athletes and officials, including Weinberg, then had their wrists and ankles bound and were forced up the stairs into the bedroom shared by Jacov Springer, a weightlifting judge, and Andre Spitzer, the Romanian-born fencing master who had arrived in Munich only the

The Israeli delegation parades during the opening ceremony on 26 August, eleven days before the attack.

previous evening. Spitzer had earlier amazed his fellow athletes by walking up to a group of Lebanese athletes in the Olympic Village to ask them about their results. Israel was at war with its northern neighbour, Lebanon, but Spitzer believed that the Olympic ideals of brotherhood and of the unifying power of sport embedded in the Olympic Charter would be more than capable of overcoming the politics of division and hate. The Lebanese group greeted Spitzer warmly, asking him about his results and wishing him well. It was exactly how Andre Spitzer had always dreamed the Olympic Games would be, and he returned to his teammates full of optimism and hope for a better world.

After securing the hostages in the first apartment the terrorists began their search for more hostages. Inexplicably walking past apartment 2, which housed five athletes including Shaul Ladany, a race walker who had survived the horrors of the Bergen-Belsen concentration camp, they moved on to apartment 3, cocked their weapons and burst in.

Further hostages—and an escape

Inside apartment 3 were the weightlifters David Berger, Zeev Friedman, Eliezer Halfin, Yossef Romano, Gad Tsabari and the most gifted and youngest member of the team, eighteen-year-old Mark Slavin, who in 1972 prior to emigrating to Israel had become the top middleweight Greco-Roman wrestler in the Soviet Union. Some had been woken by the gunshot that had injured Weinberg but had failed to recognise the sound for what it was. As the group was being led back to apartment 1, Tsabari, with no way of knowing whether he would be murdered or simply be used as a bargaining chip in a political

LEFT: Dramatic images of the siege were broadcast around the world as the hostage crisis was played out.

negotiation, made a bold bid for freedom. As the group passed a stairway that led down to an underground parking lot, Tsabari shoved aside one of the masked gunmen and threw himself down the stairs. With a terrorist in hot pursuit, the pillars and support columns of the car park provided Tsabari with the cover he needed to make good his escape. Attempting to take advantage of the melee, Weinberg also tried to break free, but was not as fortunate. Despite disarming one of his captors Weinberg was killed in the ensuing scuffle. As the hostages were being taken into apartment 1, Yossef Romano, a Libyan-born weightlifter and hero of the 1967 Six Day War, was killed as he too attempted to disarm one of the terrorists.

At 5.08 am two sheets of paper were thrown from the apartment's second-storey balcony. They listed the names of 234 prisoners who were incarcerated in Israeli gaols. The terrorists demanded that they be released by 9 am—a hopelessly unrealistic demand—and warned that if this were not done they would begin to execute their hostages at the rate of one every hour and throw the bodies into the street for the world to see.

West Germany's response to the crisis

The immediate West German response was to gather together a crisis team comprising the interior minister Hans-Dietrich Genscher, his Bavarian counterpart Bruno Merk and Munich chief of Police Manfred Schreiber. Together they struggled to formulate a response. Schreiber offered the terrorists an exorbitant amount of money. Genscher pleaded with them not to cause the spilling of yet more Jewish blood on German soil and even offered himself in return for the hostages' release. Hopes of sending in police disguised as chefs were abandoned when the terrorists ordered all deliveries of food and supplies to be dropped at the entrance to the building's foyer.

Discussions with terrorists prove futile

At 8.45 am the mayor of the Olympic Village, Walther Troga, Schreiber and an Egyptian International Olympic Committee (IOC) official were allowed into apartment 1 to discuss the details of the terrorists' demands and to meet the hostages. As they approached the apartment block the archetypal image of the kidnappings, the image of a terrorist on the second floor balcony with a balaclava over his head to hide his identity, was flashed around the world. Schreiber remembered being incensed that the man had pointed a machine gun directly at him. 'Towards *me*! The Munich Police Chief!' he later recounted indignantly. Once the German officials were inside, it quickly became apparent there would be no negotiating the hostages' safe release. Issa kept repeating his demands 'in a staccato-like fashion', Schreiber later recalled. 'He sounded like one of those people who aren't completely anchored in reality or totally aware'.

Plans to infiltrate via the heating ducts were also abandoned when it was realised television cameras were broadcasting police attempts to enter the building's air-conditioning system live to the entire world—including the television sets being watched closely by the athletes' captors. As negotiations progressed the initial 9 am deadline was extended, first to 3 pm and then to 5 pm, when the terrorists issued a fresh demand to be flown with their hostages to Cairo, where they believed the chances of negotiating a release of the 234 prisoners in Israel would have a greater chance of success. Issa issued his demands to the German negotiators: they were all to be taken to an airport and transferred onto a waiting plane; he expected the freed prisoners in Israel to be on the runway at Cairo airport by 8 am the following morning; and, if the prisoners were not delivered, all the hostages would be executed.

Adding to the tension, no one in the German government, including Chancellor Willy Brandt, was able to get Egyptian president Anwar Sadat to answer the phone and discuss the possibility of Egypt providing a more optimistic haven for the negotiations. Eventually Brandt got through to Egyptian prime minister Aziz Sidky, but he failed to provide Brandt with a promise that if the hostages were flown to Cairo they would not be harmed. In the absence of a guarantee of the hostages' safety, Brandt felt unable to permit them to be taken off German soil. The mood of the negotiators in Munich had become one of total despair. For better or worse, it seemed, the drama was destined to unfold before their eyes in the Bavarian capital. The negotiators were reluctantly forced to take the view that the only possible alternative to a bloodbath was to allow the kidnappers to believe a plane had been prepared for them, and hope that an opportunity to act would somehow surface.

At 10.10 pm a bus pulled up at the doors of the apartment complex and took the terrorists and their hostages to two waiting Iroquois helicopters, thus depriving the German sharpshooters the chance of any clear shots. German authorities in a third helicopter preceded the two Iroquois to the NATO airbase at Fürstenfeldbruck. Meanwhile, in the back of the aircraft waiting for the terrorists at the airfield, a so-called strike force was concealed. Incredibly, they had just taken a vote to abandon the mission—and had failed to consult or inform their superior officers about this extraordinary action. As a legacy of World War II, Germany had no special forces units trained to handle such a situation and the lack of professionalism would eventually doom the hostages. All that now threatened the terrorists at Fürstenfeldbruck were two Bavarian riot police and three Munich police officers (none of them sharpshooters) positioned on the roofs of the airport buildings, and chosen simply because they belonged to clubs that shot competitively on weekends.

Siege ends at Fürstenfeldbruck airfield

At 10.35 pm the two helicopters arrived at Fürstenfeldbruck and their pilots emerged, accompanied by six kidnappers. Issa immediately inspected the waiting jet. On discovering that the plane was crewless and realising he had been deceived, Issa ran back to the helicopters and ordered their pilots be held at gunpoint. At 11 pm the German snipers opened fire, killing two terrorists. The German pilots escaped to safety in the confusion, but policeman Anton Fliegerbauer, stationed in the airport's control tower, was hit and killed. When a number of armoured personnel carriers arrived just after midnight, Issa seemed to have realised his time was up and murdered Friedman, Springer and Halfin. He then threw a grenade into one of the helicopters, which exploded and incinerated all those inside. Although events at this point are somewhat blurry, the consensus is that another kidnapper, Adnan Al-Gashey, killed the remaining five hostages in the second helicopter. None survived.

Three hostages were arrested on the tarmac, all of them feigning death, while a fourth was cornered in a nearby parking lot and shot dead by police.

Abu Daoud, the mastermind behind the massacre, avoided all Israeli attempts to kill him and lives today in Syria. He published his autobiography, *Palestine: From Jerusalem to Munich*, in 1999.

1974

WATERGATE SCANDAL BRINGS DOWN THE PRESIDENCY

During the 1972 US presidential campaign five burglars were arrested in the Democratic Party headquarters at the Watergate office complex in Washington, DC. They were subsequently linked to the White House. At first President Richard Nixon downplayed the scandal but journalistic investigations gained momentum, and the government also ran its own investigation. On 5 August 1974, a secret tape was released showing that Nixon had tried to use the CIA to block the FBI's work in investigating the Watergate scandal. Within days Nixon was forced to resign—the only president in American history to have done so.

THE NIXON RESIGNATION

When the President does it, that means that it's not illegal.

PRESIDENT NIXON INTERVIEW, 19 MAY 1977

Richard Milhous Nixon entered public life in America as a congressman from California in 1946, before being elected to the Senate in 1950. Chosen as Dwight D. Eisenhower's running mate in 1952, he served as the nation's vice president under Eisenhower for two terms before becoming his party's choice to face the Democratic senator from Massachusetts, John F. Kennedy, in the 1960 presidential election. Defeated by Kennedy in the closest result in US history, Nixon continued to fight enthusiastically for Republican causes and candidates in the years that followed, including the disastrous and always doomed Goldwater campaign of 1964, travelling across America and speaking at countless Republican rallies and fundraisers. In 1968 he was given his party's endorsement as their presidential candidate in the upcoming November elections and defeated his Democratic opponent Hubert Humphrey by just 500,000 votes. On 20 January 1969 he was sworn in as the nation's thirty-seventh president.

Richard Nixon spent his entire adult life making speeches, and in the process gave Americans some of the most memorable moments in postwar politics. No speech, however, could compare to the one he gave on 9 August 1974, his last day in office, his presidency having been consumed and eventually destroyed by the Watergate scandal—many of his former aides were in jail, and his own reputation was in tatters.

One final, memorable speech

On his final morning in office, Richard Nixon spoke for the last time as president to his cabinet and the assembled White House staff. He said how he wished he'd been by their offices a little more, to ask them about their work, to shake their hands and ask their advice on 'how to run the world'. He just didn't have the time, he said. Sniffling continually, Nixon fought his emotions as his wife Pat and daughters Trisha and Julie looked on, realising their husband and father was at last speaking from the heart after a lifetime of rhetoric and debates, letting America see him as he really was. He spoke of how no one in his administration, not one man or one woman, profited as a result of being there. 'Not one single man or woman,' he said. His mannerisms were different. The political colossus of America's postwar years seemed close to tears.

He spoke of his father's lemon ranch with affection and a rare dose of comic timing. 'It was the poorest lemon ranch in California I can assure you. (Pause.) He sold it before they found oil on it.' The room was engulfed in laughter. His voice broke as he spoke of his mother, whom he called 'a saint', losing two sons to tuberculosis, and with a halting voice said what a tragedy it was that she would likely have no books written about her. After a lifetime of not allowing the world to see the man beneath the politician, and in the wake of his resignation speech to the nation the previous evening, Nixon was finally baring his soul. Grown men in the audience were crying. Nixon had saved the greatest speech by an American political figure in the twentieth century for his final hours as president, speaking for over twenty minutes without notes. 'Always give your best. Never get discouraged. Never be petty. Always remember: others may hate you, but those who hate you don't win unless you hate them, and then … you destroy yourself'.

Richard Nixon was the most complex, contradictory and paradoxical man ever to occupy the White House. Was this speech, as eloquent and moving as it was, an insight into the real man, or was it—as the former White House aide, author and speechwriter William Safire once said—just one last, final expression of a man with more layers than a layer cake, an enigma that defied explanation?

Nixon's 1972 landslide win

In the 1972 presidential election the incumbent Richard Milhous Nixon defeated the Democratic challenger George McGovern in a landslide. Nixon received 18 million more votes than the senator from South Dakota, won forty-nine out of fifty states, and his victory margin of more than 23 per cent was the fourth highest in US history. Almost from the moment McGovern announced his candidacy there was never any real doubt who would win. Nixon had wrestled with how best to extricate the United States from the mess that was Vietnam, had established a relationship with the People's Republic of China, and his administration was presiding over a healthy economy. The irony of what would become known as Watergate is that if ever a president *didn't* need to covertly acquire information on his opponents and engage in

political dirty tricks in order to win an election, he was the one. Nixon was always going to win in a landslide.

On 17 June 1972 five men were arrested breaking into the offices of the Democratic National Committee in the Watergate hotel and office complex in Washington, DC. The story was broken by two *Washington Post* reporters, Carl Bernstein and Bob Woodward, and the trail of laundered money, wiretapping, corruption and various abuses of power led first to the Committee to Re-Elect the President (CREEP), and eventually all the way to the White House itself.

The suspicions of the *Post* reporters were further raised in August when a cashier's cheque for $25,000 ended up in the bank account of one of the Watergate burglars, Bernard Barker. Then, in September, they broke the story that the former US attorney-general, John Mitchell, now Nixon's campaign manager, had been in control of a Republican slush fund that saw money appropriated for intelligence gathering operations. Mitchell vehemently refuted the claim. 'That's the most sickening thing I've ever heard', he was quoted as saying.

Conspiracy, burglary and wiretapping

An FBI investigation in October concluded that the break-in was the result of a larger, coordinated campaign of sabotage and excess by the Nixon re-election committee, and in January 1973 two members of the committee, G. Gordon Liddy and James McCord, were found guilty on eight charges of conspiracy, burglary and wiretapping by Judge John Sirica, Chief Justice for the US District Court for the District of Columbia. In April, the fallout reached deep into the White House itself when three of Nixon's most senior advisors, H. R. Haldeman,

John Ehrlichman and John Dean III, as well as Attorney-General Richard Kleindienst, offered their resignations. Nixon accepted them because, as he said the following day in a live telecast to the nation, 'There can be no whitewash at the White House', and promised he would act to purge American politics of the sort of abuses that had occurred on his watch. Nixon appointed his defense secretary Elliott Richardson as attorney-general in place of Kleindienst and gave him specific instructions to uncover 'the whole truth' of the scandal that was engulfing his administration. Nixon himself, however, was far more involved in the cover-up than he was prepared to admit.

On 18 May the Senate Watergate Committee, a special committee set up to investigate the burglary and other aspects of the scandal, began a series of nationally televised hearings, but the sort of explosive testimony some were hoping

President Nixon in happier times—campaigning for a second term in the 1972 election that he won in a landslide.

for was slow in coming to the surface. Jules Witcover, a *Washington Post* staff writer, likened the opening day's proceedings to watching grass grow, a boring ordeal of 'snail's pace testimony' and 'yawn-inspiring recounting'.

The Oval Office is implicated

On 3 June, however, the trail at last led directly into the Oval Office when John Dean, Nixon's former special advisor, acknowledged to prosecutors and Senate investigators that the President had discussed aspects of the Watergate cover-up with him on at least thirty-five occasions between January and April, and agreed to testify at upcoming Senate hearings, regardless of whether or not he would be granted immunity from prosecution. In another damning *Washington Post* exposé, Woodward and Bernstein quoted reliable sources as saying Dean had confessed to investigators that Haldeman and Ehrlichman had both been present in the Oval Office with Nixon when details of the cover-up were discussed. Then on 17 July it was revealed Nixon had been secretly tape-recording his conversations in the Oval Office, Cabinet room and the Executive Office Building since the spring of 1971, and that a telephone in the Lincoln sitting room in the White House and another on the presidential desk at his retreat at Camp David, Maryland, had also been modified.

Although much was made of Nixon's clandestine wiretapping, the practice was hardly new to Washington. Wiretapping began with Roosevelt in 1940 and every president since has made use of it. Truman endorsed wiretaps in matters of domestic security and presidents Kennedy and Johnson authorised wiretaps on Martin Luther King Junior. Nixon's conversations, however, would later prove to be damning indictments of his involvement in the cover-up. On 18 July he reportedly ordered the system to be disconnected, and on 23 July he refused requests to turn the tapes over to the Senate Watergate Committee.

The so-called Saturday Night Massacre of 20 October represented the most traumatic and far-reaching development in the crisis to date. Nixon discharged special prosecutor Archibald Cox (the former Harvard lawyer who had been appointed special prosecutor by Attorney-General Elliot Richardson to investigate the alleged Watergate cover-up), and on the same day accepted the resignations of Attorney-General Richardson and his deputy, William Ruckelshaus, after they refused his order to fire Cox. With the demise of the office of special prosecutor, all investigations and prosecution of suspects became the responsibility of the Justice Department. The crisis had been precipitated by a directive from Nixon to Cox not to request any further tapes beyond those Nixon had already agreed to provide. Cox replied he was unable to comply with the president's request, and Nixon, after failing in his attempts to get Richardson and Ruckelshaus to sack Cox, exercised his own executive authority and promptly discharged him. Late that night Cox issued a statement which read in part: 'Whether ours shall continue to be a government of laws and not of men is now for Congress and ultimately the American people'.

Nixon meets the press

The noose was tightening around the president. On 17 November, in the face of persistent questioning over his personal finances, Nixon was compelled to go on television in an hour-long question-and-answer forum with hundreds of journalists and editors from the Associated Press, during which he said: 'People have got to know whether or not their President is a crook. Well, I'm not a crook. I've earned everything I've got.' When asked what occupation he might pursue when he left office, after joking that that would depend upon when he left, Nixon replied that he would like to write or perhaps return to practising law. He ended the discussion claiming the White House tapes would exonerate him of any prior knowledge regarding the July 1972 break-in at the Watergate complex. In defending his personal finances he said while it was true that he paid only a nominal amount of tax in 1970–71, it was also true that he was the first occupant of the Oval Office since Harry Truman who didn't own any stock, having divested himself of his holdings in 1968. 'I made my mistakes, but in all of my years of public life I have never profited from public service.'

On 30 April 1974 the Nixon White House handed over more than 1200 pages of edited transcripts of the tapes, in two halves, to the House Judiciary Committee, a standing committee within the US House of Representatives whose duty it is to oversee the administration of justice in federal courts, transcripts which the White House claimed would offer proof that the president had not engaged in any criminal plots to obstruct justice. The White House PR machine went into overdrive, telephoning editors and others in the press to 'convince them' that the transcripts absolved Nixon of any wrongdoing. The second half of the transcripts were damning, with Nixon clearly discussing topics such as blackmail payments, abusing the 'national security' option in the defence of White House staff called to testify before the House Judiciary Committee, and the recording of continual references to the laundering of money. An extract from a 21 March 1973 meeting between Nixon and John Dean

left little room for interpretation when Nixon said, in response to the likelihood of raising $1 million in 'hush money': 'We could get that. On the money, if you need the money you could get that. You could get a million dollars. You could get it in cash. I know where it could be gotten.'

In July, Cox's replacement as special prosecutor, Leon Jaworski, no longer content with the White House–sanctioned transcripts and having unsuccessfully tried to subpoena the tapes, approached the Supreme Court to bypass the Court of Appeals (to which Nixon had gone in his attempts to deny Jaworski access to the tapes). Supreme Court Chief Justice Warren E. Burger, reading from a thirty-one-page document that reflected a unanimous 8–0 ruling, deemed that Jaworski as Special Prosecutor had the right to sue the President and ordered Nixon to hand over sixty-four tapes 'forthwith'. He rejected the president's claims of executive privilege. Nixon handed over the tapes, which included the infamous 'smoking gun' tape that led to the erosion of the last vestiges of support for Nixon in Congress. Over the next several days the House Judiciary Committee passed three articles of impeachment (sets of charges drafted against public official) on the charges of obstruction of justice, misuse of powers, failure to adequately respond to House Judiciary Committee subpoenas and violating the presidential oath of office. Nixon, realising he could no longer stave off impeachment, resigned the office of president on 8 August 1974.

A historic letter of resignation

Nixon's letter of resignation was typed on a single sheet of White House stationery and was addressed to Secretary of State Henry Kissinger, the man who, together with Nixon, had engineered some of the greatest foreign

A humble President Nixon gives his farewell speech to White House staff on 9 August 1974.

policy triumphs in American history, triumphs few American politicians possessed either the instincts or the daring to even attempt.

Dear Mr. Secretary:

I hereby resign the Office of President of the United States.

Sincerely,

The Honorable Henry A. Kissinger
The Secretary of State
Washington, D.C. 20520

Aftermath

Watergate had many victims, but none more so perhaps than Nixon himself. After his record-breaking election victory in 1972 he seemed to have garnered the will of the people, his Silent Majority, and was looking at a second term full of challenges and opportunities to grow in stature, to mend old political fences, perhaps achieve a rapprochement with the nation's press, which he always felt had unfairly maligned him, and to become the statesman that seemed so befitting the man. Instead he allowed his own foibles, insecurities, decades of accumulated political baggage, and his need to vanquish enemies, both real and imagined, to rouse his inner demons and blur his judgement. For those who supported him to the end, how they must have wished that the humanity, grace and eloquence that he displayed as he haltingly bade farewell to his White House Staff on 9 August had been perceived as strength rather than weakness and not been kept hidden from the American people.

On 8 September new president Gerald Ford granted Richard Nixon a 'full, free, and absolute pardon', thus bringing to an end any possibility of indicting the former president over his involvement in the Watergate affair.

1986

MELTDOWN AT CHERNOBYL

On 26 April 1986 at 1.23 am a reactor at the Chernobyl Nuclear Power Plant in Ukraine exploded, causing the worst nuclear power plant accident in history. Further explosions and the resulting fire sent a plume of highly radioactive fallout into the atmosphere and over parts of the western Soviet Union, eastern and western Europe, northern Europe and eastern North America. Large areas in Ukraine, Belarus and Russia were badly contaminated, resulting in the evacuation and resettlement of over 336,000 people. Only fifty-six people have been reported as dying as a direct result of the explosions but final casualty figures for those who were contaminated have not been agreed on. The UN states that 4000 people may eventually die as a result of the accident, while a Greenpeace report from 2006 says that as many as 270,000 cancers and 93,000 fatal cancer cases may in fact have been caused by Chernobyl—but we will never know the precise numbers.

THE NUCLEAR REACTOR ACCIDENT IN THE USSR

Chernobyl was, is and will be one of Ukraine's biggest problems.

OLEH ANDREEV, SPOKESMAN FOR UKRAINE'S EMERGENCY SITUATIONS MINISTRY

In the 1980s it would have been difficult to imagine the citizens of any nation in the world, nuclear or not, being quite as enthusiastic and at ease at the prospect of living alongside nuclear reactors as the citizens of the Soviet Union. Ever since the USSR's first reactor came on line in 1954 at Obninsk, 110 kilometres (66 miles) southwest of Moscow, the Soviet government and its scientists had been assuring the people of the safety and unlimited benefits of the 'peaceful atom' that was nuclear energy. Concerns raised about the dangers and environmental impact of nuclear power plants were deemed to be attacks on science itself, and government and academic assurances that the industry was all but accident proof went largely unchallenged for more than thirty years.

The magazine *Ogonyok*, which first went to press in Russia in 1899, was for generations at the very centre of Moscow's intellectual and literary life. In 1980 *Ogonyok* carried a story by the academic M. A. Styrikovich that was typical of the over-simplified and condescending approach the nuclear industry had towards the public it was meant to be serving. 'Nuclear power stations', he wrote, 'are like stars that shine all day long … they are perfectly safe'. Styrikovich likened nuclear reactors to steam engines, and characterised the technicians who ran them as little more than stokers. It was an outrageous comparison, but by simplifying the technology in the eyes of the public it not only helped lessen concerns over the technology, but also meant the government could pay nuclear technicians much the same as they paid employees at a steam-fired thermal power station.

Early nuclear accidents

The disaster that would soon unfold at Chernobyl was without a doubt the world's worst nuclear accident, but it was by no means the first. The accidental removal of control rods at the Chalk River reactor near Ottawa in Canada in 1952 resulted in a partial meltdown of its uranium fuel core. In 1957 a fire in the reactor of Windscale Pile 1 (north of Liverpool, England) led to the contamination of more than 518 square kilometres (200 square miles) of the surrounding countryside, and the sale of milk products from cows in the fallout zone was banned for a month. At the Three Mile Island plant in Harrisburg, Pennsylvania, in April 1979, a sudden loss of coolant in two of the reactors caused radioactive fuel to overheat, resulting in a partial core meltdown and the release of radioactive material into the atmosphere. In the face of these highly publicised incidents in the West it must have seemed, in comparison, as though the Soviet nuclear program was after all the clean, cheap, incident-free operation its government had always said it was. In reality, of course, the Soviet nuclear program was an accident waiting to happen.

In September 1957, at a nuclear power plant at Chelyabinsk, a city to the east of the Ural Mountains on the Miass River, a chain reaction in some spent fuel rods resulted in a large amount of radioactive material being released into the atmosphere. The residents of Chelyabinsk were evacuated and a barbed wire fence was erected around the exclusion zone. In 1966 there was a power surge at a reactor in Melekess (now Dimitrovgrad). In October 1975 a partial core meltdown at a nuclear power station outside Leningrad resulted in the temporary closure of the reactor and, in 1977, a meltdown of fuel assemblies at the Byeloyarsk power plant in Sverdlovsk Oblast irradiated the plant's staff. Though the irradiation levels were low and nobody died, the meltdown resulted in repairs having to be made to the reactor that took more than a year to complete.

Unlike Canada, Great Britain and the United States, the Soviet Union had little trouble in keeping its nuclear misadventures well hidden from the prying eyes of the world's media. The time was coming, however, when the accident to end all nuclear accidents would, by its sheer scale, force its disclosure to the world. Even so, at 1.23 am on 26 April 1986, when Chernobyl's No. 4 reactor exploded and started a chain reaction that released more than thirty times the amount of radiation into the atmosphere than was released by the Hiroshima and Nagasaki atomic bombs combined, the outside world was not informed that a radioactive cloud was spreading across the landscape until two days after the event.

Chernobyl's genesis in the 1970s

Construction of the Chernobyl plant had begun in the early 1970s and would include a total of four nuclear reactors, each capable of generating 1 gigawatt of electricity. The first reactor was commissioned in 1977, and No. 4 reactor came on line in 1983. At the time of the accident two more reactors were under construction, but in the wake of the explosion were never completed.

Chernobyl is located in northern Ukraine in an area known as the Belorussian–Ukrainian Woodlands. In early 1986, 110,000 people lived within a 30 kilometre- (18-mile) radius of the plant in seventy-six towns and villages. As many as 50,000 of these lived in the town of Pripyat, 2 kilometres (just over a mile) away, with the stacks of the power station easily visible in the distance. Chernobyl was a high power channel-type reactor, or RBMK 1000. RBMK reactors were 1950s technology built around a massive graphite block assemblage known as the 'moderator' which slowed the neutrons produced by fission. These 'boiling water reactors' used the radioactive steam produced from nuclear fission to power massive turbines. There were, however, many flaws inherent in the RBMK design, chief of which was the absence of the concrete containment structure common to other reactors. Such a structure wrapped around the reactor and would act as a final barrier to the release of any radioactive material in the wake of a core meltdown or other accident.

On 25 April 1986, Chernobyl's number 4 reactor was shut down in preparation for the testing of an emergency core cooling procedure. In the event of an external power failure that would cut power to the reactor's cooling pumps, it was thought the plant's slowing steam turbines could be harnessed to produce enough electricity for 45 seconds, that is, until the plant's diesel-powered generators could come on line to compensate for the loss of power. Approval for the test came only from the Chernobyl plant director, without consultation with either the reactor's designer or its scientific heads.

At 1.06 am on 25 April, technicians began to gradually reduce the power level of the number 4 reactor by inserting control rods into the core of the reactor to control the rate of fission. For the purposes of the test the reactor output should have fallen to between 700 and 1000 megawatts but, due to an oversight by a plant operator who forgot to properly set a controller, the output by 12.30 am on 26 April, nearly twenty-four hours later, had fallen to just 30 megawatts. Attempts to increase the reactor's power were hampered by a combination of graphite cooling and xenon poisoning, but by 1.03 am the reactor had been stabilised at about 200 megawatts which, despite being far lower than was considered ideal, was nonetheless thought high enough for the experiment to be continued. The reactor's automatic shutdown system was taken off line to permit the reactor to continue operating under abnormally low conditions.

A massive steam explosion

In an RBMK reactor, about thirty control rods are required to maintain control of the reactor's temperature, but, on this occasion, most were removed to compensate for the xenon buildup and only six rods were actually used—which led to the reactor becoming extremely unstable. To maintain steam pressure the operators also decided to reduce the feedwater rate. This resultant loss of cooling increased the reactor's instability and led

to a massive power surge that ruptured the fuel and hot fuel particles and, at 1.23 am, culminated in a steam explosion. The explosion tore apart fuel channels, causing the reactor to suffer a catastrophic water loss. This water loss contributed to a second and far more powerful explosion, the precise cause of which is still a matter for debate, but which many scientists believe could have been a small nuclear explosion caused by the rapid release of neutrons. The explosions were so violent that the foundations of the reactor fell by 4 metres (13 feet).

Approximately 25 per cent of the graphite blocks from inside the reactor, as well as various pieces of substructure and core components, were ejected through the reactor's roof—along with radioactive material and smoke that reached more than a kilometre (over half a mile) into the atmosphere and began to be carried by the prevailing winds in a northwesterly direction. Radiation levels soared dramatically, immediately reaching levels as high as 20,000 roentgen per hour. With a lethal dose calculated at around 500 roentgen over a five-hour period of exposure, it took only a few minutes for any unprotected workers in the reactor to receive a fatal dose. Radiation dosimeters, devices used to measure exposure to ionising radiation, were either unavailable or lacked the capacity to read anything over 0.01 roentgen. They would simply have been interpreted as being off the scale—though no one could have possibly imagined the levels of contamination that were now invisibly swirling about them as more than 180 tonnes of irradiated fuel was being released into the atmosphere.

More than a hundred firefighters from Chernobyl and Pripyat attended the fire, with the first arriving within five minutes, and it was this group that suffered the greatest degree of exposure and the highest casualties. The first firefighters to arrive were not even warned that the smoke and debris were radioactive. None of them had any idea what graphite was, and several later commented how they picked up chunks of graphite that had been ejected form the reactor off the ground.

There were not only fires in and around number 4 reactor itself but also on the roof of the adjacent turbine hall, and various spot fires were burning in fuel storage areas and other areas throughout the plant. These external and conventional fires were mostly under control by 5 am, but the graphite fire in the reactor itself was another matter. It continued burning until 10 May.

In excess of 5000 tonnes of sand, clay, lead and boron to absorb neutrons were dropped into the reactor by more than eighteen hundred helicopter sorties in an effort to extinguish the fire and prevent any further contamination. An unintended side effect, however, was that much of the material failed to be deposited on its intended target. In fact, it may have provided an insulative effect that a week after the event led to an increase in the fire's temperature and another sudden, though isolated, discharge of radionuclides (atoms with an unstable nucleus) into the atmosphere.

The following announcement was aired on Pripyat local radio in the hours preceding the town's evacuation. The wording was deliberately vague and intended to convey the impression that the 'accident' and any after-effects were confined to the plant and posed no immediate threat.

An accident has occurred at the Chernobyl Nuclear Power Plant. One of the atomic reactors has been damaged. Aid will be given to those affected and a committee of government enquiry has been set up.

The world's first radioactive highway

The town of Pripyat had been built to house the families of those who worked at Chernobyl. Within two days the entire population of 50,000 was evacuated in 1100 buses, a massive column that stretched for more than 20 kilometres (12 miles) along the Pripyat–Chernobyl road. What nobody paused to consider as the convoy took the residents of Pripyat away forever, effectively turning their home into a ghost town, was that the vehicles' tyres were picking up radioactive material from the road and were about to transform the Pripyat–Chernobyl road into the world's first radioactive highway.

Seven days after the evacuation of Pripyat, Chernobyl was abandoned. A 30-kilometre (19-mile) exclusion zone known as the Zone of Alienation was established, and remains in force to this day. In the absence of human activity, populations of wild boar, deer, wolves and the rare lynx have exploded in recent years in what has become a people-free enclave, save for the few hundred mostly elderly residents who either refused to be relocated or moved back to their homes in the months that followed. In 2009 the population inside the Zone of Alienation was estimated to be between 350 and 400.

Widespread contamination

As the radioactive cloud made its way across Europe, governments urged their citizens to remain indoors. In the German state of North Rhine–Westphalia, parents were told to stop their children from playing in sandpits. The London Festival Ballet voted to cancel an upcoming tour of the Soviet Union. It took just four days for the cloud to reach Monaco and the French Riviera.

RIGHT: A helicopter surveys the devastation at the Chernobyl plant on 26 April.

In the 2006 Torch Report, an independent report commissioned by the European Greens, it was found that those parts of Europe most contaminated were Belarus (22 per cent of its total land area) and Austria (13 per cent). High levels of radiation were also found in Finland, Sweden and Ukraine. Lower levels of contamination fell across 80 per cent of Moldovia, Slovenia, the Slovak Republic and Switzerland.

The aftermath

The hasty construction of a ferroconcrete shelter around number 4 reactor was begun almost immediately in an attempt to prevent further contamination. Also known as the 'sarcophagus' it was completed on 19 November 1986 and, out of necessity, was constructed in part using remote control methods, which immediately led to questions over its structural integrity. There

Liquidators, wearing suits that offer no protection against radiation, set up 'No Entry' signs in the no-go zone.

was a massive amount of hardware and fuel to contain: 10,000 tonnes of irradiated metal, 10 tonnes of radioactive dust, core fragments, more than 180 tonnes of fuel, and 20,000–25,000 litres (4400–5500 gallons) of contaminated water in the basement of the reactor. Not all of its seams were properly sealed, however, and its exterior walls are already showing signs of cracking. A new Safe Confinement Structure, made possible with funds from the European Bank for Reconstruction and Development and the Chernobyl Shelter Fund, is scheduled for completion in 2012, and ongoing work inside the original sarcophagus has stabilised its rate of decay.

The region's rivers and lakes were made bitter with radioactive fallout. Across the western Soviet Union rain became contaminated as it fell through the radioactive cloud, and sediments became so thick at the bottom of the Pripyat River by 1988 that the sludge was officially classified as radioactive waste. It took a decade for the swift-flowing currents in those rivers within the exclusion zone to disperse their waste and be declared clean.

More than four hundred and forty employees were present at Chernobyl at the time of the explosion and, of those, three hundred were admitted to hospital. One hundred and thirty-four were diagnosed with Acute Radiation Syndrome (ARS) consistent with exposure to iodine-131, cesium-134 and various plutonium isotopes, and twenty-eight died of their injuries. In the absence of a universally accepted methodology to calculate the final, continuing number of deaths, estimates range from a United Nations figure of between four thousand and nine thousand to a Greenpeace study that suggest the final toll could be as high as ninety-three thousand.

1989

SOLDIERS FIRE ON PROTESTERS IN BEIJING

A series of demonstrations led by labour activists, students, and intellectuals was held in China between 15 April and 4 June 1989. While the protests lacked a unified cause or leadership, participants were generally critical of corruption in Chinese Communist Party and voiced calls for democratic reform within the structure of the government. The protests centred on Tiananmen Square in Beijing, and the resulting military crackdown left many civilians dead or injured. The death toll ranged from the official figure of 200–300 to the Chinese Red Cross estimate of 2600. The army tanks that confronted the protesters were seen in news bulletins around the world.

THE TIANANMEN SQUARE INCIDENT

You mean well, and have the interests of our country at heart, but if this goes on, it will get out of control ...

ZHAO ZIYANG TO HUNGER STRIKERS IN TIANANMEN SQUARE, 19 MAY 1989

Tiananmen Square lies in the geographical centre of Beijing and is the largest city square in the world. Its 440,000 square metres (526,000 square yards) can accommodate in excess of one million people. It was on the rostrum of the Tiananmen Gate (Gate of Heavenly Peace) on the square's northern perimeter that Mao Zedong declared the establishment of the People's Republic of China on 1 October 1949. There are few places in modern China that possess greater cultural and social significance.

Death of a reformer

Beginning in 1978, a new era of economic and political reforms was initiated throughout China by Premier Deng Xiaoping, the ageing comrade of Chairman Mao and a hero of the Long March. The economic reforms proved popular among China's peasants who saw increases in real wages and demonstrable improvements in their day-to-day lives. Political reform, however, was proving more elusive, and the intelligentsia and student organisations in the country's large cities were becoming increasingly impatient for change. When the progressive political reformer Hu Yaobang, the Communist Party's sixth general secretary, died of a heart attack on 15 April 1989 many viewed his death as extinguishing the last hopes for real democratic reform. Hu's funeral was to take place in Tiananmen

Square on 22 April, and fifty thousand students planned to participate, using the occasion to deliver a petition to Premier Li Peng critical of the Party's veiled disapproval of Hu's support of both freedom of speech and freedom of the press. The Party saw Hu as uncomfortably close to the nation's 'bourgeois liberals' and left-leaning middle-class intelligentsia. Hu had been forced by Party hardliners to resign his position as general secretary in January 1987, and compelled to write a humiliating letter of 'self-criticism' of his reformist principles.

Hu's funeral arrangements, along with official government pronouncements of his importance in helping shape modern China, seemed to many to be a little subdued. He had after all fought to rehabilitate those who had suffered under the communists during the Cultural Revolution, and was a supporter of greater autonomy for Tibet, from which he once ordered the withdrawal of thousands of Chinese soldiers and ordered those who remained to learn the Tibetan language. Although Hu's official death announcement contained all the usual communist rhetoric, such as saying he had been a 'staunch communist warrior' and a 'proletarian revolutionist', he was also said to have made unspecified 'mistakes'.

On the eve of the funeral, in excess of a million people had gathered in Tiananmen

Square and its approaches. The events that were to follow, known within China as the June Fourth Movement, would be the culmination of a protest movement that first began in earnest in December 1986. Students began to take advantage of the first loosening of political control to ask for the right to study abroad as well as greater accessibility to Western culture and influences. Speeches against the slow pace of reform were suddenly being made across the country by leading figures such as Professor Fang Lizhi of the University of Science and Technology in Anhui Province, one of the founders of the pro-democracy movement who had been expelled from the Communist Party in 1987. Fang and his wife took refuge in the US embassy in Beijing on 5 June 1989 and remained there for more than a year before fleeing to England and then on to the United States.

Massacre—or protest?

'The Tiananmen Square Massacre' has become one of those phrases that has entered the world's lexicon and refuses to go away, despite the historical fact that although there were undeniably protesters killed in the square on 4 and 5 June, video footage of the melee shows little actual fighting. CBS news correspondent Richard Roth, who was standing on the south portico of the Great Hall of the People that constitutes one of the square's boundaries, was driven in a jeep through the square together with another journalist, Derek Williams, just 40 minutes after they had both heard the sound of gunfire. But they saw no bodies, no injured students or soldiers, and no ambulances. Live on air later that day with the celebrated news anchor Dan Rather of CBS, Roth stuck to his story and referred to the violence that he had witnessed in the square as an 'assault' rather than a massacre. Roth, of course, spoke only of

what he himself had seen, and had no first-hand knowledge of the violence that had occurred throughout the city. Historians have long shied away from the term Tiananmen Square Massacre and now speak instead of a broader Beijing Massacre.

So what exactly did happen in the Chinese capital on 4 and 5 June 1989?

Although portrayed in the Western media as largely a student movement, the demonstrations that began on 27 April touched a nerve with the Chinese populace. In cities across China millions began to appear in their streets in open revolt. They were elderly people, children, labourers, people representing every level of society, who took their lead from the students and dared to show dissent. It was almost a 'carnival' of protest. Large-scale protests that erupted in Guangzhou, Hong Kong and Shanghai included doctors, nurses, scientists—even elements of the Chinese navy were protesting. The Chinese press was reporting events freely and relatively unhindered, and hundreds of thousands of protesters were converging on the capital. What had begun as a student protest was evolving into a country-wide phenomenon.

On 4 May one hundred thousand protesters converged on Beijing to march in support of freedom of the press and to open a dialogue between their own elected representatives and the government. The government rejected their overtures, claiming it would speak only to the leaders of recognised, pre-existing student organisations. On 13 May, just two days before a state visit by the architect of the Soviet Union's own period of openness and reform, Mikhail Gorbachev, the students decided that in order to maintain the momentum they had generated so far, they would initiate a hunger strike. Initially involving just hundreds, the hunger strike soon took on a life of its own. Protesters from regional cities flocked to Tiananmen Square to join it. The protesters were for the most part peaceful, even cooperative with the soldiers and authorities who were monitoring them. When three students threw ink over the portrait of Chairman Mao that overlooks the square, students assisted police in arresting them.

The students meet with Premier Li Peng

It was a time of unprecedented freedoms in which confrontations between the communist leadership and ordinary citizens that would have been considered unthinkable just days earlier were played out on television screens across the nation. On 18 May the Chinese media televised a meeting between Premier Li Peng and two of the student movement's most prominent advocates, Wu'er Kaixi and Wang Dan. Wang was a history student at Peking University, one of the birthplaces of the student movement. Wu'er, an ethnic Uyghur and student of Beijing Normal University, interrupted the premier in the midst of his opening remarks and promptly made history: 'I understand it is quite rude of me to interrupt you, Premier, but there are people sitting out there in the square, being hungry, as we sit here and exchange pleasantries.'

Li broke in to accuse Wu'er of being impolite, but Wu'er realised he must seize the moment and speak not only his own mind, but also on behalf of all those in China who were seeking freedom: 'Sir, you said you are here late, but we've actually been calling you to talk to us since 22 April. It's not that you are late, it's that you're here *too* late. But that's fine. It's good that you are able to come here at all …'

At 5 am on 19 May, without warning, the general secretary of the Communist Party, Zhao Ziyang appeared among the students in Tiananmen Square and delivered a speech that had not been sanctioned by the Party leadership. Zhao asked the students to end their hunger strike and their protest before the Party's patience ran out. He promised them that the leadership would continue to discuss their grievances and said that it was wrong for them to put their young lives in jeopardy over issues that he believed could be settled in time through negotiation. It was an extraordinarily conciliatory speech, but the students did not abandon their protest. The following day Zhao was stripped of his position and placed under house arrest. His motivations for pursuing such a unilateral act in defiance of his party have remained a subject of debate ever since.

Martial law introduced across Beijing

On 20 May, the day after Zhao's speech, Premier Li Peng imposed martial law across Beijing. Three hundred thousand troops were ordered to occupy Tiananmen Square, but as the armoured personnel carriers and trucks laden with troops moved into the city they found their way forward blocked by hundreds of thousands of protesters. Columns of army transports filled with troops were mobbed by citizens demanding to know why they were entering their city. 'Brother soldiers, you should be defenders of the people!' one elderly woman cried out to a group of seated soldiers. After four days of this impasse, enduring an unprecedented loss of face in the process, the army withdrew to bases outside the city. The protesters had won a memorable triumph. The authorities, however, had not only lost face but were beginning to wonder how long it would be

FOLLOWING PAGES: A sea of student protesters gather in Tiananmen Square on 4 May.

until they lost control—and were determined that such a humiliating event, in full view of the world's media, would not happen again.

Meanwhile the demonstrations continued to spread. Three hundred thousand people thronged Hong Kong's famous Happy Valley Racecourse on 27 May to sing democratic songs of encouragement for the Beijing protesters, and the following day a rally involving 1.5 million people, representing 25 per cent of the territory's population marched through its streets.

On 1 June troops from the 27th and 28th Armies were despatched from their barracks outside Beijing and ordered into the city, this time with orders to clear the square by dawn on 4 June. In the western suburbs of the capital, every time the troops broke through a blockade, the protesters would fall back and form another blockade further down the street. But inexorably the armed forces—the People's Liberation Army (PLA)—forced their way through blockade after blockade, making their way toward Tiananmen Square.

Ordinary citizens shot by their countrymen

On the night of 3 June the troops entered the city proper from the surrounding provinces. In response, protesters barricaded the streets leading to the square with buses, trucks and earthmoving equipment. In comparison, the atmosphere in Tiananmen Square itself seemed almost surreal. It was a scene of relative peace on the evening of 3 June compared with the carnage unfolding in the surrounding streets, a place of order and calm in the midst of a gathering cyclone. At around 9.30 pm armoured personnel carriers began to ram and break through the barricades, and the populace could not believe that the PLA was firing live ammunition upon the very people it

was meant to defend. Beijing's citizens were shocked, looking down from their balconies onto troops using battlefield weapons against ordinary men, women and children. Away from the square, in the streets of the capital, people were being shot. Large numbers of casualties were ferried to local hospitals on bicycles, on carts, on anything that moved. Western journalists were being begged to take photos and to film what was happening, and to show the images to the world.

At 5.40 am on 4 June, armoured personnel carriers and soldiers with bayonets fixed entered Tiananmen Square *en masse*; several incidents of indiscriminate fire were reported by Western journalists and other eyewitnesses. Some students took refuge in buses but were pulled from them and set upon. The troops effectively blockaded access to the square, and the protesters made several attempts to enter, only to be shot at. Many were shot in the back as they first rushed and then retreated from the soldiers, who were now under orders to have the square cleared of protesters by 6 am on 5 June (the following morning).

On the morning of 5 June a line of eighteen tanks was making its way from Tiananmen Square along the Avenue of Eternal Peace. An unidentified man suddenly appeared from nowhere, in the full view of the international media. Carrying what looked like shopping bags, he stood defiantly in front of the advancing tanks, forcing them to stop. After several attempts were made by the lead tank to go around the man, the engine was turned off. Those behind it did the same. Tank Man (as he is now known) climbed on top of the lead tank and seemed to yell at its crew to turn around. A soldier emerged and after a brief conversation the man climbed down from the tank but again stood before it. He was eventually taken from the scene by what looked like ordinary civilians concerned for his safety. He has never been located or identified. Four photographers—Jeff Widener of the Associated Press, Stuart Franklin of Magnum Photos, Charlie Cole of *Newsweek* and Arthur Tsang Hin Wah of Reuters—all captured the Tank Man's defiance on film, and the next day the image made headlines across the world. In 1998 *Time* magazine named the man one of the one hundred most important people of the century.

Protesters eventually leave the square

Inside the square, meanwhile, a debate had broken out between two student factions, one wanting to stay, the other wanting to leave. The soldiers held their fire and offered amnesty if the protesters agreed to vacate the square. Thousands left Tiananmen Square by its southeast corner, singing the 'Internationale', the great revolutionary song of workers and communists, and vowing to carry on the fight. A wholesale massacre had been avoided.

Tank Man blocks the path of a military convoy along the Avenue of Eternal Peace near Tiananmen Square.

Estimates of the number of dead and injured will forever be debated as the Chinese government never made public its record of the incident. The Chinese Red Cross put the figure at twenty-six hundred people killed and more than thirty thousand injured, a total that was of course disputed by the government, which put the number killed at three hundred with seven thousand injured. Perhaps the most accurate assessment comes from the assembled foreign media who witnessed the attacks from a range of differing perspectives and whose estimates were three thousand killed, close enough to the Red Cross estimate as to represent the most plausible outcome.

The student leaders of the rebellion, many of whom were from affluent and well-connected families, largely escaped execution or long-term prison sentences. Wu'er Kaixi escaped to live in Taiwan and Wang Dan was imprisoned but permitted to emigrate to the United States. Others were imprisoned but released after serving relatively short sentences. Chai Ling, one of the leaders in the latter stages of the protest and one of the chief organisers of the hunger strike, escaped to France in 1990 and eventually settled in the United States.

As to what extent the Tiananmen Square protests affected government policy and acted as a catalyst for real change, the answer is: very little. The government continued its repressive policies and, even today, the subject of the student protests of 1989 is a taboo subject in the media. The notion of freedom of speech in China remains elusive.

1990

AFTER 27 YEARS MANDELA WALKS FREE

On 12 June 1964, Nelson Mandela, leader of the African National Congress in South Africa, was sentenced to life imprisonment. Convicted of sabotage and treason for opposing the government, he was sent to Robben Island and held under harsh conditions along with other political prisoners. During his incarceration he became a potent symbol of resistance to the official government policy of apartheid—the forced segregation of the races—and he consistently refused to compromise his political position to obtain his freedom. Meanwhile the anti-apartheid movement gathered strength, and international condemnation of the South African government grew. On 11 February 1990 the government finally bowed to domestic and international pressure, and Nelson Mandela was released after spending twenty-seven years in prison.

NELSON MANDELA RELEASED

Only free men can negotiate.
Prisoners cannot enter into contracts.

NELSON MANDELA, 10 FEBRUARY 1985

Rolihlahla Mandela was born in the small village of Mvezo in the Transkei region of South Africa on 18 July 1918. He became the first in his family to attend school when he was sent to the Clarkebury Boarding Institute, then on to a Wesleyan secondary school in Healdtown. A teacher at Clarkebury gave him the name Nelson, which in time came to be used in place of his birth name Rolihlahla, which colloquially means 'troublemaker'.

Early years with the ANC

In 1940 Mandela ran away to Johannesburg to escape an arranged marriage. There he met Walter Sisulu, a future African National Congress (ANC) collaborator, who helped him find work as a clerk in a local law firm. The ANC had been formed in 1912 as a broad-based coalition of concerned black South Africans, including tribal chiefs, church leaders and various community organisations. They were determined to fight for equality and freedom for black South Africans in the face of decades of increasing racial segregation.

It wasn't until 1948, however, in the wake of the South African general elections, that the process of segregation became enshrined as an official policy of the newly elected Nationalist Party. This official policy became known as apartheid.

In 1941 Mandela completed a bachelor of arts degree by correspondence from the University of South Africa. When he began legal studies at the University of Witwatersrand he met future anti-apartheid activists, such as the former German-Jewish refugee turned lawyer Harry Schwarz, the future ANC theoretician Joe Slovo and activist Ruth First. It was people like these, along with others such as Oliver Tambo and William Nkomo, who realised it was necessary to transform the ANC from a conservative organisation content to work within the law into a radicalised movement prepared to pursue civil disobedience and violence to achieve their aims.

In 1952 the ANC initiated its Campaign for the Defiance of Unjust Laws, and Mandela crisscrossed the country organising opposition to South Africa's discriminatory legislation. That same year Mandela and Oliver Tambo opened their own law firm in Johannesburg and, throughout the 1950s, were involved in a series of highly publicised trials. These included representation of blacks forcibly resettled under the government's Western Areas Removal Scheme and opposition to the *Bantu Education Act* (1953), which forced separation of all races in the country's schools and universities.

Nelson Mandela first saw Nomzamo Winnie Madikisela in 1957, albeit briefly, as she waited for a bus while he sped past driving a friend to hospital. Even so, he couldn't help but notice her. She was a beautiful and confident-looking twenty-two-year-old, a social worker, and he was thirty-eight. Mandela had divorced his first wife, Evelyn Mase, with whom he had four children, earlier that year, and shortly after the divorce was finalised he and Winnie were married. Winnie involved herself intimately in the ANC's struggle and soon became accustomed to police raids on her home, enforced separations from her new husband, and the endless routine of political gatherings. While pregnant with their first child she was arrested during a demonstration on behalf of the ANC Women's League and almost miscarried in prison.

Mandela's first prison sentence

The ANC was outlawed in 1960. The following year Mandela was elected leader of the ANC's armed wing, Spear of the Nation (*Umkhonto we Sizwe*—the term was Mandela's). This was a significant development in the history of the ANC which had been for the most part a non-violent organisation. But within the ANC there was growing scepticism that peaceful protests would bring effective change; in fact, each confrontation with the police seemed only to result in further erosion of black rights.

In 1962 Mandela travelled abroad for several months, speaking and generating political support for the ANC cause in Ethiopia, Sierra Leone, Senegal and Ghana. He then flew to London where he sought out former comrades and met with ANC recruits about to travel to Ethiopia to begin training in guerilla tactics. On his return to South Africa on 5 August 1962 Nelson Mandela was arrested and found guilty of illegally leaving the country and of incitement to strike. He was sentenced to five years' imprisonment and sent to Robben Island.

Robben Island's isolation, 19 kilometres (12 miles) out from Table Bay, had always made it an ideal human dumping ground. Just 5 kilometres by 2.5 kilometres (3 miles by a mile and a half) in size, the windswept, low-lying island was first seen by Europeans when Vasco da Gama's fleet sailed by in 1498; twenty-seven years later, it became a prison when the first Portuguese convicts were sent there. South Africa was subsequently colonised by both Britain and the Netherlands. From 1652 to 1795 the Dutch East India Company used Robben Island as a prison and added a quarantine station, while during the British colonial period from 1806 to 1910 it served first as a prison, then as a hospital for lepers, the mentally ill and the chronically sick. From 1939 to 1959, the island was used by the South African army and navy as a training centre. In 1960 it was transformed into a maximum security prison for political and criminal prisoners.

Mandela's second prison sentence

Nelson Mandela had been on Robben Island only a few months when he was taken back to Pretoria as a defendant in the Rivonia Trial, which saw Mandela and nine other ANC leaders tried on a total of 221 counts of sabotage and 'fomenting violent revolution'. The trial began on 26 November 1963 and the defendants, realising from the outset that it was a show trial, endured it with stoicism and strength. Three of the accused, Mandela, Govan Mbeki and Walter Sisulu, made a pact that if at the trial's conclusion they were given the death penalty, none of them would lodge an appeal. The verdict was delivered on 11 June 1964. Mandela and seven other ANC leaders, including Walter Sisulu, were all found guilty and given life sentences. Nelson Mandela was found guilty on four charges of sabotage, and most of the prisoners were flown to Robben Island the next day.

Life on Robben Island

Although Mandela was to spend the next twenty-six years behind bars, his time there was crucial in forming the man who, in the wake of his release on 11 February 1990, would become the first president of a free and democratic South Africa. He was the 466th prisoner to be incarcerated on Robben Island and was given the prisoner number 466/64. Mandela's cell, in a purpose-built part of the prison called Section B, measured just 1.8 metres square (6 feet x 6 feet) with a straw mat for a bed, a bucket for a toilet, and a small barred window. Breakfast was usually corn porridge, with just a few vegetables for dinner. Suffering almost daily harassment from the prison guards, who were anything but sympathetic to his cause, he nevertheless continued his struggle and was constantly at odds with the prison authorities over demands for better food, clothing and conditions.

Nelson Mandela was a Category D prisoner, which was the most restrictive category, reserved for political prisoners. Category D prisoners were permitted just one letter and one visit every six months. All mail was subject to extensive censorship and could be a maximum of only five hundred words in length. Nevertheless, Winnie's letters and visits sustained him, and Mandela later praised her for the love and encouragement she provided him. In a letter written from his cell in May 1979 he said to her: 'Had it not been for your visits, wonderful letters and your love, I would have fallen apart many years ago'.

The daily routine of life on Robben Island was harsh and repetitive. At 5.30 am the guards would wake the prisoners and the next hour was spent cleaning their cells, washing and shaving, and emptying their sanitary buckets into a communal toilet. A few minutes were allowed for exercise in the prison courtyard prior to breakfast, which was washed down with a roasted maize and hot water mixture that the prison guards called 'coffee'. Mandela and the other prisoners then spent the bulk of their day seated in rows, smashing the island's ubiquitous limestone rocks with small hammers weighing around 2.2 kilograms (5 pounds). The work was relentless. A one-hour lunch break may have been a welcome respite from the tedious labour but not from the boredom and sour aftertaste of prison food, with lunch consisting of a mixture of maize and yeast added to water to make a broth only slightly thicker than water. After lunch work continued until 4 pm when the prisoners were marched to their communal shower, then dinner at 5 pm. There was no such thing as 'lights out' on Robben Island, with each cell lit by its own 40-watt light bulb. Prisoners such as Mandela, who was studying to complete his law degree by correspondence, were permitted to work as late as 11 pm. Reading newspapers was forbidden, although Mandela and others found ways of bribing the guards so they could keep abreast of political developments on the mainland.

Beginning in 1965, Mandela and several other prisoners were made to extract lime from a nearby quarry using nothing but a pick and shovel and with no protection from the island's hot summer winds or the ice-cold northwest gales that blew in throughout the winter. The sun reflected harshly off the white limestone, but repeated requests for sunglasses to shield their eyes from the glare went unheeded for years until the prisoners were eventually given permission to purchase their own glasses. The glare was so intense that it damaged Mandela's tear ducts. Despite the conditions and the exposure to the elements, Mandela preferred working the limestone seams to the four

Women demonstrate in front of the Law Courts in Pretoria after the verdict in the Rivonia trial.

monotonous walls of the prison courtyard, and he looked forward to the daily 20-minute walk to and from the quarry.

Opposition to apartheid grows

In 1968–69 Mandela's mother and his son from his first marriage passed away, but on neither occasion was he permitted to attend the funeral. In 1980 the ANC and the exiled Oliver Tambo began a Release Mandela campaign, and in 1982 Mandela was transferred from Robben Island to Pollsmoor Prison on the mainland. During the 1970s he rejected various offers of early release because of the conditions attached.

Anti-apartheid demonstrations gathered strength throughout the 1980s, and by 1985 massive protests opposing the South African regime were occurring across the United States and Europe, raising awareness of its injustices and of the continuing imprisonment of Mandela and other ANC leaders. Mandela continued to remain resolute, refusing to renounce violence in exchange for another offer of early release. By June of 1986 increased violence in black townships forced President P. W. Botha to declare a state of emergency; in 1987 Mandela began a series of personal negotiations with an increasingly politically and economically isolated

South African government, a development that angered many of the ANC hierarchy who were living in exile in Zambia.

Mandela is released from prison at seventy-one

After being treated for tuberculosis in December 1988, Mandela was transferred from Pollsmoor Prison near Cape Town to Victor Verster Prison near Paarl, where he swapped a prison cell for a small cottage with a swimming pool and vegetable garden. Persistent high blood pressure saw him provided with his own personal chef who prepared a special low-sodium diet, and he began receiving visits from old friends such as Harry Schwarz. Botha suffered a stroke and was forced to resign as president in August 1989. He was succeeded by the conciliatory Frederik Willem de Klerk, who released many of those who had been imprisoned in the wake of the infamous Rivonia Trial. De Klerk was very different from the white South African politicians who had come before him. In discussions with Mandela he came to accept the principle of power sharing, and opposed the settlement of blacks into certain designated homelands. De Klerk engineered the transformation of South Africa from a racially segregated state into a respected multi-racial democracy, reversing the ban on the ANC on 2 February 1990 and at the same time announcing Nelson Mandela's imminent release. On 11 February 1990, at 4.15 pm, Nelson walked free from Victor Verster Prison—twenty-seven years, six months and five days after his arrest outside Durban for illegally having left the country. The historic event was televised live across the world, and

LEFT: Nelson Mandela addresses an ecstatic crowd in Cape Town the day after he is released.

Mandela made a speech that left the millions listening in no doubt that the struggle was far from over:

Our resort to the armed struggle in 1960 with the formation of the military wing of the ANC was a purely defensive action against the violence of apartheid. The factors which necessitated the armed struggle still exist today. We have no option but to continue. We express the hope that a climate conducive to a negotiated settlement would be created soon, so that there may no longer be the need for the armed struggle.

Nelson Mandela was already a great leader when he began his period of imprisonment on Robben Island in 1964. At forty-six he was also arrogant, easily embittered and impatient for change. The man who emerged from prison in February 1990 was very different. He had undergone a metamorphosis. His years in prison had given him humility, patience, an inner peace and an abiding certainty that things were about to change. He was at once more restrained yet every bit as determined, had 'begun to feel the power of prayer', and slowly, almost imperceptibly, had evolved into a statesman. Mandela admitted as much, saying upon his release: 'I came out mature'.

In the days that followed, the world's media all but besieged Mandela's home in the Johannesburg suburb of West Orlando. Supporters of the ANC thronged the streets, singing songs of protest and celebration day after day, from dusk until dawn. But despite the buoyant mood, there was much that needed to be done. Over the term of his imprisonment, conditions not dissimilar to anarchy had come to reign in many of South Africa's black townships. Children were refusing to go to school and vigilantism was rife, particularly by blacks on blacks. In his speeches over the coming days Mandela was openly critical of those fellow blacks 'who use violence against our people'.

Mandela elected president of the ANC—and of South Africa

On 27 February Mandela flew to the exiled ANC leadership in the Zambian capital of Lusaka and assured them he would not seek to become a lone voice in the cause of freedom. In the months to come he flew to more than twenty countries, building up incalculably valuable reservoirs of goodwill and admiration wherever he went and, despite receiving pressure from foreign dignitaries to renounce the use of violence, he never once stepped back from the ANC's stated aim of using armed struggle to attain political objectives. In 1991 Mandela was elected president of the ANC at its first national conference held inside South Africa since the organisation was banned in 1960. The following year he divorced Winnie Mandela in the wake of her conviction on charges of accessory to assault and kidnapping. In 1993 Nelson Mandela and Frederik Willem de Klerk were awarded the Nobel Peace Prize.

He voted for the very first time in his life on 27 April 1994 at the age of seventy-five. The ANC won a landslide victory with 62.6 per cent of the vote, and Nelson Mandela was elected president of South Africa on 10 May 1994.

DIANA DEAD IN HIGH SPEED PAPARAZZI PURSUIT

On 31 August 1997, Princess Diana died after a high-speed car accident in Paris, when she and her lover Dodi Fayed were pursued by paparazzi after a dinner engagement. Blood analysis showed that her driver for the night, Henri Paul, who also died in the crash, was three times over the French legal limit for alcohol. News of Diana's death caused an amazing outpouring of grief around the world, and hordes of people laid flowers outside Kensington Palace. This grief culminated in a state funeral at Westminster Abbey on 6 September for which over 1 million people gathered in London; an estimated 2.5 billion people watched it broadcast worldwide.

THE DEATH OF PRINCESS DIANA

*Since last Sunday's dreadful news we have seen,
throughout Britain and around the world,
an overwhelming expression of sadness at Diana's death.
We have all been trying in our different ways to cope.*

SPEECH BY QUEEN ELIZABETH II, 9 SEPTEMBER 1997

On 30 August 1997, Diana, Princess of Wales and her companion Dodi Fayed, son of Mohamad al-Fayed millionaire Egyptian businessman, were dining at the exclusive Hôtel Ritz in Paris. Mohamad al-Fayed was the owner of the landmark Parisian hotel, and Diana and Dodi, who had spent the previous nine days holidaying together on Mohamad al-Fayed's yacht *Jonikal*, in the waters off the French Riviera, had arrived in Paris earlier that day. They planned to spend the night at Dodi's apartment not far from the Arc de Triomphe on the Rue Arsène Houssaye, with Diana due to return to her Kensington Palace home, and to her sons, William and Harry, the following day.

Escaping the paparazzi

Diana was the most photographed woman in the world, and the ever-present paparazzi were circling outside the hotel. Dodi sent two decoy cars to the hotel's front entrance in an attempt to distract them while he, Diana, their chauffeur Henri Paul and Dodi's bodyguard Trevor Rees-Jones left by a rear exit on the Rue Cambon in a black Mercedes S280. Initially followed by at least one photographer on a motorcycle, the car drove past the Jardin de Tuileries and Place de la Concorde before turning right onto

the Cours la Reine, which runs parallel to the River Seine.

At 12.23 am, approaching the underpass beneath the Pont de l'Alma, and now with three motorcycles in hot pursuit, Henri Paul picked up speed and sped into the tunnel, coming up quickly behind a Citroen BX sedan and a white Fiat Uno. The driver of the Citroen, Mr Medjahdi, saw the car 'slewing out of control' as it was 'hurtling towards me'. He accelerated in an attempt to put some distance between the two cars, and the next thing he heard was the deafening sound of impact as the car carrying the Princess of Wales slammed into the substructure of the underpass. It was reported that part of the Fiat's taillight had been found in the tunnel, which raises the possibility that it may have been struck by the Mercedes as Henri Paul attempted to swerve around it, and that this may have contributed to his losing control of the vehicle. The Mercedes hit the right wall of the tunnel as it attempted to pass the Fiat, ricocheting across the two west-bound lanes of the tunnel and into a bridge pylon.

The Fiat Uno was the accident's 'mystery car'. Scratches of paint from it were found on the Mercedes S280 so there is no doubt the two vehicles came into contact but, despite an extensive search by French authorities, the car has never been found. Dodi Fayed's father maintained that its driver was a French photo-journalist, Jean-Paul Andanson who, he believed, was in fact a British secret agent involved in the so-called 'plot' to kill Diana. Andanson, however, had an alibi for the night of the crash, and he committed suicide in 2000. The driver of the Fiat Uno, whoever he or she may have been, has never come forward.

The Mercedes ploughs into the thirteenth pylon

The Pont de l'Alma's concrete support pylons were not protected by guardrails and the Mercedes ploughed headlong into the thirteenth

pylon. The impact was so severe the car was turned around 180 degrees before careering across the tunnel into the concrete wall on the other side and coming to rest over the centre dividing line. The front half of the car had been crushed beyond recognition and the engine pushed almost into the front seat. The rear of the car, by comparison, remained relatively secure—it was later determined that if Diana and Dodi had been wearing their seatbelts at the time of the accident both of them would probably have survived.

Henri Paul, 41, was the Ritz's assistant director of security and the man upon whom much of the blame for the accident was to fall. Although he had been employed at the Ritz

Newspapers in London the morning after the accident.

since 1986 he was not working as Dodi Fayed's personal chauffeur, despite recently receiving training in defensive driving. He was not meant to be driving Diana and Dodi anywhere that night. At 7 pm he had left the hotel, thinking he had finished for the night, but was called back because Dodi wanted to use his usual driver to drive a decoy car so he and Diana could elude the paparazzi. Thinking he was free for the evening, Paul had been indulging his fondness for a drink with other employees, something he almost certainly would not have done if he had been able to foresee the whims of Dodi Fayed.

In the wake of the accident his blood alcohol level was tested and shown to be 1.75 grams per litre, three times over the legal limit of 0.5. In the hour or so before the accident Paul had drunk two Ricards, an anise-based liquor equivalent to four shots of whisky. Forensic tests also showed high levels of prescription drugs in Paul's system, including the anti-depressant Prozac, and Tiapridal, an anti-psychotic drug often used to suppress mood disorders, which led the English toxicologist Dr Robert Forrest to remark: 'If I knew that I was going to be driven by someone in that condition, I would not get into the car with them. No way'.

Witnesses to the chase agreed that the Mercedes was travelling at 145 kilometres per hour (90 miles per hour) or more as it entered the tunnel, at least three times the speed limit of just under 50 kilometres per hour (30 miles per hour). Though it seemed to dash the hopes of conspiracy theorists the world over, it appeared the accident was the result of the very same two ingredients that lead to road deaths every other day—speed and alcohol.

James Huth, a former dental surgeon turned feature filmmaker, had been watching scenes from his first film in his parents' apartment on the Cour's Albert Premier when he heard the sound of screeching tyres followed by three loud impacts. He ran outside where a friend told him there had just been a car accident in the Pont de l'Alma tunnel. Huth ran to investigate. With no idea who the victims were, he approached the mangled wreckage of the Mercedes and saw Henri Paul slumped forward in an airbag in the driver's seat, dead. Aware of the danger of moving injured people suffering spinal injuries, Huth advised others who had arrived seconds before him not to touch the bodies. Reports by other witnesses claimed, at about this point, they had heard the woman in the rear of the car murmur: 'Oh my God' and 'Leave me alone'. Huth told Trevor Rees-Jones, who was in a state of near panic in the front passenger seat, to stay quiet, that someone would be there shortly to help him. Rees-Jones' wrist was broken and his jaw was, according to Huth, 'hanging off'.

Diana still conscious

Huth moved around to the rear of the car and saw Dodi Fayed's lifeless body slumped between the car's two front seats, his leg broken in two places below the knee the only obvious sign of trauma. The only occupant of the car he didn't clearly see was Princess Diana herself. Diana, still conscious, was thrown to the floor by the impact and lay crumpled in the rear footwell, largely obscured from Huth's view by Dodi's body. Neither Diana, Dodi Fayed nor Henri Paul were wearing seatbelts at the time of the accident.

Physician Frederick Mailliez was among the first on the scene and used his mobile phone to call for an ambulance. He too failed to recognise the woman in the rear footwell, later testifying that she seemed unconscious but at the same time was able to move her limbs. Photographers had by this time surrounded the car and were taking pictures. None of them offered to assist. Mailliez lifted up the head of the princess and placed an oxygen mask over her mouth to help her breathe. Although her internal injuries were life threatening she showed few external injuries save for some lacerations about the face. Jack and Robin Firestone, two American tourists on holiday in the French capital, also arrived in the seconds after the crash and were horrified to see photographers standing less than a metre away from the car taking pictures of a blonde woman lying on the back seat.

Within seven minutes of the accident a military emergency vehicle arrived and treatment of the injured began. At 12.40 am a SAMU ambulance (a hospital-based emergency service) arrived and its physician immediately inserted an intravenous drip into Diana, who was able to move her right leg and left arm. Dodi Fayed was pronounced dead at 1.32 am. Henri Paul was declared dead not long after being dragged from the wreckage. Both he and Dodi had suffered a ruptured aorta. Trevor Rees-Jones was taken to Pitié-Salpêtrière Hospital, a teaching hospital and one of the largest hospitals in Europe, with injuries to his brain and chest, and although initial reports suggested he might have been wearing his seatbelt, two subsequent inquiries both determined that he had not.

At 1 am Diana was removed, still conscious, from the wreckage but immediately went into cardiac arrest. External chest massage saw her cardiac rhythm return and she was transferred to the waiting ambulance at 1.18 am. Diana's injuries were horrific—the impact would almost certainly have caused major deceleration injuries such as internal lesions. Yet the ambulance crew treated her only for the outward measurable symptoms, namely falling blood pressure, while ignoring its cause. They attended her for almost an hour.

The force of the impact had shifted her heart from the left side of her chest to the right, tearing her pericardium (the double-walled sac inside which the heart rests) and partially, though not wholly, rupturing the pulmonary vein. The ambulance left the tunnel at 1.41 am and arrived at Pitié-Salpêtrière at 2.06 am, a twenty-five-minute trip to a hospital just over 6 kilometres (4 miles) away on a largely deserted expressway that should have taken just five to ten minutes. Diana was fast running out of time, but the ambulance driver, unaware of the extent of her internal injuries, deliberately drove slowly so as not to subject the patient to unnecessary bumps and movement. At one point the ambulance had to stop when her blood pressure fell to a dangerously low level.

Diana finally reaches the emergency room

Diana didn't arrive in the emergency room of Pitié-Salpêtrière until 104 minutes after the crash. Ten minutes after arriving she suffered a second cardiac arrest. Epinephrine was injected directly into her heart and an incision was made in the chest so the attending surgeons could gain manual access to the heart. Diana's left pulmonary vein was haemorrhaging where it came into contact with the left atrium, and had been losing blood for more than an hour and a half. Unlike the aorta, however, which takes blood out of the heart and where the pressure is high, the pulmonary is a 'low pressure' vein and can often partially clot if ripped. This is almost certainly what happened with Diana and is the reason she was able to survive as long as she did. The tragedy was that in Diana's case she had an injury that was impossible to repair in the field, and the French emphasis on treating people at the scene, as distinct from the US approach of 'scope and run' and of getting patients to an

In an overwhelming outpouring of grief, mourners left over one million bouquets of flowers at Kensington Palace.

emergency room as soon as possible, probably cost Diana her life. Despite being sutured, and with the haemorrhaging brought under control, two hours of open heart massage and electric shock therapy could not reestablish a heartbeat. The Princess of Wales was pronounced dead at 4 am, and her death was announced at a news conference ninety minutes later. If she had arrived at Pitié-Salpêtrière an hour earlier, would she have survived? It is a moot point.

Prince Charles and the rest of the royal family were on their traditional summer holiday at Balmoral Castle in Scotland when the accident occurred. Charles and his mother, Queen Elizabeth, decided not to tell his sons, William and Harry, the news of their mother's death until they woke the next morning. Charles and Diana's two sisters, Lady Sarah McCorquodale and Lady Jane Fellowes, travelled to Paris and accompanied Diana's body back to England.

Princess Diana's death caused an outpouring of grief around the world but particularly in Britain. More than a million people lined the route of her funeral procession from her home at Kensington Palace at the western end of Hyde Park to Westminster Abbey, throwing flowers in front of the gun carriage, drawn by six horses, that bore her coffin. On top of the coffin were three wreaths placed there by her brother, Earl Spencer, and her two sons, Prince William (fifteen) and Prince Harry (twelve). It was mostly a silent procession, or as quiet as a million people can be, a silence broken only by the tolling of Westminster Abbey's Tenor Bell, once every minute, and the sounds of the horses' hooves as they struck the pavement. A particularly memorable and heart-rending image is of Diana's two sons walking solemnly behind their mother's coffin, displaying a quiet dignity that belied their tender years and flanked by their father, Prince Charles, their grandfather Prince Philip, and their uncle, Earl Spencer.

Millions attend Diana's funeral

Two thousand people had been invited to attend the funeral, with some having to be ushered into St Margaret's Church adjacent to Westminster Abbey in order to accommodate everyone. Luciano Pavarotti, a personal friend of Diana, had been asked to sing at the service but had refused, saying he would have been unable to make it through any song without breaking down in tears. Elton John, who was to perform his song 'Candle in the Wind' with reworked lyrics in honour of Diana, entered the abbey alone.

The funeral service began at 11 am. An hour later, after a minute's silence, Diana's coffin was placed in a hearse and for the next two hours was taken on a prearranged route through the streets of London before it began its final, 128-kilometre (80-mile) journey to Althorp Estate in Northamptonshire, the Spencer family home for more than five hundred years. Twenty generations of Diana's family are buried in the cemetery of the Church of St Mary the Virgin in the nearby town of Great Brington, but it was decided the Princess of Wales' final resting place would be in the gardens of the estate itself, to spare the residents of Great Brington the inconvenience of the presence of the millions of well-wishers that would have transformed her shrine into a place of pilgrimage.

2003

COALITION FORCES INVADE IRAQ

In February 2003, one hundred thousand US troops assembled in Kuwait for an assault on Iraq. Their objective was to 'to disarm Iraq of weapons of mass destruction [WMDs], to end Saddam Hussein's support for terrorism, and to free the Iraqi people'. On 18 March they launched their attack. The invasion, supported by troops from the so-called Coalition of the Willing, and was opposed by some traditional US allies, including France and Germany, who argued that there was no real evidence for the existence of WMDs. It is estimated that between January and April 2003, 36 million people across the world took part in protests against the war. No WMDs were ever found but the occupation of Iraq continues.

THE BATTLE OF IRAQ

My fellow citizens, the dangers to our country and the world will be overcome. We will pass through this time of peril and carry on the work of peace. We will defend our freedom. We will bring freedom to others and we will prevail.

GEORGE W. BUSH 19 MARCH 2003

What possible connection could an urbane Swedish diplomat and politician, from a family of scholars, have with the US invasion of Iraq? Hans Martin Blix was born in Sweden on 28 June 1928. He studied at the University of Uppsala in Sweden and New York's Columbia University, and earned a PhD from the University of Cambridge in England. Through the 1960s and 1970s he rose through Sweden's diplomatic ranks, and became foreign minister in 1978. In 1981 he was appointed head of the International Atomic Energy Agency, an independent international organisation with links to the United Nations, and held this position until 1997. In March 2000 he was chosen to be the head of the new United Nations Monitoring, Verification and Inspection Commission (UNMOVIC), and in 2002 was ordered to focus his agency's efforts on disarming Iraq. According to American and British intelligence, Saddam Hussein had been stockpiling weapons of mass destruction (WMDs) that threatened the strategic interests of the West. Hans Blix was ordered to find them.

Hussein 'playing games of cat and mouse'

On 8 November 2002, United Nations Security Council Resolution 1441 required that Iraq compensate Kuwait for widespread looting by Iraq's troops after its invasion of 1990 and that it halt its continuing importation and acquisition of prohibited weapons. The resolution also provided Saddam Hussein with one last opportunity to comply with a string of previous resolutions calling for full disclosure of the presence of WMDs. UN inspection teams under Hans Blix were running out of patience with Saddam's stonewalling, and Blix was quoted as saying that had Saddam complied with UN resolutions after the 1991 Gulf War he would have saved his country ten years of harsh economic sanctions. Hussein had been 'playing games of cat and mouse' with UNMOVIC, Blix said, and he had warned the Iraqi government there would be serious consequences if his disarmament teams continued to be harassed and fed bogus information on the whereabouts of the country's WMDs.

Nevertheless, Blix came to believe that the case arguing for the presence of WMDs was, at best, flimsy. Despite Iraq's intransigence Blix's teams had managed to search more than seven hundred suspected WMD sites across the country in the months leading up to the invasion—and had uncovered nothing of substance. UNMOVIC's lack of evidence of WMDs was, however, in stark contrast to what was coming out of the intelligence agencies of Britain and the United States, and at odds with the talk of war coming from the White House and No. 10 Downing Street. Unable to see the case for war, Blix later confided that he thought British prime minister Tony Blair and US president George W. Bush were behaving 'like seventeenth-century witchfinders' in their determination to remove the Iraqi dictator.

In the two years following the tragedy of 9/11, it is estimated that George W. Bush and seven of his most influential aides—including his defense secretary Donald Rumsfeld, his national security advisor Condoleezza Rice and his secretary of state Colin Powell—made more than nine hundred false or misleading statements regarding the threat posed by Iraq and its supposed links to the terrorist group Al-Qaeda. Examples of the deliberate pattern of so-called irrefutable facts that Bush administration officials were using to bolster its case for war are legion. On 26 August 2002 Vice President Cheney declared: 'Simply stated, there is no doubt that Saddam Hussein now has weapons of mass destruction. There is no doubt he is amassing them to use against our friends, against our allies, and against us.' In September 2002 President Bush declared on radio: 'The Iraqi regime possesses biological and chemical weapons, is rebuilding the facilities to make more and, according to the British government, could launch a biological or chemical attack in as little as forty-five minutes after the order is given. This regime is seeking a nuclear bomb, and with fissile material could build one within a year.' In February 2003 secretary of state Colin Powell said: 'What we're giving you are facts and conclusions based on solid intelligence.' No matter that, years later, the Duelfer Report concluded that Saddam Hussein had virtually terminated Iraq's nuclear program in 1991 and had made no attempt whatsoever to resurrect it. The American people and the world

were being psychologically prepared for war, and there wasn't anything they, or Hans Blix and his dedicated teams of weapons inspectors, could do about it.

Coalition prepares for invasion

The coalition of armed forces led by the United States and Great Britain, assisted by troops from Australia, Poland, Spain and Denmark, had spent months assembling at staging posts in neighbouring countries in and around the Persian Gulf, and were poised to invade Iraq with the aim of achieving three stated objectives: to end the regime of Saddam Hussein and its support of terror, to locate and neutralise once and for all its 'weapons of mass destruction', and to free the Iraqi people from tyranny and oppression.

The beginning of the invasion, codenamed Operation Iraqi Freedom, was under the command of US army general Tommy Franks. It involved more than three hundred thousand troops and an estimated seventy thousand Kurdish troops, and its intent was signalled on 19 March 2003 with a US air strike on the Presidential Palace in Baghdad. Forty-five minutes later, at 10.15 pm Eastern time in the United States, President George W. Bush addressed the nation, declaring that the US and coalition forces were in the early stages of a campaign to disarm Iraq and free its people, that the United States was going into Iraq 'with respect for its citizens, for their great civilization, and for the religious faiths they practice'. It would be a swift campaign based on mobility, superior technology and the precise application of overwhelming force. And it would begin in the south around Basra.

RIGHT: US Marines from the 3rd Battalion engage Iraqi troops on the outskirts of Baghdad.

On 20 March coalition troops entered Basra Province in the south from their assembly points within Kuwait while commandos launched a seaborne strike to capture the port city of Basra itself. More than eight hundred cruise missiles rained down on Iraqi targets in and around Baghdad and the cities of Mosul and Kirkuk in the invasion's first forty-eight hours in a tactic known as 'shock and awe'. This tactic was designed not merely to hit designated targets but also to deal a psychological deathblow to the Iraqi armed forces and extinguish their will to fight. In the first two days of the conflict more missiles were launched against Iraqi targets than were fired during the entire forty days of the 1991 Gulf War. Unlike the 'dumb bombs' of 1991, however, these were satellite-guided high-precision bombs, and their targets were not the Iraqi army so much as its leadership—in accordance with a US battle plan that was expressly designed to bypass Iraqi divisions rather than confront them, to instead eliminate the ability of Saddam Hussein and his generals to communicate with and coordinate their armies.

As US troops headed towards Basra on 21 March, Iraq's 51st Mechanized Infantry Division, a force of eight thousand to ten thousand soldiers sent to the south of the country to guard the area bordering Iran, surrendered virtually without a fight. It was typical of the many poorly equipped regular army units encountered by coalition forces. The US 5th Corps and the 1st Marine Expeditionary Force converged upon Baghdad from the east and south. In the north, a late decision by Turkey not to allow coalition forces to use its territory to mount an assault meant that the fifteen thousand troops of the 4th Mechanized Infantry Division had to be redeployed to the south, and in their place the US 173rd Airborne Brigade was to be airdropped on the outskirts of Kirkuk, linking up with Kurdish forces to help secure the north of the country and keep the thirteen divisions Saddam had deployed there at bay.

Bombing missions dismantle Iraq's air defence

Coalition ground forces were able to advance with relative impunity due in no small part to the cover provided by coalition aircraft. The success of the air war had reduced by hundreds the number of targets that ground forces would otherwise have had to deal with and kept the Iraqi air force out of the sky. The US air force alone flew more than fifteen hundred sorties on 21–22 March, and another fifteen hundred on 22–23 March, of which more than eight hundred were bombing missions that dismantled Iraq's air defence network, command bunkers and control centres.

The coalition's advance slowed on 23–24 March and twenty-six soldiers were killed in what would be the worst single day's fighting in terms of casualties. Another two thousand sorties flown by coalition aircraft saw approximately eight hundred precision-guided bombs dropped onto five hundred targets. The Iraqi air force, as it had been from day one, was nowhere to be seen. Meanwhile, in the south, the Basra airfield had been secured and mine-clearing operations in the waterways surrounding Umm Qasr were progressing well.

On 24–25 March the 5th Corps and 1st Marine Expeditionary Force were continuing their push towards Baghdad and the Iraqi army was already showing clear signs that it was no longer functioning as a cohesive fighting force. The Iraqi leadership started stripping Republican Guard units from wherever it could gather them and redeploying them to the south of Baghdad in a desperate attempt to slow coalition progress. Their deployment, however, brought them out into the open and made them vulnerable to coalition air strikes throughout 25–26 March.

US forces had been advancing on average 125 kilometres (78 miles) a day over the first four days of the campaign, one of the most rapid armoured advances in military history. They achieved this by avoiding, where possible, large concentrations of the enemy's armed forces as well as large towns and cities.

The noose around Baghdad starts to tighten

On 30 March sandstorms that had been hampering air sorties for two days finally cleared and more than twelve hundred precision-guided bombs were dropped on specified targets, more than half of which were the rapidly disintegrating units of the Republican Guard positioned in and around the Iraqi capital. The 3rd Infantry Division secured a bridge across the Euphrates River at Al Handiyah while the 101st Airborne Division captured the airfield at An Najaf 160 kilometres (100 miles) south of Baghdad. The way to Baghdad opened on 2 April with the near-destruction of the Medina Division of the Republican Guard by the 5th Corps. The coalition advance was relentless. Fifteen hundred sorties were being flown every day, focusing on eliminating Republican Guard units and clearing the way for land forces to continue their advance on the capital. The much anticipated Battle for Baghdad was, thanks to the coalition's massive air superiority, little more than a series of smallish skirmishes fought against Iraqi troops who had been deprived of their will to fight. Helicopters were able to fly in close support to slow-moving A-10 attack aircraft in the face of almost non-existent anti-aircraft fire.

The 5th Corps took Baghdad Airport in the face of demoralised defenders and, together with the 1st Marine Expeditionary Force, was now able to initiate raids by armoured vehicles deep into Baghdad itself, further sapping the morale of those scattered Republican Guard units that had managed to escape the carnage from the air and ground and had fallen back into the hoped-for safety of the suburbs. The air campaign by now was routinely flying fifteen hundred sorties every day and mercilessly targeting the Republican Guard around the clock.

By 5 April US forces had consolidated their hold on Baghdad and its airport, and controlled both the southeastern and southwestern approaches to the city. The following day, 6 April, a coalition announcement claimed it now enjoyed air supremacy over all Iraqi airspace and the 5th Corps and 1st Marine Expeditionary Force had all but surrounded the Iraqi capital, preventing any reinforcement of Iraqi positions from its forces to the north of the city.

Fedayeen Saddam among the last to surrender

The International Institute for Strategic Studies estimated that the Iraqi forces opposing the invasion totalled approximately 536,000, of which 375,000 were regular army, eighty thousand were Republican Guards, with a further forty thousand belonging to the *Fedayeen Saddam*, literally 'Saddam's Men of Sacrifice', an ultra-loyal paramilitary force that reported directly to Saddam and operated outside of the normal parameters of the military hierarchy. Although hopelessly outgunned and outnumbered, the *Fedayeen Saddam* were among the last to surrender and continually hampered the advance of coalition forces towards Baghdad using subterfuge and guerilla tactics.

President George W. Bush addresses the nation on Iraq beneath a banner reading Mission Accomplished on 1 May.

In the end it seemed as though the US and coalition forces had achieved a magnificent victory. The Iraqi government and its military, the world's twelfth-largest standing army, had completely and utterly collapsed in just three weeks. Baghdad fell on 9 April and Saddam Hussein fled the city as US forces took control of Ba'ath Party government and administrative buildings. A successful amphibious assault by the British Royal Marines on the Al-Faw Peninsula and around the outskirts of Basra had seen the country's vast network of southern oil fields seized relatively intact, and Polish commandoes had successfully taken all of Basra's offshore oil platforms.

Fighting continued in the country's north after the fall of Baghdad, with Kurdish forces capturing the town of Kirkuk on 10 April and Mosul the following day. The invasion came to an 'official' end with the fall of Saddam Hussein's home town of Tikrit on 15 April. Saddam's Ba'ath Party and its military apparatus had been toppled with significantly less loss of life than had been anticipated, and the overwhelming technology possessed by the US punished any Iraqi mistakes in the field with overwhelming severity. Coalition casualties included one hundred and thirty-nine US personnel and thirty-three from Great Britain, as opposed to an estimated nine thousand two hundred Iraqi soldiers and almost seven thousand three hundred civilians killed.

'Mission accomplished'

An undeniable and spontaneous outpouring of gratitude towards coalition personnel was evident on the streets of Baghdad and few seemed immune from the euphoria of victory. On 1 May President George Bush flew in to address sailors aboard the aircraft carrier USS *Abraham Lincoln*. In a speech that would later be pilloried in the world media when it became apparent that any thought of victory was premature to say the least, the president made his famous declaration: 'In the Battle of Iraq, the United States and our allies have prevailed'. As if to emphasise the point, a giant banner hung on the carrier's superstructure behind him read MISSION ACCOMPLISHED. While Bush had nothing to do with the banner's deployment (it was requested by the navy and the banner itself was made by members of the White House staff), its very existence made it seem that the president clearly associated himself with the sentiments it expressed. For the war's critics, the speech summed up the arrogance of an administration that had raced into a war the critics felt America had no right to wage, then prematurely declared its closure without regard to any need to 'win the peace'.

Saddam Hussein went into hiding and was finally dragged out of a hole in the ground by soldiers of the US 4th Infantry Division at a farmhouse in Tikrit. He was found guilty of crimes against humanity and the former dictator was hanged on 30 December 2006.

BIBLIOGRAPHY

Ackerman, Peter and DuVall, Jack, *A Force More Powerful: A Century of Non-Violent Conflict*, Palgrave Macmillan, 2001.

Aikman, David, *Great Souls: Six Who Changed the Century*, Rowman & Littlefield, 2003.

Auboyer, Jeannine, *Daily Life in Ancient India*, Phoenix, 1965.

Beevor, Antony, *Stalingrad*, Viking, 1998.

Boulnois, Luce (trans. Loveday, Helen), *Silk Road*, Airphoto, 2005.

Brent, Peter, *The Mongol Empire*, Weidenfeld & Nicolson, 1976.

Bullock, Alan, *Hitler: A Study in Tyranny*, Penguin, 1975.

Burn, A.R. *The Penguin History of Greece*, Penguin, 1985.

Campbell, Bruce, *The SA Generals and the Rise of Nazism*, University Press of Kentucky, 2004.

Capek, Michael, *Emperor Qin's Terracotta Army*, Twenty-First Century Books, 2008.

Cordesman, Anthony, *The Iraq War: Strategy, Tactics, and Military Lessons*, Greenwood Publishing Group, 2004.

Cotterell, Maurice, *The Terracotta Warriors: The Secret Codes of the Emperor's Army*, Headline, 2003.

Dando-Collins, Stephen, *Cleopatra's Kidnappers*, Wiley, 2006.

David, Rosalie, *Discovering Ancient Egypt*, Michael O'Mara, 1993.

Davies, Norman, *Europe: A History*, Oxford University Press, 1996.

Davis, Paul, *Besieged: 100 Great Sieges from Jericho to Sarajevo*, Oxford University Press, 2003.

Day, David, *Conquest: A New History of the Modern World*, HarperCollins, 2005.

De Hartog, Leo, *Genghis Khan, Conqueror of the World*, Tauris Parke, 2004.

Easwaran, Eknath, *Gandhi, the Man: The Story of his Transformation*, Nilgiri Press, 2001.

Edsforth, Ronald, *The New Deal: America's Response to the Great Depression*, John Wiley & Sons Ltd, 2000.

Hill, David, *The Brutal Truth of the First Fleet*, William Heinemann, 2008.

Hill, Frances, *The Salem Witch Trials Reader*, Da Capo Press, 2000.

Hughes, Robert, *The Fatal Shore*, Collins Harvill, 1987.

Inglis, James, *Fighting Talk*, Pier 9, 2008.

Jack, Homer (ed.), *The Gandhi Reader: A Sourcebook of his Life and Writings*, Grove/Atlantic Incorporated, 1994.

Jones, Howard, *The Bay of Pigs*, Oxford University Press, 2008.

Kitto, H.D.F. *The Greeks*, Penguin, 1973.

Knight, Ian and Hook, Adam, *Isandlwana 1879: The Great Zulu Victory*, Osprey Publishing, 2002.

Knight, Ian, *The Zulu War 1879*, Osprey Publishing, 2003.

Lomax, Milton, *Great Lives: Exploration*, Macmillan, 1988.

Mackay, James, *William Wallace: Brave Heart*, Mainstream, 1995.

McClain, James L. and Wakita, Osamu, *Osaka: The Merchant's Capital of Early Modern Japan*, Cornell University Press, 1999.

Maharaj, Mac and Kathrada, Ahmad M., *Mandela: The Authorized Portrait*, Andrews McMeel Publishing, 2006.

Man, John, *Genghis Khan: Life, Death and Resurrection*, Thomas Dunne Books, 2004.

Matthews, John and Stewart, Bob, *Warriors of Christendom*, Firebird, 1988.

Medvedev, Grigori, *The Truth About Chernobyl*, IB Tauris & Company, 1991.

Montefiore, Simon Sebag, *101 World Heroes*, Quercus, 2007.

Mould, Richard, *Chernobyl Record: The Definitive History of the Chernobyl Disaster*, Institute of Physics Publishing, 2000.

Pellegrino, Charles, *Her Name, Titanic*, Robert Hale, 1990.

Rabe, Stephen, *Eisenhower and Latin America: The Foreign Policy of Anticommunism*, University of North Carolina Press, 1988.

Raychaudhuri, Tapan, Kumar, Dharma, Desai, Meghnad and Habib, Irfan, *The Cambridge Economic History of India*, vol. 2, Cambridge University Press, 1983.

Reeve, Simon, *One Day In September: The Full Story of the 1972 Munich Olympics Massacre*, Arcade Publishing, 2000.

Regan, Geoffrey, *Battles that Changed History*, Guiness Publishing Limited, 1992.

Reid, Struan, *The Life and World of Montezuma*, Heinemann Library, 2002.

Sancton, Thomas and MacLeod, Scott, *Death of a Princess*, St Martin's Press, 1998.

Sharp, Mike, Westwell, Ian and Westwood, John, *History of World War I*, Marshall Cavendish Corporation, 2002.

Staten, Clifford, *The History of Cuba*, Greenwood Publishing Group, 2003.

Strathloch, Robert, *Marco Polo*, Heinemann, 2002.

Terrill, Ross, *Mao: A Biography*, Stanford University Press, 2001.

Thornton, Ian, *Krakatoa: The Destruction and Assembly of an Island Ecosystem*, Harvard University Press, 1997.

Turnbull, Stephen, *Osaka 1615: The Last Battle of the Samurai*, Osprey Publishing, 2006.

Tyldesley, Joyce, *Cleopatra: Last Queen of Egypt*, Profile, 2008.

Washington Post, www.washingtonpost.com, original reported stories

Weir, Alison, *Henry VIII: King and Court*, Jonathan Cape, 2001.

Weir, William, *50 Military Leaders Who Changed the World*, Career Press, 2007.

Weldon, Fay, *The Shrapnel Academy*, Hodder & Stoughton, 1986.

Xiao Hong Lee, Lily and Wiles, Sue, *Women of the Long March*, Allen & Unwin, 2008.

PICTURE CREDITS

INDEX

Published in 2010 by Pier 9, an imprint of Murdoch Books Pty Limited

Murdoch Books Australia
Pier 8/9
23 Hickson Road
Millers Point NSW 2000
Phone: +61 (0) 2 8220 2000
Fax: +61 (0) 2 8220 2558
www.murdochbooks.com.au

Murdoch Books UK Limited
Erico House, 6th Floor
93–99 Upper Richmond Road
Putney, London SW15 2TG
Phone: +44 (0) 20 8785 5995
Fax: +44 (0) 20 8785 5985
www.murdochbooks.co.uk

Publisher: Diana Hill
Developmental Editor: Emma Hutchinson
Cover design and design concept: Hugh Ford
Designer: Susanne Geppert

Contributing authors: James Inglis (chapters 1–17, 20–21, 25, 32), Barry Stone (Introduction, chapters 18–19, 22–24, 26–40)

Original cover image Corbis Images, reworked by Hugh Ford.

National Library of Australia Cataloguing-in-Publication entry

Author:	Stone, Barry.
Title:	History's greatest headlines / Barry Stone and James Inglis.
ISBN:	978-1-74196-453-0 (pbk.)
Notes:	Includes bibliographical references and index.
Subjects:	World history.
Other Authors/Contributors:	Inglis, James.
Dewey Number:	909

A catalogue record for this book is available from the British Library.

Printed by 1010 Printing International Limited, Hong Kong.